The Anglican Tradition from a Postcolonial Perspective

The Anglican Tradition from a Postcolonial Perspective

KWOK PUI-LAN

Seabury Books
19 East 34th Street
New York, New York 10016

Seabury Books is an imprint of Church Publishing Incorporated.

Cover design by David Baldeosingh Rotstein.
Cover image: He Qi, The Great Commission. Courtesy of James Qi He. www.heqiart.com.
Typeset by Nord Comp.

A record of this book is available from the Library of Congress.
Library of Congress Control Number: 2023943597

ISBN 978-1-64065-629-1 (hardcover)
ISBN 978-1-64065-630-7 (paperback)
ISBN 978-1-64065-631-4 (ebook)

To the faculty, students, and staff of Episcopal Divinity School,
Cambridge, Massachusetts, USA

Contents

Acknowledgments

I **would like to thank colleagues** at the Episcopal Divinity School in Cambridge, Massachusetts, who have discussed ideas in the book with me, especially Ian T. Douglas, Christopher Duraisingh, Fredrica Harris Thompsett, Sheryl Kujawa-Holbrook, William M. Kondrath, Susanna Snyder, and Stephen Burns. With Douglas, who later became bishop diocesan in the Episcopal Church in Connecticut, USA, I coedited the book *Beyond Colonial Anglicanism*, which sowed the seeds for writing the present volume. I am grateful to the students at the Episcopal Divinity School for their probing questions and conversations. I dedicate this book with gratitude to the faculty, students, and staff at the school, which has provided a stimulating environment for me to develop my career and scholarship.

I am grateful for the friendship and collaboration with colleagues in different parts of the Anglican Communion, including Jenny Te Paa Daniel, Esther Mombo, Beverley Haddad, Gerald West, Denise M. Ackermann, Daniela Gennrich, Gloria Mapandol, Judy Berinai, Renie Chow Choy, Anderson Jeremiah, Mark Nam, Jane Shaw, Jennifer Strawbridge, Kapya John Kaoma, Judith A. Berling, Dan Joslyn-Siemiatkoski, and Scott MacDougall. I am indebted to my colleagues at the Candler School of Theology, particularly Joy McDougall, Musa Dube, Emmanuel Y. Lartey, Kyle Lambelet, Gabrielle Thomas, and Danielle Tumminio Hansen, who have supported my work and served as dialogical partners.

I had the privilege of participating in the Working Group that produced the project "Being Anglican: Learning from Global Perspectives" sponsored by Theological Education for the Anglican Communion. The project included a YouTube channel and a study guide. Working on this project with colleagues for two years and gathering resources for the study guide convinced me of the usefulness of a book like this. I want to express my appreciation to Stephen Spencer, Muthuraj Swamy, Marcus Throup, and Paulo Ueti for their vision and collaboration.

I thank the students who have taken the course "Critical Issues in the Anglican Communion" with me at the Episcopal Divinity School and Candler School of Theology. The students who took the course at Candler in the spring of 2023 have read part of the manuscript and offered helpful comments, and their presentations in class and papers have enriched the contents of the book. I am very grateful to Jennifer Snow and Stephen Spencer who took the time to provide thoughtful and constructive comments on chapters of the book. I would like to acknowledge research assistance by Carmie McDonald and Junmey Wang, who combed through bibliographies and databases for relevant sources. As the book wants to showcase the voices of scholars from the Global South, their help has saved me much time and broadened my knowledge. Special thanks to McDonald and Michael Yorke for editing the manuscript with attention to detail and making the book more precise and consistent. Yorke's assistance helped me cross the finish line as I worked on and revised the last chapters. I am grateful to Candler School of Theology for providing the funds to support research and editorial assistance.

My editor at Church Publishing Justin Hoffman expressed interest in the book from the beginning and wanted to include it in the Seabury Books imprint. I thank him for his vision and encouragement and the editorial and production team for their efficient work in bringing the book out in a timely manner. This book draws from my previous publications and I am grateful to Church Publishing for permission to use material from "The Legacy of Cultural Hegemony in the Anglican Church," in *Beyond Colonial Anglicanism: The Anglican Communion in the Twenty-First Century*, ed. Ian T. Douglas and Kwok Pui-lan (New York: Church Publishing, 2001), 47–70; and Morehouse Publishing for "From a Colonial Church to a Global Communion," in *Anglican Women on Church and Mission*, ed. Kwok Pui-lan, Judith A. Berling, and Jenny Plane Te Paa (Harrisburg, PA: Morehouse Publishing, 2013), 3–20.

CHAPTER

1

Introduction

When I was a teenager growing up in the former British colony of Hong Kong in the mid-1960s, a neighbor brought my sister and me to the Holy Trinity Church, a beautiful Anglican church built in a traditional Chinese architectural style. My neighbor was a descendant of one of the early Chinese Anglican ordained pastors in the colony. A few years later, Deacon Hwang Hsien-Yuin arrived and began serving as the vicar of the church, even though she was not yet ordained to the priesthood. In December 1971 at the St. John's Cathedral in Hong Kong, Deacon Hwang and Deacon Joyce Bennett, a missionary from the Church Mission Society (CMS),[1] were ordained women priests in the Anglican Communion. The first woman ordained in the Communion was Li Tim-Oi (1907–1992), also from Hong Kong. In 1944, Bishop Ronald Owen Hall ordained Li to the priesthood so that she could celebrate communion during the emergency caused by the Japanese occupation in World War II.

Today, women's leadership and ministry have increasingly been recognized in the Anglican churches. Female priests can be found in many parts of the Communion, and a growing number of women have become bishops, serving as diocesan or suffragan bishops in various dioceses. In addition to female bishops in the Global North, female bishops have been consecrated in Anglican churches in Kenya, Southern Africa, South Sudan, Cuba, Brazil, and the Church of South India, which is a united church and a member of the Communion. Bishop Maria Grace Tazu Sasamori was consecrated in 2022 on the island of Hokkaido in northern Japan as the first female bishop in Japan. Bishop Katharine Jefferts Schori was elected and served as the presiding bishop of the Episcopal Church, USA, and Archbishop Linda Nicholls serves as the primate of the Anglican Church of Canada. The primate is the most senior bishop or archbishop of a member church of the Anglican Communion.

Another major change in the Anglican Communion in the past several decades has been the demographic shift from the Global North to the Global South. The Anglican Communion is a worldwide fellowship of churches with more than 90 million people speaking more than 2,000 languages in more than 165 countries. Currently, it is made up of 42 provinces, which are autonomous member churches, and five other national or local churches known as Extra Provincials.[2] In the second half of the twentieth century, the Communion has undergone significant growth and demographic change. As countries in Africa and Asia regained political independence after World War II, churches founded as colonial and missionary outposts by Britain and the United States have become autonomous Anglican provinces. According to Todd M. Johnson and Gina A. Gurlo, the number of Anglicans doubled from 47 million in 1970 to 86 million in 2010. They write, "In 1970, 62% of all Anglicans were found in Europe. By 2010 this had dropped to just 31%. During the same period, Africa grew from 16% of all Anglicans worldwide in 1970 to 59% in 2010. In essence, Europe and Africa changed positions over the 40 years. Northern America fell from 9% of global Anglicans in 1970 to 3% in 2010."[3]

While the term "Anglican" originally comes from Medieval Latin and means "of the English people," Anglican churches today are no longer defined by its English heritage, as more than half of Anglicans live in Africa and speak a language other than English. Roughly a quarter of the provinces, such as Congo, Japan, and Brazil, that are current members of the Anglican Communion have never been part of the British Empire.[4] The *World Christian Database* provides data for Anglicans in different continents and countries. In 2015, there were about 90 million Anglicans worldwide, with 57 million living in the African continent (22 million in Nigeria, 14 million in Uganda, and 6 million in Kenya). Both the Church of England and the Episcopal Church have seen a steady decline in membership in the past decades. Membership of the Church of England dropped from 29 million in 1970 to 24 million in 2015, while that of the Episcopal Church fell from 3.1 million to 1.9 million in the same period.[5]

The changes in Anglican churches are consistent with the shift in Christian demographics in the past century. Whereas in 1900, 83 percent of the world's Christians lived in Europe and North America, today the majority of Christians live in the Global South.[6] In 1900, Africa had only about 10 million Christians, about 9 percent of the population. A century later, the number has increased to 383 million, roughly 47 percent of the population. According to the most recent data, in mid-2021, about 1.71 billion Christians live in the Global South (685 million in Africa, 617 million in Latin America, and 383 million in Asia), whereas 833 million live in the Global North (564 million in Europe and 269 million in North America).[7] The shift of demographics has a gender dimension as well, as Anglican missiologist Cathy Ross pointed out in 2008: "Christianity is not only becoming increasingly nonwhite; it is also becoming increasingly female. The average Anglican in our world today is black, female and in her late teens or early twenties."[8]

This demographic shift means that we can no longer use a North Atlantic framework to interpret the Anglican tradition and must adopt a postcolonial approach to wrestle with both the colonial legacy and current controversies over race, gender, sexuality, and authority. By the Anglican tradition, I refer to the theologies and practices that can be traced to the English Reformation, which had their roots in earlier times. The Australian historian Bruce Kaye uses the term "conversation" to describe the Anglican tradition. He says, "I will be treating Anglicanism as a tradition. By this I do not mean a set of fixed habits from the past, but rather the more dynamic sense of being a conversation over time amongst a community of people held together by sets of practices and beliefs."[9] The conversation had been full of debates and contestations since the beginning—from the Elizabethan settlement, antislavery debates, the Oxford movement, the Christian Socialist movement—up to our present time. In *The Promise of Anglicanism*, Robert S. Heaney and William L. Sachs encourage us to see contestation positively, as a mark of the dynamic of Anglican history and development. They write, "Contestation reveals a faith tradition that is unfolding, that is reshaping itself through lived experience in multiple contexts, facing social challenges amid societies in political and economic disarray. . . . It should not be surprising that there is difference, nor that no particular formulation of Anglican identity encompasses the breadth of contextual life."[10] The contestation in the Communion shows that "Anglicanism proves unfinished; it is ever in the process of becoming."[11]

It is an opportune time to deepen the conversations about the Anglican tradition from a postcolonial perspective. While past scholarship on Anglicanism has focused on the history and theological tradition of the British Isles, we have more works on Anglican churches from a global perspective, such as Kevin Ward's *A History of Global Anglicanism* and Bruce Kaye's *An Introduction to World Anglicanism*.[12] Books on the history and practices of Anglican churches outside the North Atlantic have been published in the past decades, such as those focusing on the church in Burma, China, Malaysia, Nigeria, Sierra Leone, South Sudan, Zimbabwe, Australia, and the Maori church in Aotearoa New Zealand.[13] These books have substantially enriched our understanding of the relationships between Anglicanism and colonialism in the past and the adaptation of Christianity to local cultures and practices.

In recent years, both the Church of England and the Episcopal Church have renewed their efforts to address global racism as an integral part of the legacy of slavery and colonialism. In February 2020, the General Synod of the Church of England voted to apologize for racism experienced by Black and minority ethnic people in the Church and reiterated an earlier apology for the Church's role in the slave trade. Later that year, a new antiracism task force was formed to prepare for the launch of the Archbishops' Racism Action Commission.[14] Commission members were appointed in 2021 and the Commission was charged to promote racial justice, equality, and inclusion in the Church.

In the United States, after the murder of George Floyd, an unarmed Black man, and the protests spurred by the Black Lives Matter movement, the Episcopal Church announced a new churchwide racial truth and reconciliation effort in 2021. The Presiding Bishop Michael Curry said the church needs to "reckon with our church's historic and current complicity with racial injustice, make commitments to right old wrongs and repair breaches and discern a vision for healing and reconciliation."[15] A new working group was formed, charged with conducting a review of the past and present truth and reconciliation processes within the Episcopal Church and the wider Anglican Communion and drawing lessons from efforts taken in South Africa, Rwanda, and New Zealand.

In addition to the renewed efforts by these two churches, there are also Communion-wide projects which aim to showcase the racial and cultural diversity of members of the Communion. For example, in preparation for the Lambeth Conference in 2022, Theological Education for the Anglican Communion, an initiative set up by the Anglican Primates, produced a project "Being Anglican: Learning from Global Perspectives."[16] The project aimed to produce a set of videos and a study guide on Anglican identity and the Anglican Communion for Anglican theological colleges and seminaries for their teaching and training. I had the privilege of serving on the working group for this project. We interviewed clergy and laypeople across the Communion to produce short multilingual and multicultural videos about their views on Anglican discipleship, worship, mission, ecumenical and interfaith relations, the Communion, and spirituality. The project foregrounds the faces and voices of Anglicans from the Global South to highlight the rich, dynamic, and pluralistic nature of the Communion. Over the years, I have had the opportunity of collaborating with Anglican scholars and church leaders on several projects, which greatly expanded my knowledge about the diversity and issues facing the Communion. As I was born and grew up in Hong Kong, I have also developed a keen interest in postcolonial theory and theology, especially around the time Hong Kong was returned by the British to China in 1997. This book combines my interests in studying the Anglican tradition and postcolonial theory and theology. By means of this book, I hope to highlight the issues and concerns of Anglican churches from the Global South and the contributions of Southern Anglican scholars and racial and ethnic minority scholars in the United States. I hope my research will stimulate more conversation and critical inquiries in the future.

The Postcolonial Optic

The meaning of the term "postcolonial" is contentious because the prefix "post" can have various meanings. If "post" is understood in a chronological sense, "postcolonial" means the period after colonialism and the transition of political power from the colonizers to the colonized. However, even as many countries have regained political independence, many people argue that we have not entered a postcolonial period, because neocolonialism continues to dominate much of the world. Apart from a temporal sense, "post" can also refer to reading strategies, practices, and actions that challenge colonialism and its legacy. I have defined postcolonial imagination as "a desire, a determination, and a process of disengagement from the whole colonial syndrome, which takes many forms and guises."[17] Cameroonian political theorist Achille Mbembe delineates three different phases in the development of postcolonial thought.[18] The first phase is the emergence of anticolonial thought by seminal figures such as Léopold Senghor, C. L. R. James, Aimé Cesaíre, and Franz Fanon during the struggles for political independence. The second phase began in the late 1970s with the publication of Edward Said's *Orientalism*.[19] Following Said's lead, many postcolonial critics study the colonial imprint and logic expressed in literature, history, and anthropology. The third phase moves beyond the study of colonial discourse and literature to confront social and economic inequities brought by globalization and the neoliberal economy. It has been used to study capitalist formation, struggle over land, coloniality of gender, racial and ethnic politics, queer resistance, migration, statelessness, and global environmental crisis.[20]

Edward Said, a Palestinian American, is generally hailed as the pioneer of postcolonial theory. Said grew up in a religious Palestinian household with close ties to the church. His father studied at the Anglican St. George's School in Jerusalem, and he grew up in Cario attending Sunday school in an English preparatory school, followed by matins at All Saints' Cathedral for many years.[21] He read the Book of Common Prayer (BCP) and the Anglican tradition had a cultural imprint on him. In his 1978 pioneering text, *Orientalism*, he argues that colonization implies not only political and military domination, but also cultural hegemony and colonial representation of the Other. Analyzing British and French writings on the "Orient," Said links directly the structures of colonialism with Western knowledge production and cultural representation. The "East" was presented in these writings stereotypically as female, passive, despotic, backward, and irrational, while the "West" represented the masculine, aggressive, democratic, progressive, and rational. Such skewed misrepresentation contributed to the creation in the public mind of the prejudice that the "East" was inferior: these people could not rule themselves and had to be ruled. From his own experience as a Palestinian boy growing up in Cairo, Said demonstrates the significant roles played by mission schools, churches, English soccer, Western music, and fashion in furthering colonial cultural domination.

In analyzing the cultural and religious dimensions of colonialism, Said builds on the theory of hegemony by Italian Marxist thinker Antonio Gramsci. Said writes: "It is hegemony, or rather the result of cultural hegemony at work, that gives Orientalism the durability and the strength I have been speaking about."[22] The word "hegemony," in its etymological sense of "leadership" and in its derived sense of "dominance," usually refers to relations among social groups and states. Facing the ascendancy of Fascism in Italy, Gramsci was concerned to challenge the apparatus or mechanisms of the hegemony of the dominant class, unmask the contradictions in religion, ideology, and arts, and create a popular culture that promotes the interests of workers and their political allies. He astutely observed that hegemony of the ruling class was maintained by both the civil and political society. While civil society taught and propagated ideas and values of how people should think and behave according to bourgeois interests, the state had the disciplinary power to coerce by force when people rebelled or resisted. Gramsci's theory was borrowed by Said in his discussion of how cultural hegemony facilitated colonial rule:

> Gramsci has made the useful analytic distinction between civil and political society in which the former is made up of voluntary (or at least rational and noncoercive) affiliations like schools, families, and unions, the

> latter of state institutions (the army, the police, the central bureaucracy) whose role in the polity is direct domination. Culture, of course, is to be found operating within civil society, where the influence of ideas, of institutions, and of other persons works not through domination but by what Gramsci calls consent.[23]

Said's critiques of cultural hegemony and biased representation of other cultures and societies are useful in looking at the Anglican tradition, given its inseparable connections with colonialism. In 1800, the British Empire consisted of 1.5 million square miles and 20 million people. By 1900, the Victorian empire was made up of 11 million square miles and about 390 million people.[24] Wherever the crown went, the cross went. As the products of their own time, many church leaders and missionaries during the expansion of the empire shared the attitude of cultural superiority that Said chastised. For example, Samuel Wilberforce, the bishop of Oxford, noted in 1853 that the vocation of the British people was to

> leave as an impress of their intercourse with the inferior nations, marks of moral teaching and religious training, to have made a nation of children see what it was to be men—to have trained mankind in the habits of truth, morality and justice, instead of leaving them in the imbecility of falsehood and perpetual childhood; and above all, to have been instrumental in communicating to them, not by fierce aggression and superior power—but by gentle persuasion, that moral superiority, that greatest gift bestowed by God upon ourselves, true faith in his Word and true belief in the revelation of His Son.[25]

After Said, postcolonial critics have developed and elaborated on cultural representation, colonization as a transcultural and transnational process, racial and sexual politics, cultural hybridity, social temporality, and subaltern speech. I will briefly introduce some of the key postcolonial theorists and their contributions since they provide a valuable interpretive framework to examine the ways the Church of England participated in and continued to maintain cultural hegemony during and after the colonial era.

Stuart Hall, a Jamaican-born British postcolonial thinker, was also widely acclaimed as a pioneer in cultural studies, for he was the founder of the Birmingham University Centre for Contemporary Cultural Studies. As a Black sociologist living in England, Hall maintained that one of the myths that sustain the cultural hegemony of the West is none other than the construction of "the West" itself. He argued that discourses that deploy the binarism of "the West and the Rest" undergirded the ascendancy of Europe, shaping "its image of itself and 'others,' its sense of 'us' and 'them,' its practices and relations of power towards the Rest."[26] Instead of treating "the West" as infinitely superior to and different from the rest of the world, Hall investigates the intricate relationship between the cultures of the colonizers and the colonized. On the one hand, the colonizers superimpose their language, schools, churches, marriage systems, and legal codes onto those they rule. On the other hand, the colonized raise issues the colonizers must face, and provide a rich diversity of customs, food, arts, and music that form an integral part of metropolitan culture. Colonization, for Hall, is never a one-way street, but a transcultural and transnational "global" process that challenges an easy binary construction of "here" and "there," "then" and "now," and "home" and "abroad."[27]

Hall has written extensively on race, ethnicity, and identity, and has commented on Black popular culture and Black cinema. Well-versed in Marxist thought, Hall finds Gramsci's ideas relevant in theorizing racism, though Gramsci had not written explicitly on the subject. Specifically, Hall regards Gramsci's discussion of the roles of the state and civil society, his reflections on ideology and popular consciousness, and his emphasis on historical specificity and regional differences as important for any discussion of race, especially regarding its complex relationship to class.[28] Commenting on the cultural representation of Black people in the British media, Hall laments that in literary, visual, and cinematic forms, Blacks have typically been the objects and rarely the subjects of representation. He condemns the fetishization, objectification, and negative figuration of the Black subject in popular culture. Black cultural politics thus consists of the struggle for access to the rights of representation by Black artists and cultural workers and for the creation of "positive" Black imageries to counteract the dominant stereotypes.[29]

Hall's work helps us to see the Anglican tradition not from a center and periphery model, as if colonialism was a one-way street. Anglican histories in metropolitan areas and colonies were overlapped and mutually inscribed, for even as Anglican missionaries and colonial officials sought to impose their English culture onto the indigenous peoples,[30] what happened in the colonies also affected metropolitan culture. A clear example was that the ordination of Li Tim-Oi stimulated discussion of women's ordination in the Church of England. Hall's work on Black cultural politics provides food for thought as the Anglican Communion grapples with its long legacy of racism, cultural superiority, and the marginalization and oppression of indigenous populations.

Similar to Hall, the Indian-born postcolonial critic Homi Bhabha critiques British colonialism and pays attention to race, culture, and history. His densely argued book, *The Location of Culture*, explains why the culture of Western modernity must be critiqued from the postcolonial perspective.[31] The beliefs in rationality, liberty, and liberal humanism failed to challenge racism, slavery, and colonization in the modern period, he argues. The racist and colonial discourses were based on the fantasy of the difference of the other, constructed often in racial and sexual terms. Colonial discourse assumes the identity of the subjected people as fixed and unchanging, and the difference between them and the colonizers as unbridgeable. For Bhabha, the necessity of the creation of stereotypes points to the unstable psyche of the colonizers and the contradictory nature of colonial authority.[32]

Besides the concept of colonial fantasy, Bhabha contributes significantly to postcolonial theory through his articulations of mimicry, hybridity, and ambivalence. He notes that since colonialism violently impinges one culture upon another, the colonial subjects have to learn a foreign tongue and the cultural idioms of their oppressors. In the colonies, one can easily discern imitations of the colonizers' writing and speaking styles, social habits, customs, and religious practices. Instead of simply treating such cultural practices as identifying with the colonial regime,

Bhabha argues that mimicry can also function to mock the power the colonizers hold to be a model, that power that supposedly makes it imitable. Thus, mimicry can serve as a double vision "which in disclosing the ambivalence of colonial discourse also disrupts its authority."[33] Bhabha's theory is highly relevant to the study of the spread and expansion of Anglican churches in diverse cultural contexts. We can easily see mimicry of the Church of England in many former colonies, from the popular use of the 1662 BCP to English vestments and music. On the surface, we can say these churches are simply mimicking the "mother" church. But Bhabha challenges us to look deeper, to see that colonial mimicry may not simply be passive acquiesce but can be an ongoing and ambivalent negotiation process with multiple layers of, and sometimes contradictory, meanings.

Bhabha rejects the idea that cultural boundaries are airtight, clearly demarcating the insiders from the outsiders. He insists that cultures interact with one another and that all cultures are continually in a process of hybridity.[34] Cultural hybridity challenges the myths of purity of cultural lineage, homogeneity of identity, and monolithic understandings of national cultures. He helps demystify any easy identification of religion and national identity and resist the urge to locate Anglican identity simply from its English origin, without seeing that the Anglican tradition is continuously changing. His concept of hybridity opens a space in between so that denied knowledge can be articulated and recognized.[35] Hybridity and the "in-between" spaces, for him, "provide the terrain for elaborating strategies of selfhood—singular or communal—that initiate new signs of identity, and innovative sites of collaboration, and contestation, in the act of defining the idea of society itself."[36]

Bhabha also calls for a radical reimagining of the category of time and the reconceptualization of history. At the boundaries of white, colonial, and male histories, he writes, are a range of other dissonant histories and voices—women, peasants, slaves, minority groups, and the subalterns. He destabilizes the binary construction of the "center" and the "margin," because for him "the boundary becomes the place from which *something begins its presencing*."[37] Thus, history requires a radical revision of social temporality in which emergent histories can be written and histories of different peoples can be seen and analyzed as occupying the same time frame. His arguments are insightful for Anglican studies, as the books on Anglicanism by and large focus on the history of the Church of England and present mostly white, masculine viewpoints. This book is an exercise of imagination to offer another perspective of the Anglican tradition that speaks to the demographic shift of the Anglican Communion and includes a symphony of many voices from different parts of the world.

Although most of the well-known postcolonial theorists are male, Indian critic Gayatri Chakravorty Spivak distinguishes herself by her sophisticated analyses, combining poststructuralist theory, Marxist criticism, and feminist analysis. Her most important contribution to the postcolonial discourse is her controversial essay "Can the Subaltern Speak?"[38] She refers to the debate surrounding *sati*, the custom of Indian widows immolating themselves after their husband's death. She says while the Hindu traditionalists sought to defend the custom and missionaries and colonial officials denounced it, the widows could not speak for themselves, except by their dead bodies. She argues that female subalterns, who are oppressed in multiple ways, do not have access to power and representation, and thus cannot speak. Furthermore, if the subaltern could speak, she would no longer be a subaltern. The essay created a storm, as her critics accused her of constructing the native, both male and female, as a historically muted subject. Others surmised that Spivak is not able to hear the subalterns because of her elitist position. In response to her critics, Spivak says the more important question is not "Who can speak?" but "Who will listen?" For even if the subaltern speaks, her voice will not be heard by the elites, both in the Global North and Global South. The key issue, therefore, is creating the social conditions and infrastructures so that the subalterns can speak.[39]

Spivak's question, "Can the subaltern speak?," serves as a constant reminder to pay attention to the missing voices in the study of the Anglican tradition. Far too often, we have only paid attention to the voices of male bishops, clergy, and theologians, as if they speak for the whole Anglican tradition. To enlarge our historical and theological imagination, we need to listen to voices that are left out and not so often heard. Spivak also criticizes the dominance of white women's voices in feminism and the construction of white female subjectivity. In her widely read essay, "Three Women's Texts and a Critique of Imperialism," she discusses the British imperial context in Charlotte Brontë's novel *Jane Eyre*. The novel was set in nineteenth-century England when England colonized the West Indies and profited from the plantations. Spivak asks the readers to consider the kind of subjectivity Brontë created for Jane Eyre and Bertha Mason, the madwoman in the attic who came from the West Indies. While white feminist critics have rushed to reclaim the subjectivity of the protagonist Jane Eyre, Spivak questions why they have conveniently forgotten the imperialist impulse that set the stage for the story.[40] Within the Anglican tradition, we need to pay attention to how gender intersects with imperialism and how women of the Global South have been portrayed, neglected, or completely left out of our memory.

Although postcolonial theory has significantly impacted the humanities and social sciences and has been introduced to biblical studies and theology since the mid-1990s, it has not influenced much of the study of the Anglican tradition. People in the pews have hardly heard their pastors talk about the roles Anglicanism has played in colonialism. Most of the books on the Anglican tradition have not placed colonial history at the center of inquiry or seriously engaged with postcolonial thought. In the following, I want to argue why it is important to examine the Anglican tradition from a postcolonial perspective to set the stage for the discussion in the book.

Postcolonial Thought and the Anglican Tradition

Postcolonial thought is indispensable for the study of the Anglican tradition because the Anglican Communion was formed as a result of the expansion of the British Empire and mission work in the colonies. Beginning in the seventeenth century, Anglican churches were established in the settler colonies in what would later become the United States, Canada, Australia, Aotearoa New Zealand, and South Africa. By the mid-1860s, a number of overseas Anglican dioceses were effectively independent of the

Church of England, having their own patterns of government and discipline and procedures for electing bishops. Controversy over the position of churches in the colonies led the Canadian bishops to request Archbishop of Canterbury Charles Longley to convene a meeting of all the bishops of Anglican churches, both at home and abroad. Lambeth 1867 has often been cited as the official beginning of the Anglican Communion. Of the 76 bishops gathered at Lambeth Palace, many shared very similar backgrounds, as the colonial bishops and the English bishops had mostly been educated at Oxford or Cambridge.[41]

The idea of an Anglican Communion slowly took root and was popularized in the first half of the twentieth century. After World War II, the diversity within the Communion was heightened when many African and Asian countries became independent and struggled to reclaim their cultural roots and autonomy. Lambeth 1948 endorsed the United Nations' proposed Covenant on Human Rights and declared that these rights belong to all men (sic) irrespective of race and color.[42] The Conference also discussed the relationship between the church and the modern state.

As Anglican churches in the Global South have enjoyed growth and vitality in the past decades, the global breadth of the Communion was shown at Lambeth 1998, the last Lambeth conference before a sizeable number of bishops boycotted subsequent Lambeth conferences over the issue of homosexuality. Lambeth 1998 was attended by nearly 750 bishops, including 224 from Africa, 177 from the United States and Canada, 139 from the United Kingdom and Europe, 95 from Asia, 56 from Australia, 41 from Central and South America, and 4 from the Middle East.[43] The voices of bishops and leaders from the Global South could no longer be ignored, and they have significantly impacted the discussion on the identity, mission, and authority in the Communion. The changes in Communion have prompted scholars to reflect on the colonial legacy of Anglican churches and dream of a postcolonial future, as evident in the volume *Beyond Colonial Anglicanism*.[44] A growing number of anthologies have been published, featuring contributors from diverse cultures, regions, and backgrounds in the Communion.[45]

The controversies and schisms over gender, sexuality, and authority reflect the challenges of a former colonial church seeking to become a postcolonial and multicultural Communion. The so-called bonds of affection within the Anglican Communion have been put to the test as more and more bishops do not share the English heritage and have different opinions about the Bible and tradition. Some of the vocal Southern bishops have questioned the primacy of the archbishop of Canterbury, who functions as the symbolic head but has no jurisdiction over other provinces. Lambeth no longer serves as a symbol of unity where bishops meet, but as a reminder of division. The conservative bishops who boycotted Lambeth 2008 gathered with other Anglican clergy and lay leaders at the Global Anglican Future Conference (GAFCON) in Jerusalem and formed the Fellowship of Confessing Anglicans. GAFCON has chosen to meet in Jerusalem, Nairobi, Dubai, and Kigali, Rwanda, signifying a shift of gravity away from Lambeth and London. The gatherings of Anglicans in the Global South led to the formation of the Global South Fellowship of Anglican Churches, which emphasizes biblical authority and conversative views on gender and sexuality.

Postcolonial theory illuminates the controversy on human sexuality that is ripping the Anglican Communion apart, showing how race, gender, and sexuality intersect in colonial discourse. The debate on sexuality has its roots in the discussion of polygamy in the nineteenth century. As I will discuss in chapter 5, some of the missionaries in Africa and Asia regarded polygamy as incompatible with Christianity and considered it a symptom of the inferiority of the cultures of the darker races. They taught that monogamous marriagc is thc only acceptable Christian way. Many Christians in the Global South, including their leaders, have accepted monogamous marriage between a man and a woman as synonymous with modernization and Christian custom. While their cultures are generally more inclusive of diverse sexual practices, they have learned from the colonial masters and missionaries a much narrower view of sexual propriety and acceptable codes of conduct. Thus, some African and Asian bishops consider homosexuality abominable, to be deplored because of what they have learned and internalized as the teachings of the Bible and tradition. For them, the table has been turned this time, as they want to "retain and restore the Bible to the heart of the Anglican Communion,"[46] while it is the sexual morality of the West that is under attack and scrutiny.

The clash of opinions over homosexuality is but one example of the larger culture wars in global politics today, as is evident in the discussions of human rights, ethnic cleansing, external and internal migration, religious identity, and women's rights. How can we avoid reinscribing the cultural superiority of the West on the one hand and uncritical acceptance of biblical literalism and cultural authenticity of formerly colonized peoples on the other? How can we promote genuine dialogue and mutual understanding that both learn from and go beyond the colonial past, which for some is just a generation or two away?

The debates over homosexuality and other matters touch on fundamental issues such as the crisis of Anglican identity, the relationship between the local and the global (the Communion), the nature of authority, the variety of views of biblical interpretation, and ecumenical relations with other churches. There are three major approaches to maintaining unity among member churches, as Norman Doe, a legal scholar and consultant of canon law, has pointed out.[47] The first is the institutional instruments of unity, which include the archbishop of Canterbury, Lambeth Conference, Anglican Consultative Council, and Primates' Meeting. But since these instruments enjoy moral authority but not coercive jurisdiction, they have not been able to bring unity amid the controversies. The second is the canonical instruments of unity. Each province of the Communion has a constitution, canon laws, rules, decrees, regulations, and codes of practice. The primates recognized that there is an unwritten law common to the churches in the Anglican Communion expressed in the shared principles of canon laws in member churches. However, there is no global canon law that serves as a binding legal system for the Communion. The third is the covenant as an instrument of unity. An Anglican Communion Covenant, first suggested by the Windsor Report of 2004, was drafted and finalized in 2009. It was circulated among the churches in the Communion for ratification or rejection according to each church's formal processes. The Covenant calls upon the church to live together in mutual care and affection and to be in communion in witness and mission. However, the Covenant did not succeed in bringing about unity, as the Church of England, the Episcopal Church, and other churches rejected it.

Since institutional, canonical, and covenantal instruments cannot bring about unity and resolve conflicts, I suggest looking at the Anglican tradition anew to find resources to live together as a family of churches across racial, cultural, linguistic, and regional differences. The church needs to outgrow its Anglo-Saxon captivity to imagine new patterns of interdependence. To accomplish this, postcolonial theory can help us look at our colonial history with courage and honesty, and only by wrestling with and learning from our past can we envision a new future together. Postcolonial theory's reading of culture and history and concepts such as hybridity, in-between spaces, fluid identity, and subaltern speech can offer analytical tools to point to the way forward.

The strength of Anglicanism lies in its respect for the Bible, accountability to tradition, the honor of reason, and the consideration of human experiences. Each of these constitutive elements must be brought into play and interpreted through diverse experiences when we want to articulate Anglican theology and moral vision. However, the components of these four categories—scripture, tradition, reason, and experience—have been defined in the past through the lens of Western culture alone. Today, they must be subject to postcolonial scrutiny and amplified by the cultural resources from many parts of the Communion. For example, postcolonial interpretation of the Bible helps us to lift up neglected voices in the Bible and pay attention to the racial and cultural politics in biblical times.[48] Furthermore, "tradition" must not be a coded term for the tradition of the Church of England but must include the various traditions in the Communion formed by the interaction of Anglican churches with local cultures. In order to become a hope for the future, the Anglican Communion must value different styles of reasoning and configurations of human experiences.

About This Volume

This book is based on many years of conversations with faculty colleagues and students at the schools that I have taught and other scholars in the Anglican Communion. It is divided into seven chapters; each chapter is like a piece of the mosaic contributing to the whole. After this introductory chapter, chapter 2 presents an overarching argument for decolonizing Anglican churches. It discusses the relationship between Anglicanism and colonial imagination since the turn of the eighteenth century. But the rich and diverse Anglican tradition also possesses seeds to challenge colonial expansion, the rationale for the development of autonomous churches, and arguments for raising local church leaders and workers. The chapter argues that the decolonization of Anglican churches requires a theological imagination that challenges the legacy of English cultural hegemony, confronts the legacy of slavery and racism, and reimagines authority and leadership in the Anglican tradition beyond a clerical, hierarchical, and patriarchal model.

Colonialism is based on unequal social, economic, and political relations. Chapter 3 discusses Anglicanism and the global order, examining the theological justifications for and against colonialism in the past and the formation of empire in the present. Although theologians such as Frederick Dennison Maurice (1805–1872) had criticized social inequity in nineteenth-century England, he and many others during his time viewed colonialism as benevolent, bringing civilization to the "heathens." In 1942, Archbishop William Temple (1881–1944) articulated his vision for the church, state, and society in his important work *Christianity and the Social Order*.[49] This chapter expands on his thought and scrutinizes Anglican social teachings on economic justice and discusses the church's support for debt relief and the Millennium Development Goals. It also introduces theologians and church leaders who have shone a spotlight on the ways the neoliberal economy has contributed to the ecological crisis and proposed ways to address it.

As Anglican churches do not have a common confession or a set of doctrines acceptable by all, their liturgy and the BCP, in particular, have served as a unifying factor for the Communion. But the development of the BCP has been closely tied to English national identity. As the colonies sought independence, there was the need to revise the Prayer Book to adapt to local contexts. Chapter 4 presents postcolonial scrutiny of the liturgy of Anglican churches and the politics of revising the BCP in Aotearoa New Zealand, Kenya, and Brazil. Since *lex orandi, lex credendi* (the law of prayer is the law of belief) is widely held in Anglican churches, it is necessary to reimagine our worship, music, and the use of sacred space so that they are contextual and rooted in the lives of the communities.

Chapter 5 discusses the heated debates on human sexuality in the Anglican Communion, which can be traced back to the first Lambeth Conference in 1867. John Colenso was the first bishop of Natal in South Africa. His controversial position on polygamy and Zulu culture was one of the reasons that the first Lambeth was called. For over a hundred years, the Anglican Communion continued its vigorous debates about whether polygamists could be accepted into the church. In the past several decades, the issue of homosexuality threatened to divide the Anglican Communion. Taking into consideration race, gender, and sexuality, I will explain the globalization of culture wars in the United States and why sexuality, often taken as a marker of cultural and religious differences, remains a contentious issue. The chapter includes the voices of women and laypeople, who are often left out of the debates and news coverage.

Chapter 6 focuses on the leadership and ministries of Anglican women from the Global South, since their history has often been overlooked in the studies about the Anglican tradition. This chapter highlights their contribution to Christian missions as evangelists and leaders adapting the Christian message to their local situations and building spiritual communities. They joined and later transformed the Mothers' Unions to meet their local needs. Some of them take part and exercise leadership in women's organizations, which connect them with other women in the Anglican Communion. The ordination of Li Tim-Oi paved the way for women's ordination and changed the male image of Anglican priesthood. While some former colonies had already begun to ordain women, the Church of England lagged far behind and did not approve women's ordination until 1992. But ordained ministry is only one form of women's leadership, as many laywomen serve in different capacities in the church and participate in the fight against gender-based violence and the HIV/AIDS pandemic.

As the Anglican Communion was formed as a result of the success of the missionary movement, chapter 7 examines the understanding of Anglican mission in different historical periods and articulates postcolonial visions for mission by engaging the works of Cathy Ross, Christopher Duraisingh, Julio E. Murray, and many others. Converting "heathens" used to be seen as part of the civilizing mission and the white men's burden. In our religiously pluralistic world, Anglican theologians have argued for interreligious dialogue and solidarity, which are indispensable to Christian mission. Since religious persecution and intolerance have exacerbated conflict, violence, and bloodshed in many parts of the world, I will discuss the church's possible roles in peacebuilding as well as the church's responsibilities toward migrants, refugees, and asylum seekers.

The epilogue builds on the argument that has been laid out in the book to envision the future for Anglicanism that is postcolonial, polycentric, and pluralistic. This postcolonial church respects differences and is based on partnership in God's mission, mutuality, and interdependence. It understands authority to be dispersed rather than centralized, relational rather than hierarchical, and participatory rather than concentrating power in the bishops and church leaders. It anticipates an emerging Anglican ecclesiology that is creative, inclusive, and not afraid of conflict.

In the twenty-first century, the Anglican Communion must determine whether it will be a relic of the colonial past or a bridge to the postcolonial future. It must develop an understanding of the church grounded in our baptismal covenant and values the contributions of women, youth, people of darker skin color, racial and sexual minorities, and indigenous and marginalized groups. The Communion has to reexamine its old model of church-state, in which the church relies on the support of the colonial masters or the power-grabbing national elites and move toward a church that exists for Christian mission in the midst of the world's vulnerable and suffering people. It must resist the temptation to turn the Communion into a huge, bureaucratic corporation, but rather strive to be a polycentric and multicultural communion of churches. Last but not least, it must promote renewal in theological education for lay and ordained ministry, so that a new generation of leaders can be formed as global citizens with a deepened understanding of the legacy of the Anglican colonial past and the global mandate for the church at the present. The Anglican Communion will have a bright future if our leaders have a broad historical vision, cultural sensitivity, and humility to work with people with diverse points of view and faith traditions.

Notes

1. Its former name was Church Missionary Society.
2. "Member Churches," Anglican Communion, https://www.anglicancommunion.org/structures/member-churches.aspx.
3. Todd M. Johnson and Gina A. Gurlo, "The Changing Demographics of Global Anglicanism, 1970–2010," in *Growth and Decline in the Anglican Communion: 1980 to the Present*, ed. David Goodhew (New York: Routledge, 2017), 37.
4. Andrew McKinnon and Christopher Craig Brittain, "Anglicans in a Globalizing World: The Contradictions of Communion," in *Contemporary Issues in the Worldwide Anglican Communion*, ed. Abby Day (Surrey, England: Ashgate, 2016), 116.
5. Todd M. Johnson and Gina A. Gurlo, eds., *World Christian Database* (Leiden: Brill, accessed January 2020), https://www.worldchristiandatabase.org/.
6. Andrew Walls, *The Significance of African Christianity* (Edinburgh: St. Colm's Education Center and College, 1989), 3.
7. Center for the Study of Global Christianity at Gordon-Conwell Theological Seminary, "Study of Global Christianity, 2021, in the Context of 1900–2050," Gordon-Conwell Theological Seminary, December 2020, https://www.gordonconwell.edu/center-for-global-christianity/wp-content/uploads/sites/13/2020/12/Status-of-Global-Christianity-2021.pdf.
8. Cathy Ross, "Credo: The Average Anglican Is a Black, Female Teenager," *The Sunday Times*, July 19, 2008, https://www.thetimes.co.uk/article/credo-the-average-anglican-is-a-black-female-teenager-79lfhbxggdh.
9. Bruce Kaye, *An Introduction to World Anglicanism* (Cambridge: Cambridge University Press, 2008), 3.
10. Robert S. Heaney and William L. Sachs, *The Promise of Anglicanism* (London: SCM, 2019), xx–xxi.
11. Heaney and Sachs, *Promise of Anglicanism*, xxi.
12. Kevin Ward, *A History of Global Anglicanism* (Cambridge: Cambridge University Press, 2006), and Kaye, *Introduction to World Anglicanism*.
13. Edward Jarvis, *The Anglican Church in Burma: From Colonial Past to Global Future* (University Park: Pennsylvania State University Press, 2021); Philip Wickeri, ed., *Christian Encounters*

with Chinese Culture: Essays on Anglican and Episcopal History in China (Hong Kong: Hong Kong University Press, 2015); Edward Jarvis, *The Anglican Church in Malaysia: Evolving Concepts, Challenging Contexts, Emerging Subtexts* (Cham, Switzerland: Palgrave Macmillan, 2022); Akinyele Omoyajowo, ed., *The Anglican Church in Nigeria (1842–1992)* (Lagos, Nigeria: Macmillan Nigeria Publishers, 1994); Jehu Hanciles, *Euthanasia of a Mission: African Church Community in a Colonial Context* (Westport, CT: Praeger, 2002); Jesse A. Zink, *Christianity and Catastrophe in South Sudan: Civil War, Migration, and the Rise of Dinka Anglicanism* (Waco, TX: Baylor University Press, 2018); Pamela Welch, *Church and Settler in Colonial Zimbabwe: A Study in the History of the Diocese of Mashonaland/Southern Rhodesia, 1890–1925* (Leiden: Brill, 2008); Brian H. Fletcher, *The Place of Anglicanism in Australia: Church, Society, Nation* (Mulgrave, Australia: Broughton Publishing, 2008); and Hirini Kaa, *Te Hāhi Mihinare: the Māori Anglican Church* (Wellington, New Zealand: Bridget Williams Books, 2020).

14. "Anti-Racism Taskforce," The Church of England, https://www.churchofengland.org/about/policy-and-thinking/our-views/anti-racism-taskforce.

15. Egan Millard, "Presiding Bishop Announces New Churchwide Racial Truth and Reconciliation Effort during the First Day of Executive Council," Episcopal News Service, June 25, 2021, https://www.episcopalnewsservice.org/2021/06/25/presiding-bishop-announces-new-trans churchwide-racial-truth-and-reconciliation-effort-during-first-day-of-executive-council/.

16. The project has a YouTube channel, "Being Anglican: Learning from Global Perspectives," https://www.youtube.com/channel/UC-Xb_sdp8Y9guqo72m1-qhg, as well as a guidebook, https://www.anglicancommunion.org/media/465802/TEAC_Being-Anglican-Learning-from-Global-Perspectives_WEB_2022_en.pdf.

17. Kwok Pui-lan, *Postcolonial Imagination and Feminist Theology* (Louisville, KY: Westminster John Knox Press, 2005), 2–3.

18. Achille Mbembe, *Out of the Dark Night: Essays on Decolonization* (New York: Columbia University Press, 2021), 67–71.

19. Edward W. Said, *Orientalism* (New York: Vintage Books, 1979).

20. See Olivia U. Rutazibwa and Robbie Shilliam, eds., *Routledge Handbook of Postcolonial Politics* (New York: Routledge, 2018).

21. Edward W. Said, *Out of Place: A Memoir* (New York: Alfred A. Knopf, 1999), 7, 22.

22. Said, *Orientalism*, 7.

23. Said, *Orientalism*, 6–7.

24. Samuel P. Huntington, *The Clash of Civilizations and the Remaking of World Order* (New York: Simon & Schuster, 1996), 51, 91.

25. Cited in Mark Chapman, *Anglicanism: A Very Short Introduction* (Oxford: Oxford University Press, 2006), 11.

26. Stuart Hall, "The West and the Rest: Discourse and Power," in *Formations of Modernity*, ed. Stuart Hall and Bram Gieben (Cambridge: Polity Press, 1992), 318.

27. Stuart Hall, "When Was 'the Postcolonial'? Thinking at the Limit," in *The Postcolonial Question: Common Skies, Divided Horizon*, ed. Iain Chambers and Lidia Curti (New York: Routledge, 1996), 247.

28. Stuart Hall, "Gramsci's Relevance for the Study of Race and Ethnicity," in *Critical Dialogues in Cultural Studies*, ed. David Morley and Kuan-Hsing Chen (London: Routledge, 1996), 435–40.

29. Stuart Hall, "New Ethnicities," in Morley and Chen, *Critical Dialogues in Cultural Studies*, 442.
30. In this book, I use the words "indigenous" and "native" in lowercase when referring to indigenous or local people in general and capitalize "Indigenous" and "Native" when referring to the Indigenous peoples of North America.
31. Homi K. Bhabha, *The Location of Culture* (London: Routledge, 1994).
32. See the discussion of Bhabha in Bart Moore-Gilbert, *Postcolonial Theory: Contexts, Practices, Politics* (London: Verso, 1997), 117.
33. Bhabha, *Location of Culture*, 88.
34. Jonathan Rutherford, "The Third Space: Interview with Homi Bhabha," in *Identity: Community, Culture, Difference*, ed. Jonathan Rutherford (London: Lawrence & Wishart, 1990), 211.
35. Bhabha, *Location of Culture*, 193.
36. Bhabha, *Location of Culture*, 1–2.
37. Bhabha, *Location of Culture*, 5. Emphasis in original.
38. Gayatri Chakravorty Spivak, "Can the Subaltern Speak?," in *Marxism and the Interpretation of Culture*, ed. Cary Nelson and Lawrence Grossberg (Urbana: University of Illinois Press, 1988), 271–313.
39. See Gayatri Chakravorty Spivak, "Subaltern Talk: Interview with the Editors," in *The Spivak Reader*, ed. Donna Landry and Gerald MacLean (New York: Routledge, 1966), 287–308; also her *A Critique of Postcolonial Reason: Toward a History of the Vanishing Present* (Cambridge, MA: Harvard University Press, 1999), 308–11.
40. Gayatri Chakravorty Spivak, "Three Women's Texts and a Critique of Imperialism," *Critical Inquiry* 12, no. 1 (1985): 244–47.
41. W. M. Jacob, *The Making of the Anglican Church Worldwide* (London: SPCK, 1997), 151–69.
42. Lambeth Conference 1948, Resolutions 7 and 8, Anglican Communion, https://www.anglicancommunion.org/media/127737/1948.pdf.
43. Miranda K. Hassett, *Anglican Communion in Crisis: How Episcopal Dissidents and Their African Allies Are Reshaping Anglicanism* (Princeton, NJ: Princeton University Press, 2007), 71.
44. Ian T. Douglas and Kwok Pui-lan, eds., *Beyond Colonial Anglicanism: The Anglican Communion in the Twenty-First Century* (New York: Church Publishing, 2001).
45. For example, Andrew Wingate, Kevin Ward, Carrie Pemberton, and Wilson Sitshebo, eds., *Anglicanism: A Global Communion* (London: Mowbray, 1998); Kwok Pui-lan, Judith A. Berling, and Jenny Plane Te Paa, eds., *Anglican Women on Church and Mission* (New York: Morehouse Publishing, 2012); and Muthuraj Swamy and Stephen Spencer, eds., *Witnessing Together: Global Anglican Perspectives on Evangelism and Witness* (London: Anglican Communion Office, 2019).
46. "About GAFCON," GAFCON: Global Anglicans, https://www.gafcon.org/about.
47. Norman Doe, "The Instruments of Unity and Communion in Global Anglicanism," in *Wiley-Blackwell Companion to the Anglican Communion*, ed. Ian S. Markham et al. (Malden, MA: Wiley Blackwell, 2013), 47–66.
48. See R. S. Sugirtharajah, ed., *The Postcolonial Bible* (Sheffield: Sheffield Academic Press, 1998); and Laura E. Donaldson, ed., "Postcolonialism and Scriptural Reading," *Semeia* 75 (1996): 1–240.
49. William Temple, *Christianity and the Social Order* (1942; repr., New York: Seabury, 1976).

CHAPTER

2

Decolonizing the Anglican Churches

In **1534, Henry VIII** became the "supreme head of the Church of England" after the English Parliament passed the Act of Supremacy. The king had wanted to have a male heir and sought an annulment from Katherine of Aragon so that he could marry Anne Boleyn. When Pope Clement VII refused to grant his wish and prohibited him from remarrying under the penalty of excommunication, Henry VIII thought that his authority, both temporal and spiritual, was usurped by the Roman pontiff. He insisted that he had authority over the Church and that the clergy were his subjects and should not submit to Rome. He argued that the pope had no authority outside his province and over other bishops and the English Church had no obligations to accept a foreign authority.

Since the Church of England separated from Rome to become a state church, it became closely connected with the national identity. Coronations took place at Westminster Abby, the archbishops of Canterbury were selected by the Crown, and the liturgy included prayers for the monarch. When the British Empire expanded, this national identity had an imperial dimension, as Britain competed with other countries for overseas territories and sought to strengthen her connections with the colonies. In the sixteenth and early seventeenth centuries, while English traders, voyagers, and geographers had expressed interest in foreign lands, the acquisition of overseas territories and missions were not primary concerns because these would require long-term commitment and effort. During this period, there was no clear Protestant theory supporting empire, as the English Church was embroiled in the conflicts between Protestants and Catholics and in other doctrinal controversies, as well as political upheavals.[1]

Beginning in the eighteenth century, religion began to play a critical role in the formation of imperial identity as colonial expansion also brought religious expansion into foreign lands. In 1701, a royal charter inaugurated the Society for the Propagation of the Gospel in Foreign Parts (SPG), charged with bringing the gospel to the newly acquired overseas colonies.[2] Three years earlier, the Society for the Promotion of Christian Knowledge (SPCK) was formed to dispense Bibles and tracts of religion in England and other parts of the world. These societies changed the relationship between Anglicanism, mission, and empire. After the religious awakening in the mid-eighteenth century, evangelical fervor brought growing support for missionary zeal. The CMS was formed in 1799 to establish missions in Africa and the East. Within the same decade, the Baptist Missionary Society was formed in 1792 and the interdenominational evangelistic London Missionary Society in 1795. The nineteenth century was called the great century of mission, and at the same time, there was a dramatic expansion of the British Empire, such that people claimed the sun never set on the empire. Missionaries were sent to convert the "heathens," as well as to propagate the English or British way of life. Some of the Anglican church leaders and missionaries provided religious justification for colonialism based on their faith and beliefs. With a sense of cultural and religious superiority, they saw the British Empire as benevolent and instrumental in spreading the gospel and civilization.

This chapter begins by teasing out how Anglican leaders and missionaries fueled the colonial imagination through their interpretation of the Bible, history, and theology. But as postcolonial theorists have taught us, colonialism has never been a totalizing process since there are ways and possibilities to subvert empire. Within the Anglican tradition, some people challenged imperial aggression, arguing that colonialism was unjust and contradictory to the gospel. The decolonization of Anglican churches began when colonial churches asserted their authority to become autonomous churches and have the right to decide their own affairs. This chapter argues for a decolonial ecclesiology as the Church evolved from the established Church of England to become a global Anglican Communion. This ecclesiology requires a theological imagination that challenges the legacy of English cultural hegemony, debunks the ideologies undergirding slavery and global racism, and reimagines authority and leadership beyond a clerical, hierarchical, and patriarchal understanding.

Anglicanism and the Colonial Imagination

As Edward Said has argued, colonialism involves not only a contest of political and military power, but also the development of culture, media, knowledge, and ideology that shape people's worldviews and values. In *Orientalism*, he charged that it was the Christian "West" that has relentlessly constructed and promulgated negative images of the "Orient" for the sake of domination.[3] Christianity had played indispensable roles in the development of modern European colonialism, such that commerce, Christianity, colonialism, and conquest often went hand-in-hand. Beginning in the fifteenth century, the Catholic Church granted religious sanction to the Spanish and Portuguese monarchs for the colonization of the Americas and the enslavement of African peoples.[4] In subsequent centuries, different Protestant denominations had become complicit at various times with empire-building, racism, slavery, and colonialism. As the British Empire expanded to become the largest empire the world has ever known, did the Church of England contribute to fueling the colonial imagination, given its preeminent status in English society?

In the past, scholars who have studied British imperial history have usually taken a secular approach, attributing empire-building to the results of capitalist expansion and other sociological and structural factors.[5] But other historians, such as Rowan Strong and Andrew Porter, have provided in-depth studies on the complex and multifaceted ways Christianity had connected with the British Empire. Anglican church leaders and missionaries, through their sermons, speeches, reports, publications, missionary journals, and fundraising appeals, contributed to shaping a social imaginary that was favorable to empire formation. Philosopher Charles Taylor defines social imaginary as "that common understanding that makes possible common practices and a wide sense of legitimacy."[6] Colonial expansion required political and military campaigns, and religious sanctions provided legitimacy and moral persuasion for the populace. Anglican leaders' religious rhetoric in support of empire-building became part of colonial discourse. American theologian Reinhold Niebuhr said empires need gods to give them an aura of ultimacy and universality.[7] In the British case, Andrew Porter observes, "It is true that dogma, faith, and intentions, however passionate, have rarely by themselves dictated the outcomes of British expansion, but that expansion's spiritual and ethical inspiration was real enough."[8] Even if Anglican bishops, church leaders, and theologians might not represent the opinions of the whole church, their voices mattered because, by virtue of their positions, they could sway public opinions and influence a substantial portion of the British people.

Many Anglicans in the eighteenth and nineteenth centuries viewed the expansion of the British Empire in favorable terms because they thought God had chosen their country for a special mission. They believed in God's providential action in the world and that the English people were especially blessed because of their religion and culture. The Church of England, for them, represented the pristine form of Christianity because it had overcome the excesses of the Catholic Church and the heresies of the Continental Reformation. The Church provided a binding spiritual and moral force for the nation, and the church and state were united for a higher purpose. However, the constitutional revolution of 1828–1832, which allowed the Nonconformists and Catholics to sit in Parliament, undermined the old alliance between the church and state and challenged Anglican political hegemony. As a response, a group called the Tractarians—after the *Tracts for the Times* they published to share their views—argued that the Church of England had a privileged status because it was the legitimate successor to the primitive church. As the true Catholic Church of England, it stood in continuity with the teachings of the church fathers and the bishops. Rather than being subservient to Parliament, it should be the final authority, beyond the instrument of the state, in all matters of spiritual import.[9] As the political authority and influences of the Church of England were weakened, the expansion of the empire provided a renewed sense of purpose and a social and political framework for the Church to carry out its wider mission in the world.[10] Historian Edward Jarvis writes, "An ordered society, both within the Church and in the world at large, was the ideal of High Church Anglicans. They revered the bishop and the monarch and wished to see Western Christian civilization extended throughout the world. This was at the heart of their understanding of colonial expansion, and it was a perception that sat in harmony with the political understanding of colonialism as well."[11] Philip Shuttleworth, warden of New College at Oxford and later the bishop of Chichester, preached in 1840 that Britons should be awakened to their divine responsibility because "this country has been specially selected, and endowed by Providence, as an instrument for suffusing knowledge and civilisation and social happiness throughout the world."[12]

With the confidence in the superiority of Christianity and their culture, both English and colonial Anglicans created a binary between "us" and "them," treating non-Christians as ignorant and pitiful "heathens." Since the encounter with Native peoples in North American colonies, Anglican missionaries saw the heathens as living in darkness, illiteracy, and idolatry, and subject to eternal damnation. If Christians worshipped the true God incarnate in Jesus Christ, the eternally perishing heathens were under the dominion of Satan.[13] Rowan Strong writes that the heathens, seen as "enslaved by the supernatural enemy of God, were the ultimate theological Other for these Anglicans."[14] The otherness of these heathens was reinforced by the perceived superiority of the white race. Anglicans saw that they had the God-given responsibility to rescue their souls by bringing them into the Christian fold and teaching them English civilization. The evangelicals among them emphasized the confession of sin and personal salvation through Jesus Christ. The Great Commission to make disciples in all nations (Matt. 28:19) assumed new significance for many Christians. By the late nineteenth century, there was an urgency to do so because of their millennial beliefs in the second coming of the Lord. As the "great century" of missions moved into the high imperial era of the 1880s to World War I, racism, colonialism, and missions twisted together. Anglicans assumed that white people had the mandate of saving people of black or "dusty" hues (referring to the Indians), who were less developed. This was what Rudyard Kipling called "the white man's burden," in his poem originally written for the celebration of the Diamond Jubilee of Queen Victoria in 1897.

Gayatri Chakravorty Spivak has insightfully pointed out that the concept of a white man's burden has a gender dimension. Using her Indian context as an example, she formulated the masculinist-imperialistic formation as "white men saving brown women from brown men."[15] Missionaries condemned the practices of polygamy, footbinding, *sati*, veiling, and the segregation of the sexes in the colonies. Missionary literature contrasted the ignorance, backwardness, and filthiness of native women with the ideals of Christian womanhood, such as piety, purity, and domesticity, from the earliest missions to Burma and Hawai'i.[16] Using the pretext of saving brown women, colonial desire and expansion had been masked and reconstituted in a blatant reversal as a civilizing mission. As native women were hard to reach by men, CMS and other mission societies sent female missionaries to evangelize women, open schools, and teach social hygiene. Although these female missionaries did not share full equality with men at home, once in the colonies, they enjoyed authority and privilege because of their race and social status. Some of their work, such as opening schools for girls, provided greater opportunities for native women. Yet for many years, they seldom reflected on how mission work might have been complicit with the imperialistic agenda. The kind of evangelical domesticity that they introduced, focusing as it did on women's roles at home, did not meet the needs of the colonies at a time when more fundamental social reforms were necessary.

Since many Anglicans believed that they were chosen to evangelize and civilize the whole world, they embraced empire as an instrument for proselytism. Just as in the first century, the Roman Empire because of its roads, means of transport, commerce, and law and order had facilitated evangelism in the Mediterranean world, in the modern period, the British Empire was destined to fulfill similar functions so that the gospel could reach even more territories. Charles Longley, bishop of Ripon who would later become the archbishop of Canterbury in 1862, said that this meant enormous responsibilities for the nation and the British people because God had ordained that a vast portion of the world be brought under the rule of one nation, "in order that his word may have the freer course, and reach the ends of the earth through those numberless channels which our commerce and enterprise are ever opening to us."[17]

The belief in God's providential blessings of the British Empire was shared not only by people at home but also by white Anglican leaders of colonial churches. For example, Daniel Wilson, the evangelical bishop of Calcutta and Metropolitan of India, wrote in 1849 that God had spared Britain from the successive waves of revolution since the French Revolution and the political upheavals of 1848, such that the nation could vastly expand in the past sixty years. He said the country had been "raised during this very period to the possession of the most wonderful empire, and the widest influence which the world has ever seen, either in ancient or modern times."[18] He surmised that Britain had been given possession of India and colonies all over the world so that the immense blessings of the gospel could be communicated to the indigenous populations. The Church of England could help consolidate the empire in India, because through its ministry, "the Native population would be permanently gained over to our Empire; and . . . we should have intelligent, attached and obedient Christian subjects."[19] He made it clear that the Church could serve as the empire's handmaiden to inculcate compliant and dutiful colonial subjects.

Politicians and colonial officials also employed religious rhetoric to justify the doings of the government and its imperialistic outlook. For example, the colonial secretary, the third Earl Grey, justified colonial rule over overseas territories by appealing to religious providence. He publicly stated in 1853: "The authority of the British Crown is at this moment the most powerful instrument, under Providence, of maintaining peace and order in many extensive regions of the earth, and thereby assists in diffusing among millions of the human race, the blessing of Christianity and civilisation."[20] The English East India Company had forbidden missionary work for fear that Christian missions would damage trading relationships with the colony. The policy later changed, and the chairman of the East India Company at the time of the Indian mutiny in 1857 saw that divine providence had given the vast empire of India to the hands of the British such that its inhabitants would be converted to Christianity in due course.[21] Some of the colonial government officials who belonged to the evangelical wing of the church lent support to Christian churches in carrying out their mission. Others believed that churches could assist local governments in providing education and social services for the local populace. As part of the established Church of England, the churches carried prestige and amassed social capital in the colonies, and even in areas where the British Empire was not formally established, Anglican missionaries brought bishops and churches.

The expansion of the British Empire and the pervasive colonial ethos formed the backdrop for Anglican theology and biblical interpretation in the nineteenth century. As I will discuss in the next chapter, a group of Christian Socialists, led by Frederick Denison Maurice and John Malcolm Ludlow (1821–1911), denounced social inequity and the rich's exploitation of the poor. They embraced progressive social values based on God's inclusive love for all and the universality of the Kingdom of Christ. They preached the brotherhood of all men and hoped to combine Christianity with socialist ideals to work for the improvement of the social conditions of the poor, workers' rights, and education for workers and their children. Despite their progressive social teachings and activism at home, some of the early generation of Christian Socialists embraced empire and the opportunities it provided. They did not connect concerns for the poor in London with exploitation in the British colonies.[22]

John Robert Seeley was a notable historian who defended empire and presented a revisionist account of Jesus's life to justify colonialism. As continental biblical scholars were busy separating dogmas from history in their quest for the historical Jesus, Seeley published the first English book on the life of Jesus entitled *Ecce Homo: A Survey of the Life and Work of Jesus Christ* in 1865. Seeley used the model of the British Empire to describe the Kingdom of God and Jesus's ministry. He focused on Jesus's moral character and described him as a king who was the founder of a theocracy, a new Christian commonwealth. The commonwealth was open to all and through obedience to his teachings, his followers could become the citizens or subjects of the Christian republic.[23] Seeley portrayed Jesus as an enlightened king with royal power, yet he used it with empathy and self-restraint. He did not rule by force but by moral example and benevolence, and his love and self-sacrifice had great appeal to his followers. Similarly, the British did not use force to conquer the colonies, he argued, but ruled over vast territories because of the superiority of the British. He wrote, "In Christ's monarchy no force was used, though all power was at command."[24] Within the Christian commonwealth, Seeley believed that human beings were not equal, and he supported the rule of the father over the child and the husband over the wife. Even as Britain had abolished slavery in 1833, Seeley defended that Christianity had allowed slavery to exist because of its understanding that not everyone could live in a free condition. Seeley would later assume the prestigious position as the Regius Professor of Modern History at Cambridge University and penned the popular and influential book *The Expansion of England* to defend the inevitability of empire and remind readers that the colonies were not mere appendages but an expansion of the British state and British nationality. He displayed Orientalist attitudes and justified the rule over India, arguing that without British rule, the Indians would revert to anarchy and turmoil, as they were incapable of ruling themselves.[25]

The Church of England not only provided religious sanction for empire but also benefited economically, socially, and politically from its collusion with empire. It benefited from Britain's military power, which opened up mission fields in places where people were previously hostile to Christianity. After China was defeated by the British in the Opium War, it was forced to sign an unequal treaty in 1842, which ceded Hong Kong to the British, and the same treaty allowed missionaries to live and work in five coastal cities. Later in the century, Britain's occupation of Egypt in 1882 and its conquest of the Sudan in 1889 opened possibilities for new mission fields in predominantly Islamic lands. Anglican churches in the colonies were enmeshed in the social and political realities defined by unequal positions between the colonizers and the colonized. Colonial Anglicanism enjoyed status and privilege because of its association with the established church. Though the membership of these churches might be small, they had high social standing and often ran the best schools, whose purpose was to train future colonial elites. Anglican missions sought protection from the government during periods of political upheaval and instability. When there were religious and ethnic rivalries, missionaries believed that only a strong colonial rule would offer them security. When mission work faced severe resistance or backlash, they could ask the government for protection and to help open doors. Historian Stuart J. Brown writes, "There was a sense that the empire promoted the spread of Anglicanism, and that Anglicanism elevated the empire with a higher mission."[26]

However, there were also Anglican church leaders and missionaries who criticized imperialism and its devastating impact. Missionaries who lived among the people saw firsthand the injustice and cruelties inflicted upon the people by colonial officials and their policies. Sometimes, their position might be at odds with their government's, which caused difficulties with the local administration. For example, some missionaries in China objected to the opium trade, having witnessed the huge social costs of opium to the people and their families. Missionaries in Africa also spoke out against slavery and the brutality of colonial governments as they reaped plenty from the continent. CMS's first mission was to Sierra Leone, a colony established by Britain for freed slaves. Henry Venn, the influential secretary of CMS from 1841 to 1873, was a staunch supporter of the abolition of the Atlantic slave trade and pressed the government for enlightened colonial policy for Africa by providing more opportunities in education and economic development. He argued that Africans should be trained to take up more responsibility in government and commerce. As a highly respected leader of the evangelical missionary movement, Venn was ahead of his time in foreseeing that a missionary-driven model of mission would be unsustainable. He began to champion the ideal of independent native churches and the revolutionary concept that the "settlement of a native church, under native pastors, upon a self-supporting system" was the ultimate goal of a mission.[27] He developed the three-self principles for the indigenous church—self-supporting, self-governing, and self-propagating.[28] He supported a self-reliant local church with local pastors under a local episcopate. His idea of a native pastorate was first tried out in Sierra

Leone and this experiment represented an early effort at constructing an African Christian identity separate from foreign influence and control. The experiment had mixed results as the missionaries did not fully trust native pastors and give them the support they needed.[29] But his three-self principles stimulated critical reflection when churches in former colonies had to rethink their identity and mission after independence.

By the early twentieth century, the harmful effects of imperialism, including its insidious racism, were more publicized and harder to defend. Some of the Christian Socialists during this time were anti-imperialist and spoke out against racism, the Boer War, and colonialism in India and Africa. Resistance movements against colonial rule mounted as heightened political consciousness developed. In India, Gandhi began to lead a nonviolent and noncooperation campaign against the British, based on the revival of traditional Indian values. Charles Freer Andrews, a SPG missionary and a close friend of Gandhi, expressed sympathy for Indian nationalism and advocated dialogues with Hindus and Buddhists instead of converting them. He worked with Gandhi to protest against the inhumane treatment of Indian indentured laborers in South Africa. He argued that the church should recognize and minister to the poor and speak out against social and moral wrongs. His concrete experience in the colonies and witnessing the resistance movements led him to expand Anglican social thought and apply it internationally.[30] As the wave of decolonization swept across the British Empire, many Anglicans saw the necessity to disentangle the Church from the state and Anglicanism from Englishness so that a global Anglican Communion would become possible.

Challenging Cultural Hegemony

The issue of cultural difference has been present in the Anglican Communion since its inception. The first Lambeth was called in 1867 in part to settle the "Colenso Affair." John Colenso, bishop of Natal in South Africa, was more sympathetic to Zulu culture than his contemporaries and challenged their condescending attitudes toward Africans. He argued that polygamy should not be a barrier to baptism and full membership in the church. Although he did not believe in polygamy, he insisted that all wives should be cared for, otherwise they could become destitute. Other church leaders criticized his position and his use of the historical method to study the Bible, which they saw as undermining the authority and inerrancy of the scripture. Colenso insisted that God is revealed to all humanity and that revelation is not confined to one nation and one set of books. Colenso approached the Bible through wider and comparative lenses and insisted that Christ redeems all people everywhere whether they have heard his name or not.[31] He was tried for heresy by the church and appealed his case to England. The Colenso affair brought into focus questions that would engage the Anglican Communion for many years to come, such as the relationship between gospel and culture, diversity in biblical interpretation, the nature of the Church, and relations in the Communion.

Since the first Lambeth Conference, there has been much discussion on the identity, integrity, and authority of Anglicanism, issues that remain central to dialogues within the Communion today. The crisis of Anglican identity can be attributed to many causes. Anglican churches do not have the equivalent of the Augsburg Confession and a body of official doctrines similar to those of Lutheranism. It was formed more out of political expediency by Henry VIII, rather than out of rigorous theological arguments similar to those advanced by Luther and Calvin. The Thirty-nine Articles, which served to define the doctrine of the Church of England during the Reformation, are not officially normative in all Anglican churches. The Chicago-Lambeth Quadrilateral adopted by Lambeth 1888 laid out the broad consensus of the Church: the scripture as containing all things necessary to salvation, the importance of the creeds for Christian faith, the two sacraments of baptism and Eucharist as ordained by Christ himself, and the emphasis on the historic episcopacy, locally adapted to the needs of the nations and peoples as the basis for Christian unity.[32] While the Quadrilateral can serve as a foundation to discuss Christian unity and ecumenism with other churches and denominations, it does not spell out the uniqueness of Anglicanism.

Some of the prominent Anglican theologians even debated whether Anglicanism has special doctrines of its own. Several modern interpreters, such as Michael Ramsey, Stephen Neill, and Henry McAdoo, insist that Anglican churches belong to the historical Christian tradition that embraces the creeds and doctrines of the early church and do not have unique doctrines of their own. Such a claim emphasizes the intention of Anglicanism to be Catholic, to remain in the mainstream, and to be part of the whole.[33] Others, such as Stephen Sykes, argue that "the no special doctrines" claim is a fallacy, for every Church must have a doctrine of the Church to legitimize its existence and maintain its integrity. Sykes writes, "While it may have been true that there is no specifically Anglican Christology or doctrine of the Trinity, or even (though it could be disputed) doctrine of justification, it cannot be the case that there is no Anglican ecclesiology."[34]

These debates led to the publication of many volumes on Anglican identity and history to try to define the historical and theological loci of the Anglican tradition. Some of these writings harken back to the past, to the liturgy of Thomas Cranmer, the writings of Richard Hooker, the institution of the episcopacy, and the religious establishment in England to find the unique characteristics of Anglicanism. In postcolonial language, these authors look back to the "point of origin" to find the unity and identity of Anglican churches. But as Caribbean theologian Kortright Davis has forcefully argued, "The Anglican Church must everywhere come to be known as the living church with the traditions of the living; no longer must anyone dare to call it a 'Royal Society for the Preservation of Ancient and Historical Monuments.'"[35] Even if these historical monuments are constitutive elements of what it means to be Anglican, their meaning and significance would look very different if interpreted through a global and postcolonial perspective. Historian Renie Chow Choy argues that English monuments, including such landmarks as Westminster Abby, as well as English hymns, ecclesiastical arts, and literature belong not only to the British but also to those in the former British Empire who had associations with them as part of the colonial legacy.[36]

As the cultural diversity of the Anglican Communion increases, Kevin Ward, who has taught for many years in Uganda and later in England, has encouraged us to see the Anglican Communion as "not English, but

Anglican" because Anglicanism has been appropriated and inculturated into local contexts, a continuing process that has shaped the churches we find today. He set out to write a history of global Anglicanism, focusing not on the Church of England, but the churches in the Global South and the work of local agents. He points out that in the Global South, the "English" or "British" heritage constitutes but only one element, among many, in the local appropriation and expression of Anglicanism. The challenge for the Anglican Communion, he says, is to develop

> a self-understanding that enables the communion to appreciate its common heritage of faith and order, its worship and discipleship, in ways which both acknowledge and transcend Anglicanism's ethnic, national and colonial origins. It needs, further, to develop a common Christian identity and confession which does not privilege "Englishness," but which honours the distinctly local forms in which the Gospel has been appropriated and rooted, and which must constantly be interpreted anew.[37]

I suggest the postcolonial concept of cultural hybridity would help examine the negotiation, appropriation, and contestation of different cultures in the development of Anglicanism. Anglicanism was a cultural hybrid, as the Church of England assimilated elements from both Roman Catholicism and Reformed Protestantism to create a national identity. The Church later adopted a via media approach and was able to hold together the Anglo-Catholics on the one hand and the evangelicals on the other. The encounter with diverse cultures during the colonial age presented both risks and opportunities to the cultural identity of Anglicanism. But instead of continuing the process of hybridity, Anglican churches formed during the imperialistic period tended to be mimicries of churches at the metropolitan center. The report of the Lambeth Conference of 1988 laments:

> Thus when Anglicanism was exported to other continents, it came not only with the "Englishness" of certain styles of clothing, music and worship, but with certain assumptions about who made decisions, who had authority in social life, who had ultimate control in economic affairs,

> markets, production, land ownership. The dominance of the English style . . . could be seen as a reflection of the plain facts of political and economic dominance.[38]

Although we have entered the postcolonial age, Anglican churches in many parts of the world remain cultural representations of the colonial era. Africans and Asians living in tropical climates continue to wear English clerical dress even under the blazing hot sun. John Pobee of Ghana has called this phenomenon the "Anglo-Saxon captivity of Ecclesia Anglicana."[39] In many cases, such mimicry of the "mother church" serves not as a mockery of colonial authority, but as a sign of privilege by association.

To get out of this captivity, the newer churches of the Anglican Communion must take seriously their hybrid identity as both Anglican on the one hand, and African, Asian, Latin American, Caribbean, or Oceanian on the other. Postcolonial theorists have warned that the recovery of cultural identity must avoid the temptation of nativism, self-Orientalism, and narrowly defined ethnocentrism. As Indian theologian Christopher Duraisingh has warned, such an ethnocultural quest for identity can lead to new forms of ethnic nationalism and cleansing, the oppression of religious minority groups, and the breakdown of community as seen in many parts of the world today.[40] The urgent question is how to construct identity in community so that the result will not be fragmentation, fundamentalism, or balkanization. The Anglican Communion can offer a unique prophetic model. On the one hand, it should encourage the experimentation of new cultural forms among member churches. On the other hand, the different cultural hybrids are in communion with one another, so that each can serve as a mirror for others, without absolutizing one's specific cultural form.

To embrace this multicultural and plurivocal model of Anglican Communion, we need to reconceive Anglican tradition and history not in a linear fashion or using a dispersal model, as if everything emanates from the center. Many historical works on the Anglican tradition follow a chronological narrative and place heavy emphasis on the development of the Church of England.[41] From a postcolonial perspective, this is reading history from the metropolitan center, relegating the histories of other peoples to the periphery. If colonization is a transnational and transcultural process, affecting both the colonized and the colonizers, how can we reinterpret the history of Anglicanism as a continued interaction between "the center" and "the periphery," thereby destabilizing both? Furthermore, how can we reimagine a different temporality so that we can resurrect the histories and stories of people, who are either pushed to the boundary or are completely invisible in metropolitan history? Then we will hear the stories of local scholars helping the English or American missionaries translate the Bible into the local tongues or the contribution of Bible women (a common term for local female evangelists) in teaching local women to read and write and serving as community leaders in their villages. We will learn about the contribution of African local clergy, whose work was central to the missions along the Niger River, and the pioneering role of African Caribbean Anglicans in establishing the church in Latin America. This multicultural and global interpretation of Anglican history requires the collaboration of many scholars with different expertise.

I will offer a few examples as several possible directions this multicultural interpretation can take. During the colonial days, Anglican congregations in America had to coexist with those of other denominations, especially with the strong presence of Puritans in the northeast. After the American Revolution, the colonial Anglican church could no longer be part of the Church of England, as the Church of England was part of the imperial government and led by the British monarch. The Episcopal Church separated from the English Church in its first General Convention in 1785 and adopted a national structure that paralleled that of the American government. The General Convention was divided into two houses: the House of Bishops and the House of Deputies that included clergy and laity. It drew its members from the middle and upper class, as well as leaders in the public sector.[42] The Episcopal Church developed a contextualized church polity that was significantly different from that of the Church of England. As Colin Podmore argues, the two different ecclesiologies—"the traditional western catholic ecclesiology of England and Ireland and the more democratic, egalitarian ecclesiology of the American Episcopal Church"—coalesced at the Lambeth Conference of 1867 and influenced its subsequent development.[43] It would be fruitful to explore how other Anglican churches developed their ecclesiology and polity when they formed autonomous provinces.

Another example is discerning racial politics in the Anglican Communion, especially in its important gatherings. At the Lambeth Conference of 1948, Black bishops made up only 6 percent of the 37 bishops from Africa, but by 1978, they made up 80 percent of the 102 African bishops, representing almost 20 percent of all participants.[44] The increased presence and influence of bishops from the Global South during the 1998 Lambeth Conference was evident. The first Anglican Consultative Council, which met in 1971 in Limuru, Kenya, was perhaps one of the first times that a world council with nonwhites as the majority had met since before the Council of Nicaea.[45] During Lambeth 1867, churches in the Global South were referred to as "Colonial Churches," but many have become fully autonomous provinces since 1950. Archbishop Desmond Tutu, Bishop James Ottley, Bishop David Gitari, Archbishop Thabo Makgoba, Archbishop Julio E. Murray, Christopher Duraisingh, Emilio Castro, and John Pobee have each played a critical role in the Lambeth Conferences. In preparing for the Bible studies for Lambeth 2022, scholars and theologians from the Global South, both men and women, contributed their expertise. Jenny Te Paa, former principal of Te Rau Kahikatea, St. John's College in Auckland, Aotearoa New Zealand, and Esther Mombo, former deputy vice chancellor at St. Paul's University, Limuru, Kenya, served on commissions charged with drafting important reports. The contributions of these bishops and theologians to Anglican theology and gatherings have to be emphasized since many accounts failed to highlight them.

The third example regards the translation and adaptation of Anglican liturgy into different local languages and idioms. One of the defining characteristics of Anglicanism is the use of the BCP. Today, many new revisions of the BCP are available, and the question of how much diversity can be allowed without losing the identity of the church becomes urgent. In addition, there have been attempts to use cultural resources other than English. As early as 1922, the Episcopal Synod of India sanctioned the use of *The Indian Liturgy*, which received provincial authorization in 1933 and contained examples of local inculturation. The Church of South India, formed as a merger of churches after independence, composed *The Book of Common Worship* in 1950, which contained many more examples of local cultural elements.[46] The first attempt at an African indigenous liturgy came as African countries were moving toward independence. "A Liturgy for Africa" was produced in English in 1964, but it did not have African elements in it.[47] Not many dioceses or provinces ever used the service, as there were few local translations. The Anglican churches in Africa have since played a key role in the discussion of inculturation of liturgy in the Anglican Communion, including the use of spontaneous prayers, African music, body language, and other cultural elements in worship. Another example is *A New Zealand Prayer Book* of the Anglican Church in Aotearoa, New Zealand and Polynesia, published in 1989, which adopts the language, poetry, and wisdom of the Maori and Polynesian peoples.[48] It seeks to embody and honor the linguistic, cultural, and religious diversity of the people of the province.

The diversity of the Anglican Communion cannot be represented by only a small group of leaders who dominate the media and public square, while the subaltern cannot speak. The unity of the Communion is symbolized by the bishops of the churches gathering together approximately every ten years. In between the Conferences, some primates met as a consultative body of the Conference, and such gatherings became the precursor of the Primates' Meetings, which first convened in 1979. The Anglican Consultative Council was formed by the Lambeth Conference of 1968 and consisted of bishops, clergy, and laypeople. Meeting every two or three years, the Council shares information about the development of the churches in the Communion, advises on matters arising from national and regional concerns, develops Anglican policies in world mission, and guides Anglican participation in ecumenical dialogues and fellowship.[49] Two Anglican Congresses were organized in Minneapolis (1954) and Toronto (1963), which provided opportunities for a large number of priests and laypeople, as well as bishops to meet people from all parts of the world and to experience the richness of the universal church.

Except for the two congresses, the rank-and-file members of the Church seldom have opportunities to share communion with each other.

Only those laypeople who participate in the Anglican Consultative Council or serve in particular commissions appointed by the archbishop of Canterbury have any real impact on the life of the whole church. The structure of the Communion is modeled after that of the British Commonwealth, with the bishops functioning almost as governors or heads of state. The hierarchical structure and its symbolic representation diminish the participation of the laity, both at the international and local levels.

And yet the laity is the backbone of the church. As historian Fredrica Harris Thompsett has noted: "Contemporary scholarship demands that attention be paid to the common folk, to what has been described as 'popular religion.' Critical scholarship has rejected the implicit two-tiered 'producer/consumer' model of supposedly articulate clergy developing doctrine for presumably inarticulate laity."[50] But in the discussion of the authority of the church and other important matters, the voices of the laity are seldom heard. Even though the Lambeth Conferences repeatedly affirmed the ministry of all baptized and the involvement of the whole people of God in mission, there are no adequate channels, both local and international, to mobilize the masses.

The voices of women in the Global South have been particularly marginalized, even though the church is growing most rapidly in the southern continents. The Lambeth Conference of 1998 welcomed the first group of eleven women bishops, but none of them were from the Global South. Except for Bishop Barbara Harris of Massachusetts, all of them were white, though slowly a small group of women bishops from the Global South have joined the ranks. The gathering of Anglican women in Brazil in 1992 was a good beginning, but most of the participants were from the Global North, and there were few resources for follow-up work. The stories of African Anglican women fighting the HIV/AIDS crisis, and the witness of their sisters in Asia amid the fast economic changes in their societies have seldom been told to expand our historical horizons and inspire church ministry. As Spivak has asked, even when these subalterns speak, who will listen?

The old forms of cultural hegemony and political domination of the colonial period have been superseded by the information superhighway and global market economy. Using mass media, satellite technology, and the World Wide Web, the postindustrial West continues to exert its power to create a "globalized" culture defined by Western tastes and norms. The "McWorld" has extended itself exponentially in the past decades through the omnipresent tendrils of fiber optics and satellites. Even as the logic of global capitalism becomes the logic of society itself, influencing cultural productions such as arts, sports, education, entertainment, and communication, there is renewed interest and self-awareness of people searching for their cultural, ethnic, and religious identities. A section report of the 1998 Lambeth Conference notes: "In almost every part of the world, we find a search for cultural roots and tradition, a stress on cultural uniqueness, an insistence on 'difference' and the right of each group to its own specific ways of being and development."[51] Such a trend can lead to the affirmation of a plurality of cultures but can also result in violent ethnic conflicts and the persecution of minorities. In different parts of the world, various kinds of cultural and religious fundamentalisms have emerged, vehemently contesting and resisting the formidable forces of globalization. Some fundamentalists are deeply suspicious of Western liberal causes, such as the education of women, religious tolerance, and democratic political participation. In addition, conservative sectors in the Anglican churches in the Global North with more resources can easily connect with their counterparts in the Global South, promoting an agenda that is anti-gay and anti-women. The internet and social media allow more actors to play and vie for attention. Western media is fond of reporting on polarizing and sensational issues, such as the acrimonious debates on homosexuality, and seldom on meaningful partnership and collaboration across the Communion. Cultural politics within the Anglican Communion is more complicated and challenging today and requires critical judgment and analysis.

Confronting the Legacy of Slavery and Racism

In June 2022, Archbishop of Canterbury Justin Welby apologized after an investigation showed that the Church of England's investment fund had for more than a hundred years invested large sums of money in a company that had transported slaves from Africa to South America.[52] The Church of England and its overseas missions benefited financially from the Atlantic slave trade, which began in the sixteenth century. Britain was one of the most successful slave-trading countries, and together with Portugal accounted for about 70 percent of Africans transported to the Americas.[53] In the century before the Abolition of Slave Trade Act was passed in 1807, the British shipped more than three million Africans to the plantations. The slave trade brought enormous bounty to the country and slavery was generally accepted by society. Supporters of slavery justified their actions by citing the curse of Ham (Gen. 9:22–27), the fact that Abraham owned male and female slaves (Gen. 24:35), and the provision in Mosaic legislation for Israelites to buy and sell slaves and to treat them in certain ways (See, for example, Exod. 25 and Lev. 21:44–46). In the New Testament, slaves were told to obey their masters (e.g., Eph. 6:5–9; Col. 3:22–25), and Paul sent the runaway slave Onesimus back to his master Philemon (Philem. 1).[54] When SPG missionaries worked in North America, the Caribbean, and West Africa, they wanted to convert the slaves and sought better treatment for them. SPG's attitude toward the slaves was paternalistic and as time went on the Society gradually accommodated their message to the slaveowners. It argued that chattel slavery was compatible with Christianity and the two could even be mutually beneficial. SPG owned hundreds of slaves in its Codrington plantations in Barbados, where they hoped to gain profits and at the same time win souls.[55] The sugar-based profits from these plantations were sent back to the Church of England, and the Church was complicit in condoning slavery which brought so much pain and suffering to Africans.

The abolition movement did not gain traction in Britain until the last decades of the eighteenth century, though some Puritans and Quakers had spoken against slavery earlier. As many abolitionist groups and organizations were formed, the Quakers, Methodists, Baptists, and Presbyterians joined the cause and argued that slavery was fundamentally wrong and incompatible with Christian tenets.[56] In the Church of England, William Wilberforce, Thomas Clarkson, and other members of the Clapham Sect—a group of evangelicals committed to social reforms and mission work—campaigned for the abolition of slavery. Wilberforce helped found the Anti-Slavery Society and spearheaded antislavery legislation in Parliament. Thomas Clarkson traveled around the country showing the evidence of cruelty inflicted upon the slaves and campaigning against the slave trade in the British Empire. Under mounting pressure, Parliament passed the Abolition of Slave Trade Act in 1807 and finally abolished slavery in 1833. Many abolitionists were influenced by Enlightenment ideas, including the equality of all human beings, a principle popularized by the French Revolution and the American War of Independence. Wilberforce and other English evangelicals were also prompted by their Christian outrage and their broader interpretation of Christian moral responsibility that included the concern for social justice and moral righteousness. For them, slavery was against Jesus's admonition to "love your neighbor as yourself." Wilberforce wrote in his diary, "God almighty has set before me two great objects, the suppression of the slave trade and the reformation of manners."[57] He became a staunch leader against slavery as a member of Parliament and the upper class and pressed the government to enforce legislation against drunkenness and other demeanors. He took personal responsibility for the moral failings of the government and argued that Parliament and the nation were guilty of allowing the horrid slave trade to continue for so long. As a Christian politician, he saw slavery as a disgrace to the nation and formed organizations to change Britain so that it would become a more perfect Christian nation. In addition to British abolitionists, there were Africans in London, most of them freed slaves, who denounced the slave trade, bearing testimonies of living under slavery and the freedom Christianity had brought them. A notable leader was Olaudah Equiano, who recounted his story as a former slave in the Caribbean in his autobiography, and was part of the Sons of Africa, an abolitionist group of Africans living in Britain.[58] As one of the earliest slave narratives, the book fueled antislavery interest in Britain, Europe, and America.

The struggle against slavery was more tortuous in the United States because of the entrenched economic interests of slaveholders in the southern states, enshrined in the Constitution of the new nation as a topic that must effectively be kept off the table. Both supporters and opponents of slavery cited the Bible and Christian theology to support their arguments. Slaves often had to worship in segregated worshipping spaces with separate slave galleries or gather at separate worship times. The cultural and ideological differences between the north and the south over slavery divided the nation and caused schisms in the mainline denominations, particularly the Baptists, Methodists, and Presbyterians.[59]

Within the Episcopal Church, the southern slave-owning class had enormous clout in the Church, and northern Episcopalians were divided in their opinions about slavery; some leaders did not want to take a stance. Southern Episcopalians separated from the national Episcopal Church during the Civil War but reunited after the War was over. After emancipation, there was a mass exodus of Black Episcopalians to denominations that would permit Black leadership. White Episcopalians were paternalistic toward Black Episcopalians, and although there had been free Black churches since the Revolution, these churches were kept from sharing power at the diocesan and national levels. When the southern states enacted Jim Crow laws, white Episcopalians circumscribed the freedom of African Americans in the ecclesiastical spheres to echo it. Some white church leaders were influenced by the theory of social Darwinism and firmly believed in the superiority of the white race, and that Black Episcopalians could neither be equals nor be without white supervision. Facing discrimination and segregation, Black Episcopal leaders persistently called the Church to live out its mission as a church for all people and treat Black people with dignity and respect. The prominent Black Episcopal priest Alexander Crummell and other Black leaders organized the Conference of Church Workers among Colored People and advocated for a strong racial ministry. Anna Julia Cooper, a public speaker and writer, argued for education as a means of racial uplift and demanded the recruitment and ordination of more Black priests.[60] Racial segregation and paternalism in the post–Civil War era continued to affect America's racial relations and the church's mission in the following periods.[61]

During the civil rights era, the white-led Episcopal Church and other denominations gradually became involved in the fight for desegregation and equal rights for African Americans. Several prominent Black leaders who were in or linked with the Episcopal Church, notably lawyers Thurgood Marshall and Pauli Murray and psychologist Kenneth B. Clark, used their expertise to argue against segregation and the "separate but equal" assumption. Although Episcopalians had different opinions about the civil rights movement, some of them participated in protests and boycotts led by Dr. Martin Luther King Jr. In 1959, a group of clergy and laity formed the Episcopal Society for Cultural and Racial Unity, and members participated in protests and civil disobedience to overcome racial division in the Church and to promote racial unity. The Society supported "kneel-ins," which were attempts of African Americans to enter places where they were not welcome in the south. Members and supporters took part in voter registration, organized prayer pilgrimages, joined the Selma marches, and mobilized grassroots supporters to advocate for the integration of churches, schools, and camps.[62] In the 1960s, after Bishop John Hines was elected the presiding bishop, the Episcopal Church became outspoken on racial issues and authorized a special program to provide funds to support the fight for racial and economic justice, despite tensions and controversies about the program that led to its cancellation and Bishop Hines's early resignation. The civil rights era and King's legacy have had a tremendous impact on the development of Black consciousness and theology in the United States and around the globe. Kortright Davis said that the civil rights era is one of the pivotal Black prophetic moments, which "have generated not only the prophetic visionaries, and activists, and advocates for alternative historical conditions, but also the divinely inspired climate and counter-culture for a more humane and equitable communal existence."[63] Continuing the work from the civil rights movement, Kelly Brown Douglas, a leading womanist theologian and Episcopal priest, has criticized the ideology behind American exceptionalism and Manifest Destiny, which is based on white hegemony and anti-Blackness. She argues that to follow Christ means that the church must listen and respond to the cries of the crucified people of our time.[64] Harold T. Lewis, historian and former staff officer for Black Ministries in the Episcopal Church, says, "Black Episcopalians have cherished the hope that they could be recognized neither as an alien race, nor as coming from a foreign shore, but as integral and bona fide members of the Church."[65] Inspired by Black people's persistent striving for racial equality, other racial and ethnic minority groups also demanded their rightful place in the church and society. In the Episcopal Church, Asian Americans, Latinos and Hispanics, and Native Americans formed their different ministries to address pastoral and communal issues of their communities.

In South Africa, Archbishop Desmond Tutu asserted moral and spiritual authority during the long fight against apartheid. Even in the darkest days, he believed in God's faithfulness and goodness and wrote, "God is a God who cares about right and wrong. God cares about justice and injustice. God is in charge. That is what has upheld the morale of the people, to know that in the end good will prevail. It was these higher laws that convinced me that our peaceful struggle would topple the immoral laws of apartheid."[66] In his sermons and speeches, he frequently drew inspiration from scripture, which he thought to be revolutionary and subversive. In particular, he cited the Exodus, in which God liberated the Israelites from Pharoah, and the prophetic tradition for support for anti-apartheid struggles. As he was trained in Western theology, he had for a long time thought that there was one universally valid theology. But his exposure to Latin American theology and African American Black Theology convinced him that "a truly relevant theology was one that addressed the issues of a particular community."[67] He evoked the African idea of *ubuntu* (humanity to others) as he assessed the South African situation and developed his Christian ethics. After the apartheid regime ended, Archbishop Tutu served as the chairman of the Truth and Reconciliation Commission in an effort to help the deeply torn country to heal. Instead of seeking revenge and punishment, the archbishop argued that only through forgiveness, amnesty, and restorative justice could the country be brought together. In *No Future Without Forgiveness*, he pointed out that forgiveness does not mean forgetting the past nor does it imply weakness. As Christians, we forgive because God has forgiven us. Forgiveness has intrinsic moral values for the one who forgives, and it can lead to long-term interpersonal and communal reconciliation.[68] The Truth and Reconciliation Commission has served as a model for other oppressed groups seeking justice and healing.

As the struggle against racism has taken an international turn, Anglicans of African descent in different parts of the world wanted to redefine themselves and express solidarity as members of the Anglican Communion. Canon Frederick Boyd Williams, who had participated in the anti-apartheid movement and Black freedom movements, founded the Conference on Afro-Anglicanism.[69] The first meeting took place in 1985 in Barbados, where the SPG once owned profitable sugar plantations and slaves, and issued the Codrington Consensus. The document spoke not only for Afro-Anglicans but addressed Anglicans in general in an attempt to chart a new method of global Anglicanism. The two hundred participants from seventeen countries affirmed that they were both African and Anglican. Instead of the usual tripolite base of Anglican theology—Bible, tradition, and reason—they added liturgy, ministry, and social witness as sources for discerning the signs of the Kingdom in the world.[70] The Consensus also renounced all forms of racism, sexism, classism, and imperialism and expressed solidarity with all others in the struggle for global justice and human liberation. Held every ten years, the conference was held in Cape Town, South Africa, in 1995 at the invitation of Archbishop Tutu. The Toronto conference in 2005 welcomed more young people and discussed economic issues, health, HIV/AIDS, and young adults in the life of the Church.

In addition to the organizing of Afro-Anglicans, indigenous people in the Anglican Communion formed the Anglican Indigenous Network, which traced its historical beginnings to the 1991 General Convention of the Episcopal Church in Phoenix, Arizona. The Network states that they are committed to the Anglican tradition while affirming their traditional spirituality. Through this Network, indigenous Anglicans wish to protect their heritages, land rights, and the environment, and they urge the Church to accept a full partnership with indigenous peoples.[71] As indigenous cultures have been erased or suppressed in settler colonialism, indigenous Anglican leaders push for the incorporation of their cultures and languages in liturgy and life of the Church. Indigenous leaders also admonish the Church to repent for the harm that Anglican churches have done to indigenous peoples. For example, the Anglican Church of Canada apologized in 1993 for the operation of residential schools for Indigenous children, separating them from their families and cultures. The Canadian Church ran about three dozen residential schools from 1820 to 1969, educating about 150,000 Indigenous children. Mark MacDonald, the first national Indigenous bishop of the Anglican Church of Canada, participated in the Truth and Reconciliation Commission in Canada, which was formed to address abuses and harm done to First Nations people. He said the Church must recognize systemic evil, but he remained hopeful that Indigenous Anglican communities are learning to translate their concerns to the broader public.[72]

The decolonization of Anglican churches requires the dissociation from a colonial syndrome that places white people at the top of the racial hierarchy and denigrates other races and indigenous peoples, the original inhabitants of the lands. Several Lambeth conferences have denounced racial discrimination in its various forms, and Lambeth 1968 acknowledged that the churches in the Communion had not done enough to combat racism and needed to reexamine their life and structures.[73] In *The Wretched of the Earth*, Frantz Fanon spoke about the violence and psychological trauma inflicted upon colonized peoples. He chastised the Church as a colonial collaborator and wrote, "The Church in the colonies is a white man's Church, a foreigner's Church. It does not call the colonized to the ways of God, but to the ways of the white men, to the ways of the master, the ways of the oppressor."[74] Through their witness and activism, Afro-Anglicans, indigenous Anglicans, and people of different racial and ethnic groups in the Anglican Communion want to expand the colonial church and claim their rightful place in God's house with many mansions. They are committed to broadening the Church's theological imagination and religious practices such that it can truly be one, holy, catholic, and apostolic, as God has called it to be.

Reimagining Authority

The transition of a colonial Church of England to a global Anglican Communion encountered numerous questions and issues. The Anglican

Communion does not have a centralized governing body as the Roman Catholic Church does. Instead of opting for the universal primacy of Canterbury, the Anglican Communion is a fellowship of churches, each in communion with the See of Canterbury and with each other. This rather decentralized structure is rooted in the development of Anglican history. When the Church of England broke away from Rome, it formed a national church with the monarch as the secular head and the Parliament as its governing body. After independence, the Episcopal Church separated from the Church of England and ratified its consitution and developed its revised American version of the BCP. By the 1860s, both the Anglican churches in Australia and Aotearoa New Zealand adopted the form of synodical government with the rights to elect their bishops and the power to regulate the life of their churches. When the bishops gathered at the first Lambeth Conference in 1867, Archbishop Charles Longley who called the conference functioned as a *primus inter pares* (first among equals) and not as an Anglican pope. The laity was not invited because lay synodical representation was still in contention in the Church of England. The result was that the role of the bishops was heightened, even if the final resolutions called for the establishment of synods in places where Anglicanism was not established by law.[75] Over the years, there has developed a general ecclesiastical commitment to respect the provincial and regional autonomy of governance, worship, mission, and ministry.

The structure of the Anglican Communion has been tested by controversies on polygamy, women's ordination, and homosexuality at various times. The Instruments of Unity (the archbishop of Canterbury, the Lambeth Conference, the Anglican Consultative Council, and the Primates' Meeting) have not been sufficient to help member churches to find consensus or resolve conflicts. Some scholars attribute the crisis of the Communion to the difficulties of the transition of an English church to a global multiracial, multicultural, and multilingual Communion. In *The Transformation of Anglicanism*, William L. Sachs notes: "The deepening of local influences upon the Church brought forth a profusion of religious forms, all claiming historic precedent and religious validity, which shattered the unity of Anglican identity. The modern question became one of mediating between diverse forms of Anglican experience."[76] Ian T. Douglas, a scholar of Episcopal missions and later a bishop in Connecticut, has gone one step further in his critique of the cultural domination and the continued colonial patterns of power in the Anglican Communion. For him, the crisis in the Anglican Communion is not so much about structure and Instruments of Unity, but about relationships and mission. In order for the Church to advance God's mission of reconciliation and restoration, the Church must respect and embrace what he has called "different incarnational realities."[77] He writes, "Communion is thus primarily based upon relationships of mutual responsibility and interdependence in the body of Christ across the differences of culture, location, ethnicity, and even theological perspective to serve God's mission in the world."[78]

The conflict of opinions between some of the bishops from the Global North and Global South came to the fore at Lambeth 1998. While some had gone to the conference to discuss how the Communion could respond to global economic issues and the Millennium Development Goals, the debates on human sexuality dominated the media and occupied much attention. Scholars have observed the shift of power and the increasingly vocal bishops from the Global South in various ways. Some have described this as a postcolonial backlash. Mark Chapman, for instance, states that "the global shift in Anglicanism was asserting itself," and describes what happened at Lambeth 1998 as a postcolonial "fight-back," with support from Western conservatives.[79] On the surface, such an analysis has its appeal because polygamy and other sexual practices in Africa had been under scrutiny and attack for more than a hundred years. Amid the homosexuality debate, several African bishops have turned the tables and called the American Church an unruly child that needs discipline. By so doing, they reversed the "civilizing mission" of the West and claimed moral authority in expressing their righteous indignation.

Yet even as the commentators use the term "postcolonial," they have not applied postcolonial theories or insights to examine the postcolonial condition. Postcolonialism is not just about power reversal, but also about an engaged critique of the structures, ideologies, symbols, mentality, and legacy of colonialism. Some seasoned observers question whether colonial and neocolonial domination continues to operate within the Communion. Assessing Lambeth 1998, Ian T. Douglas and Julie Wortman asked whether there is the rise of a truly postcolonial world Anglicanism, in which the Southern Anglicans can participate fully alongside their Northern colleagues, or whether the Communion is still dominated by Northerners, who determine the rules of engagement for Southerners.[80] Miranda K. Hassett, an anthropologist and Episcopal priest, elucidates the material dependence of the Southern churches on the Northern churches and the asymmetry in the transnational Anglican alliances. She concludes that "the relative wealth of the Northern churches continues to shape North/South relationships within the Communion. Southern Anglican moral dominance, so eagerly advocated by Northern conservatives, is balanced against, and limited by, continued Northern Anglican material dominance."[81]

Postcolonial theorists not only point their fingers at the colonizers but also painstakingly study the many ways the colonized have adapted to and collaborated with empire. Albert Memmi, a Tunisian-Jewish writer and a forerunner of postcolonial theory, argued that colonization is not possible without the collaboration of the colonized in *The Colonizer and the Colonized* published in 1956.[82] Drawing from his experience in Tunisia, he described in vivid terms the mutual dependence between the colonizers and colonized. Spivak and other postcolonial scholars, including those affiliated with the Subaltern Studies Group, have questioned the rise of postcolonial elites and their use of nationalistic language to assert power after independence. Likewise, we should question the colonial church structures that granted much power to the bishops appointed by Britain during the colonial era and how such privileges have been passed on to the local bishops who succeeded them. The race and ethnicity of the bishops might have changed, but the colonial church structures may have remained. As a result, some bishops continue to hold enormous economic power and political clout because of their church's past association with empire. While the Southern bishops speak with a sense of moral authority, they do not have a concomitant self-critique of their own privileged positions enabled by the colonial legacy in the past and association with conservative American allies in the present. This dynamic cannot be overlooked when we examine the politics and authority in the Communion today. Though the conservative Southern bishops often claim to speak for the majority of the Church who are "orthodox Anglicans," they do not represent the diversity of opinions within their churches, let alone speak for the Communion. One cannot just listen to what the loudest and most vocal bishops have said, without paying attention to other voices and the wide spectrum of perspectives.

For example, while some African and other conservative bishops threatened to boycott Lambeth 2008, members of the International Anglican Women's Network attending a United Nations Conference reiterated their commitment to remaining always "in communion" with and for one another amid deep divisions over sexuality in the Communion. The more than 80 women from 34 countries acknowledged global tensions in the Church, and their statement said, "Given the global tensions so evident in our church today, we do not accept that there is any one issue of difference or contention which can, or indeed would, ever cause us to break the unity as represented by our common baptism. Neither would we ever consider severing the deep and abiding bonds of affection which characterize our relationships as Anglican women."[83]

After Lambeth 1998, the Communion continued to be plagued by divisions and acrimony, exacerbated by the election of the first openly gay bishop Gene Robinson in 2003. Archbishop of Canterbury Rowan Williams acknowledged the divisions and mistrust in the Communion and tried to find ways for reconciliation. He recognized that the issues that threaten to divide the Communion are not limited to human sexuality, but could include "developments about how we understand our ordained ministry; how we understand our mission; the limits of diversity in our worship; even perhaps in the public language we use about our doctrine."[84] That Anglican churches have not come to some common understanding on so many fundamental aspects of the Church and mission points to profound challenges to mutual relationships and accountability. In his first presidential address at Lambeth 2008, Archbishop Williams described four different approaches people have suggested for relationships in the Communion. The first is a loose federation, with different expressions of Anglicanism existing side-by-side with little coordination in mission. Since different positions can compete with each other with little moderation, this approach would encourage all kinds of division. The second is a family of regional and national churches with independent systems of government, like sovereign states, that come together from time to time to address common concerns. This approach ignores the complexity of living in a globalized context and economy and hinders the churches from learning from and challenging one another. The third is to have a firmer and more consistent control of diversity, empowering a set of bodies to govern the affairs of local communities in the Communion. This would lead to a centralized and homogenized Communion at the mercy of powerful bodies and groups which would define the rules of belonging. He preferred the fourth, which is defined by council and covenant. He said, "It is the vision of an Anglicanism whose diversity is limited not by centralised control but by consent—consent based on a serious *common* assessment of the implications of local change."[85] The covenantal process would allow member churches to consent to a common set of beliefs and principles to resolve conflicts when controversies that threaten to divide the Communion occur.

The archbishop appointed a Covenant Design Group in 2006 and several drafts were circulated for feedback from the churches.[86] The final version, released in December 2009, was sent for adoption by constituent provinces through appropriate processes.[87] The Anglican Covenant is disappointing in that it is more concerned about resolving conflicts and disciplinary procedures than about meeting the challenges of mission in the twenty-first century. Its theology of the Church hearkens back to the past and shows curious neglect of liberative impulses across churches around the globe in the second half of the twentieth century. Many people have criticized how the Covenant elevates the role and power of bishops, especially primates, to the neglect of the work and ministry of the laity. "The proposed Anglican covenant says little about the role of the laity," Episcopal scholar Ruth Meyers notes.[88] The Covenant mentions baptism as one of the sacraments but says little about the baptismal ministry that all who are baptized in Christ are called to do. The Covenant also recommends that the Standing Committee of the Anglican Communion, consisting of members of the Primates' Meeting and the Anglican Consultative Council, become the organ to maintain the Covenant and resolve disputes. Fredrica Harris Thompsett calls this new bureaucratic structure "a concentration of power at the highest levels of the Anglican Communion."[89] As a church historian, she argues that such a development will not solve the present crisis, but acts against Anglican tradition, which understands authority to be dispersed throughout the Communion.

Ellen K. Wondra, an Episcopal theologian who has been active in ecumenical dialogues, offers several insightful suggestions to reimagine authority. She argues that the Anglican Covenant and other church reports far too often focus on the bishops to the eclipse of the laity. The bishops are not treated as members of and a part of the *laos* (people of God) and are seen as primarily relating to each other, in isolation from the rest of the church body.[90] Such a view is rooted in a hierarchical and patriarchal ecclesiology and ignores relationships in church life in actual practice. She insists that we must overcome

> the split between ecclesiology and ecclesial life and practice so that ecclesiology not only shapes but is shaped by the lives and witnesses of ordinary Christians who are gendered, sexual, and postcolonial subjects whose race and ethnicities are integral to who they are and how they live. Only when ecclesiology is explicitly shaped by actual ecclesial life with all its difference can it serve its purpose of informing reflection and stimulating imagination and vision of what it means to be a faithful community following Christ.[91]

Instead of a top-down, hierarchical conception of authority, Wondra argues for an understanding based on a relational theology centered on the creativity and dynamism of the Triune God. Within the Trinity, the three persons are different and distinct, but without separation.[92] She points out that there are different kinds of authority in the church. While the bishops and priests have authority in worship and teaching, others may know more about church finance and property. There is a distinction between formal authority, vested in the person with a certain status, and informal authority, which is often shared among persons and groups through consultation and deliberation. The conflicts facing the Communion cannot be resolved by more concentration of power and authority, but by cooperative and participatory forms of governance that are synodical and conciliar. Conciliarity means "the whole church sharing responsibility for its well-being and is an ongoing activity of the church."[93] Within this model, authority is exercised for the benefit of the church and the well-being of all. Legitimate authority is received with consent and exercises in communal and collegial ways. All are invited to participate in shaping the mission and direction of the future of the Church either directly or through delegation.[94]

Authority issues arise when conflicts occur and compromises are difficult. Archbishop Thabo Makgoba, the primate of Southern Africa and archbishop of Cape Town, describes the Anglican Communion as a family where "we don't hide our differences and we are real with one another."[95] Since the Communion has people from so many cultures and nations, conflicts are bound to occur. He hopes that the Communion will work together to discern what God is calling this family to be. Just as in any family, relationships can be messy. He does not think the structures of the Communion are set in stone and if the Instruments of Unity are not working, we can change or modify them to ease the tensions. He suggests that the best way for resolving conflicts is for people with different views to gather around the table for dialogue, instead of boycotting. He recognizes that the issue of same-sex unions is highly contentious but argues that it should not be treated "as a church-dividing matter but as one of Pastoral accommodation to the needs of each individual Province: we can do this by adopting a new Anglican via media, a middle way that bridges the divide."[96]

The crisis of the Anglican Communion can mean the danger of schism, but also opportunities for reflection and renewal. The second half of the twentieth century was marked by liberation movements within the Church and society. Formerly oppressed and marginalized groups, such as women, the poor, the youth, the Dalits, the indigenous, racial and ethnic minorities, and lesbian, gay, bisexual, transgender, and queer (LGBTQ) people have demanded their voices be heard and changed the ways that theology has been done. The renewal movements of the Church have emphasized the role of the laity. The basic Christian communities in Latin America have inspired many Christians in the world to find new models of being Church. A leading Brazilian theologian, Leonardo Boff, writes, "Christian life in the basic communities is characterized by the absence of alienating structures, by direct relationships, by reciprocity, by a deep communion, by mutual assistance, by communality of gospel ideals, by equality among its members."[97] He calls this new experience of being Church *Ecclesiogenesis*.

Anglican churches need their *Ecclesiogenesis*. The danger of the Anglican Communion today is that it will adopt expedient measures to avoid schism and shortchange the process of deep thinking about what the Church can become. Steeped in colonial history, Anglican churches have much to learn to rid their colonial vestiges. This does not mean turning the tables so that more power is given to the Southern churches over the Northern churches. This means reimagining a Communion that is truly global, multicultural, respecting differences, and remaining in conversation and fellowship even when it becomes difficult. It means asking the difficult question of how the Church can come together as "disciples of equals,"[98] given the massive inequity of wealth and power in the world. If the Church can find a way to live out its commitment to mutual responsibility and interdependence, it can offer hope to a broken world and a foretaste for God's Kingdom. Many Anglicans would like to see the birth of such a new church: a church that is more concerned about God's mission than policing sexuality, a church that is not afraid of cultural differences but welcomes diversity as its strength, and a church that is not centralized or hierarchal but celebrates democracy and participation of all who together constitute the Body of Christ.

Notes

1. Rowan Strong, *Anglicanism and the British Empire, c.1700–1850* (Oxford: Oxford University Press, 2007), 2.
2. Strong, *Anglicanism and the British Empire,* 1–9.
3. Edward W. Said, *Orientalism* (New York: Vintage Books, 1979).

4. Pope Nicholas V issued a series of papal bulls in the fifteenth century and granted Portugal the right to enslave Sub-Saharan Africans. See "Pope Nicholas V and the Portuguese Slave Trade," Low Country Digital History Initiative, https://ldhi.library.cofc.edu/exhibits/show/african_laborers_for_a_new_emp/pope_nicolas_v_and_the_portugu.
5. Andrew Porter, "Religion and Empire: British Expansion in the Long Nineteenth Century, 1780–1914," *Journal of Imperial and Commonwealth History* 20, no. 3 (1992): 374–75.
6. Charles Taylor, *Modern Social Imaginaries* (Durham, NC: Duke University Press, 2004), 23.
7. Reinhold Niebuhr, *The Structure of Nations and Empires* (New York: Charles Scribner's Sons, 1959).
8. Porter, "Religion and Empire," 386.
9. Mark D. Chapman, *Anglican Theology* (London: T & T Clark International, 2012), 12–13, and Diarmaid MacCulloch, "The Myth of the English Reformation," *Journal of British Studies* 30, no. 1 (1991): 1.
10. Stewart J. Brown, "Anglicanism in the British Empire, 1829–1910," in *The Oxford History of Anglicanism*, vol. 3, *Partisan Anglicanism and Its Global Expansion, 1829–c.1914*, ed. Rowan Strong (Oxford: Oxford University Press, 2017), 46.
11. Edward Jarvis, *The Anglican Church in Burma: From Colonial Past to Global Future* (University Park: Pennsylvania State University Press, 2021), 124.
12. Philip Shuttleworth, bishop of Chidester, *Sermon* (1840), quoted in Strong, *Anglicanism and the British Empire*, 280.
13. Rowan Strong, "Rescuing the Perishing Heathens: The British Empire versus the Empire of Satan in Anglican Theology, 1701–1721," *Studies in Church History* 45 (2009): 323–35.
14. Strong, *Anglicanism and the British Empire*, 284.
15. Gayatri Chakravorty Spivak, "Can the Subaltern Speak?," in *Marxism and the Interpretation of Culture*, ed. Cary Nelson and Lawrence Grossberg (Urbana: University of Illinois Press. 1988), 296–97.
16. Dana L. Robert, "Evangelist or Homemaker? Mission Strategies of Early Nineteenth-Century Missionary Wives in Burma and Hawaii," *International Bulletin of Missionary Research* 17, no.1 (1993): 4–6, 8–10, 12.
17. Charles Longley, bishop of Ripon, *A Sermon* (1841), quoted in Strong, *Anglicanism and the British Empire*, 281.
18. Daniel Wilson, *A Charge Delivered to the Clergy of the Four Dioceses of Calcutta, Madras, Bombay, and Colombo* (London, 1849), 10, quoted in Brown, "Anglicanism in the British Empire," 45.
19. Wilson, *Charge Delivered to the Clergy*, 21, quoted in Brown, "Anglicanism in the British Empire," 45.
20. Earl Grey, *The Colonial Policy of Lord John Russell's Administration* (London: R. Bentley, 1853), vol. 1, 12–14, quoted in Bernard Porter, *The Lion's Share: A History of British Imperialism 1850 to the Present*, 6th ed. (New York: Routledge, 2021), 25.
21. Porter, *Lion's Share*, 37.
22. Philip Lockley, "Social Anglicanism and Empire: C. F. Andrews's Christian Socialism," *Studies in Church History* 54 (2018): 420. See also Peter Jones, *The Christian Socialist Revival, 1877–1914: Religion, Class, and Social Conscience in Late Victorian England* (Princeton, NJ: Princeton University Press, 1968).

23. J. R. Seeley, *Ecce Homo: Life and Work of Jesus Christ* (1865, repr., New York: E. P. Dutton, 1908), 56–57.
24. Seeley, *Ecce Homo*, 86.
25. J. R. Seeley, *The Expansion of England* (1883, repr., Boston: Little, Brown, and Company, 1905), 226–27.
26. Brown, "Anglicanism in the British Empire," 66.
27. Henry Venn, "Minute upon the Employment and Ordination of Native Teachers," 1851, cited in Jehu J. Hanciles, "Anatomy of an Experiment: The Sierra Leone Native Pastorate," *Missiology* 28, no. 1 (2002): 64.
28. Wilbert R. Shenk, "Henry Venn's Legacy," *Occasional Bulletin of Missionary Research* 1, no. 2 (1977): 16–19. Venn originally used the term "self-extending." See Wilbert R. Shenk, "Rufus Anderson and Henry Venn: A Special Relationship?" *International Bulletin of Missionary Research* 5, no. 4 (1981): 170–71.
29. Jehu J. Hanciles, *Euthanasia of a Mission: African Church Autonomy in a Colonial Context* (Westport, CT: Praeger, 2002).
30. Lockley, "Social Anglicanism and Empire," 407–21.
31. R. S. Sugirtharajah, *The Bible in the Third World: Precolonial, Colonial, and Postcolonial Encounters* (Cambridge: Cambridge University Press, 2001), 120–21.
32. "The Chicago-Lambeth Quadrilateral," Anglicans Online, last updated May 9, 2019, http://anglicansonline.org/basics/Chicago_Lambeth.html.
33. Paul Avis, "Anglican Ecclesiology," in *The Routledge Companion to the Christian Church*, ed. Gerard Mannion and Lewis S. Mudge (New York: Routledge, 2008), 214.
34. Stephen Sykes, *Unashamed Anglicanism* (Nashville, TN: Abingdon, 1995), 125.
35. Donald Henry Kortright Davis, "Present and Future Trends in Anglicanism," in *Anglicanism: Present and Future*, ed. Michael P. Hamilton (Washington, DC: Washington National Cathedral, 1992), 25.
36. Renie Chow Choy, *Ancestral Feelings: Postcolonial Thoughts on Western Christian Heritage* (London: SCM, 2021).
37. Kevin Ward, *A History of Global Anglicanism* (Cambridge: Cambridge University Press, 2006), 17–18.
38. Lambeth Conference, *The Truth Shall Make You Free: The Lambeth Conference 1988* (London: Church House Publishing, 1988), 88.
39. John Pobee, "New Dioceses of the Anglican Communion," in *The Study of Anglicanism*, ed. Stephen Sykes and John Booty (London: SPCK, 1988), 395–98.
40. Christopher Duraisingh, "Editorial: Gospel and Identity in Community," *International Review of Mission* 85 (1996): 6–7.
41. Stephen C. Neill, *Anglicanism* (Harmondsworth: Penguin, 1958); William L. Sachs, *The Transformation of Anglicanism: From State Church to Global Communion* (Cambridge: Cambridge University Press, 1993) also follows a chronological narrative, but he devotes half of the book to a global perspective.
42. Sachs, *Transformation of Anglicanism*, 67–68.
43. Colin Podmore, "Two Streams Comingling: The American Episcopal Church in the Anglican Communion," *Journal of Anglican Studies* 9, no. 1 (2011): 12–37.
44. John Howe, *Anglicanism and the Universal Church* (Toronto: Anglican Book Center, 1990), 14.

45. Howe, *Anglicanism and the Universal Church*, 19.
46. The original form of the Indian liturgy drew from the Liturgy of St. James of the Syrian Christians and the 1662 BCP, and it had rarely been used outside the diocese of Bombay. M. E. Gibbs, *The Anglican Church in India 1600–1970* (Delhi: ISPCK, 1972), 397. See also Shawn Strout, "Prayer Book Uniformity: Myth or Icon?" *Anglican Theological Review* 105 (2023): 36.
47. The introduction to "A Liturgy for Africa" along with its text can be found in Colin Ogilvie Buchanan, ed., *Modern Anglican Liturgies 1958–1968* (Oxford: Oxford University Press, 1968), 48–69.
48. *A New Zealand Prayer Book =He Karakia Mihinare O Aotearoa* (Auckland: Collins, 1989).
49. Howe, *Anglicanism and the Universal Church*, 87–88.
50. Fredrica Harris Thompsett, "The Laity," in Sykes and Booty, *The Study of Anglicanism*, 245–46.
51. Mark Dyer et al., eds., *The Official Report of the Lambeth Conference 1998* (Harrisburg, PA: Morehouse Publishing, 1999), 186.
52. Aleem Maqbool and Harry Farley, "Archbishop of Canterbury Apologises over Church Fund's Link to Slavery," BBC News, June 16, 2022, https://www.bbc.com/news/uk-61834511.
53. "Slavery and the British Transatlantic Slave Trade," The National Archives, https://www.nationalarchives.gov.uk/help-with-your-research/research-guides/british-transatlantic-slave-trade-records.
54. Richard A. Burridge, "Being Biblical? Slavery, Sexuality, and the Inclusive Community," *Sewanee Theological Review* 52, no. 1 (2008): 17.
55. Travis Glasson, *Mastering Christianity: Missionary Anglicanism and Slavery in the Atlantic World* (New York: Oxford University Press, 2012).
56. James Walvin, "Slavery, the Slave Trade, and the Churches," *Quaker Studies* 12, no. 2 (2008): 191.
57. Robert Isaac Wilberforce and Samuel Wilberforce, eds., *The Correspondence of William Wilberforce*, vol. 1 (London: John Murray, 1838), 149, quoted in John White, "Christian Responsibility to Reform Society: The Example of William Wilberforce and the Clapham Sect," *Episcopal Review of Theology* 32, no. 2 (2008): 167.
58. Olaudah Equiano, *The Interesting Narrative of the Life of Olaudah Equiano, or Gustavus Vassa, the African* (1789; repr., Chicago: Lakeside Press, 2004).
59. C. C. Goen, *Broken Churches, Broken Nation: Denominational Schisms and the Coming of the Civil War* (Macon, GA: Mercer University Press, 1985).
60. Gardiner H. Shattuck Jr., *Episcopalians and Race* (Lexington: University Press of Kentucky, 2000), 7–29.
61. Jennifer C. Snow, *Mission, Race, and Empire: The Episcopal Church in Global Context* (New York: Oxford University Press, 2023).
62. Shattuck, *Episcopalians and Race*, 98–134.
63. Kortright Davis, "The Legacy of Black Prophetic Moments: Dynastic Monuments versus Dynamic Movements," *Anglican Theological Review* 97 no. 3 (2015): 452.
64. Kelly Brown Douglas, *Stand Your Ground: Black Bodies and the Justice of God* (Maryknoll, NY: Orbis Books, 2015).

65. Harold T. Lewis, *Yet with a Steady Beat: The African Struggle for Recognition in the Episcopal Church* (Valley Forge, PA: Trinity Press International, 1996), 180.
66. Desmond Tutu, *God Has a Dream: A Vision of Hope for Our Time* (New York: Doubleday, 2004), 2.
67. Desmond Tutu, "Dark Days: Episcopal Ministry in Times of Repression, 1976–1996," *Journal of Theology for Southern Africa* 118 (2004): 32.
68. Desmond Tutu, *No Future Without Forgiveness* (New York: Doubleday, 1999).
69. "Afro-Anglicanism: Ending Global Racism," Episcopal Archives, https://episcopalarchives.org/church-awakens/exhibits/show/awakening/afro-anglicanism.
70. "The Codrington Consensus: Agreed Statement from the Conference on Afro-Anglicanism," *Journal of Religious Thought* 44, no. 1 (1987): 84–93; Kortright Davis, "The Codrington Consensus," *Anglican Theological Review* 89, no. 1 (2007): 35–43.
71. "Anglican Indigenous Network," Anglican Communion, https://ain.anglicancommunion.org.
72. Jeanne Person, "Bp. MacDonald's Keynote for Practical Peacebuilding Is Featured in the Living Church Magazine," General Theological Seminary General News, February 7, 2013, http://news.gts.edu/2013/02/bp-macdonalds-keynote-for-practical-peacebuilding-is-featured-in-the-living-church-magazine.
73. Lambeth Conference 1968, Resolution 16, Anglican Communion, https://www.anglicancommunion.org/resources/document-library/lambeth-conference/1968/resolution-16-racism.aspx.
74. Franz Fanon, *The Wretched of the Earth*, trans. Richard Philcox (New York: Grove Press, 1963), 7.
75. Mark D. Chapman, *Anglicanism: A Very Short Introduction* (Oxford: Oxford University Press, 2006), 114–15.
76. Sachs, *Transformation of Anglicanism*, 336.
77. Ian T. Douglas, "Authority, Unity, and Mission in the Windsor Report," *Anglican Theological Studies* 87, no. 4 (2005): 573. This "mutual responsibility and interdependence in the body of Christ" was heralded in the 1963 Anglican Congress. See Stephen Fielding Bayne, *Mutual Responsibility and Interdependence in the Body of Christ* (New York: Seabury Press, 1963).
78. Douglas, "Authority, Unity, and Mission," 573.
79. Chapman, *Anglicanism*, 139.
80. Ian T. Douglas and Julie Wortman, "Lambeth 1998: A Call to Awareness," *Witness* 81 (September 1998): 24–25.
81. Miranda K. Hassett, *Anglican Communion in Crisis: How Episcopal Dissidents and Their African Allies Are Reshaping Anglicanism* (Princeton, NJ: Princeton University Press, 2007), 241.
82. Albert Memmi, *The Colonizer and the Colonized*, trans. Howard Greenfeld (New York: Orion Press, 1965).
83. "Anglican Women Gathered at the 51st Session of the United States Commission," Anglican News Service, March 6, 2007, https://www.anglicannews.org/news/2007/03/anglican-women-gathered-at-the-51st-session-of-the-united-nations-commission.aspx.
84. Rowan Williams, "Why the Covenant Matters," Dr. Rowan Williams, 104th Archbishop of Canterbury, March 5, 2012, http://rowanwilliams.archbishopofcanterbury.org/articles.php/2380/archbishop-why-the-covenant-matters.html.

85. Rowan Williams, "Archbishop's First Presidential Address at the Lambeth Conference," Dr. Rowan Williams, 104th Archbishop of Canterbury, July 28, 2008, http://rowan williams.archbishopofcanterbury.org/articles.php/1353/archbishops-first-presidential-address-at-lambeth-conference.html.

86. Marilyn McCord Adams provides an astute analysis of the first two drafts of the Covenant. See "Unfit for Purpose—or, Why a Pan-Anglican Covenant at This Time Is a Very Bad Idea!" *Modern Believing* 49, no. 4 (2008): 2–45.

87. "The Anglican Communion Covenant," Anglican Communion, http://www.anglican communion.org/commission/covenant/final/text.cfm.

88. Ruth Meyers, "The Baptismal Covenant and the Proposed Anglican Covenant," in *The Genius of Anglicanism: Perspectives on the Proposed Anglican Covenant*, ed. Jim Naughton (Chicago: Chicago Consultation, 2011), 13, http://www.chicagoconsultation.org/site/1/docs/Genius_of_Anglicanism_final.pdf.

89. Fredrica Harris Thompsett, "Inquiring Minds Want to Know: A Layperson's Perspective on the Proposed Anglican Covenant," in Naughton, *Genius of Anglicanism*, 30.

90. Ellen K. Wondra, "Problems with Authority in the Anglican Communion," in *Anglican Women on Church and Mission*, ed. Kwok Pui-lan, Judith A. Berling, and Jenny Plane Te Paa (New York: Morehouse Publishing, 2012), 23.

91. Wondra, "Problems with Authority," 25.

92. Ellen K. Wondra, *Questioning Authority: The Theology and Practice of Authority in the Episcopal Church and Anglican Communion* (New York: Peter Lang, 2018), 218–25.

93. Paul Avis, "Anglican Conciliarism: The Lambeth Conference as an Instrument of Communion," in *The Oxford Handbook of Anglican Studies*, ed. Mark D. Chapman, Sathianathan Clarke, and Martyn Percy (Oxford: Oxford University Press, 2015), 50.

94. Wondra, *Questioning Authority*, 14.

95. Archbishop Thabo Makgoba, "The Anglican Communion—A "Real" Family," Anglican Communion News Service, September 27, 2017, https://www.anglicannews.org/blogs/2017/09/the-anglican-communion-a-real-family.aspx#:~:text=The%20Primate%20of%20Southern%20Africa%2C%20Archbishop%20of%20Cape,differences%20and%20we%20are%20real%20with%20one%20another.%E2%80%9.

96. Anli Serfontein, "Makgoba: Lambeth 2020 Boycotts Will Not Help Anyone," *Church Times*, June 28, 2019, https://www.churchtimes.co.uk/articles/2019/28-june/news/world/makgoba-lambeth-2020-boycotts-will-not-help-anyone.

97. Leonardo Boff, *Ecclesiogenesis: The Base Communities Reinvent the Church*, trans. Robert R. Barr (Maryknoll, NY: Orbis Books, 1986), 4.

98. Elisabeth Schüssler Fiorenza, *In Memory of Her: A Feminist Theological Reconstruction of Christian Origins*, 10th-anniv. ed. (New York: Crossroad, 1994), 140, 150.

CHAPTER

3

Anglicanism and the Global Order

In **early 1942 during** World War II, Archbishop William Temple published an influential tract, *Christianity and the Social Order*, which sold an astonishing 139,000 copies and was read by people in the Church of England and beyond.[1] In this tract, the archbishop explained the reasons the Church needs to be involved in social and political issues and outlined practical proposals for British post-war society. Temple's work stands in the tradition of Anglican social thought that can be traced back to Frederick Dennison Maurice and Charles Gore (1853–1932). This Anglican tradition of social thought is relevant for thinking about contemporary issues and developing a Christian social theory for today.

The world we live in and the social, economic, and political issues we face today are very different from Temple's. Many former colonies in Asia and Africa became politically independent after World War II. In the 1950s and 1960s, various development theories were introduced, which resulted in a growing dependence of the Global South on the Global North. The Cold War divided the world into capitalist and communist blocs, with the nuclear arms race threatening the survival of human beings and the planet. Since the end of the Cold War, the tendrils of capitalism have reached deeper into the far corners of the earth. Globalization and the neoliberal economy have created a transnational capitalist class that amasses tremendous wealth, while the poor become poorer and many live at or below the subsistence level. According to a study by Oxfam in 2020, the world's richest 1 percent have accumulated twice as much wealth as

6.9 billion people, and much of that wealth is built on the backs of women doing unpaid and underpaid work.[2]

The coronavirus pandemic has further shone a spotlight on the social and economic disparity of the world. As of July 2023, 676 million in the world have contracted the virus with more than 6.8 million people dying from it. In the early months of the pandemic, we saw poor countries struggle to combat the virus with meager resources and the lack of essential medical supplies, including oxygen. The bodies of COVID victims were hastily buried in mass burial sites or burnt on funeral pyres that cramped New Delhi's sidewalks and car parks. After vaccines were developed, richer Western countries hoarded their vaccines and gave their citizens booster shots, while low-income countries faced an unconscionable shortage of vaccines. In the United States, the coronavirus has disproportionally affected Black and brown communities, because of poverty, ill health, and the lack of adequate access to health care and social supportive networks. The pandemic has shown how interconnected the world is and how we depend on each other for our survival. We can ill afford to go back to life as usual and must commit to building a more just and sustainable world order.

Postcolonial theory is helpful to illuminate the relationship between Anglicanism and the global order because it offers insights into the complex entanglement between culture, ideology, and religion on the one hand, and political economy and material conditions of peoples on the other. Since the 2000s, there has been growing interest in bringing postcolonial thought into dialogue with political science and economics through global perspectives.[3] For example, in the book *Postcolonial Economies*, contributors use postcolonial approaches to question Eurocentric understandings of economic theory and political-economic categories such as land, labor, and capital. They scrutinize Western economic concepts and emphasize cross-cultural differences in their conceptualization, pointing to more hybrid and grounded theorization. They argue that political economy and its justification are always shaped by social relations and cultural meanings, including those molded by colonialism and postcolonialism. These scholars criticize development policies and urge us to examine Western economic theories through an international frame, paying attention to the critical voices, concepts, and economic spaces emerging in the non-Western world.[4] Using some of these insights, this chapter begins by examining the contributions and limitations of the Christian Socialist movement in England and moves on to the critique of global economic order. In the final section, I will discuss the social and economic consequences of an unsustainable global order, plagued by climate change, deforestation, pollution, rising sea levels, and tsunamis.

The Christian Socialist Movement

The British Empire and its colonial expansion were built on a constellation of factors, including the industrial revolution, the development of mercantile trades and capitalism, and the strength of the navy and military power. The colonial project and capitalist development transformed the life worlds of the colonized while at the same time creating economic inequity and social ills at home. The Christian Socialist movement in Britain, which emerged in the mid-nineteenth century, offered an important critique of the economic order and its exploitation of workers. Unlike Marxism, which championed a classless society and revolutionary changes, British Christian Socialism advocated less radical reforms and promoted the formation of cooperative societies. The fact that the Church of England was an established church influenced its social teaching. The Church contributed to the common life and upheld the nation's traditions, moral values, and spiritual life. Anglican Christian Socialists argued that the Church had the responsibility to address injustice in society and teach what a good social life was.

The Christian Socialist movement began in England in 1848 with the trio Frederick Denison Maurice, John Malcolm Ludlow, and Charles Kingsley (1819–1875) as its leaders. When Maurice and his companions used the term "socialism" in mid-Victorian Britain, its meaning was quite different from the dominant usage of the term in later generations, and it was not seen as antithetical to Christianity. Maurice was born into a Unitarian family and later became an Anglican cleric, theologian, and professor. His interest in Christian Socialism was based on his continuing preoccupation with the social role of the church and his ecclesiological convictions. Maurice believed that God is love and Jesus's incarnation ushered in the Kingdom of Christ on earth. He saw the Bible as "the history of the establishment of a universal and spiritual kingdom, of that kingdom which God has ever intended for men."[5] He emphasized the abiding unity of human beings in God, but human egotism often stands in the way and creates division and competition. In the divine order, all human societies should live together in community and fellowship. His understanding of universal brotherhood or fraternity meant that humans are not created as separate creatures but are meant to have fellowship with and love one another.[6] The Church should be comprehensive and unifying and bear witness to the Kingdom of Christ and the goodness of the divine order. It had a role in social reform against the injustice of capitalism. For him, socialism meant the cooperative principle of society. He regarded socialism as a development and outcome of Christianity, and for it to be successful, it had to build on the Christian foundation. Therefore, he wanted to engage and challenge "the unsocial Christians and the unChristian socialists."[7]

Several social and cultural factors in mid-nineteenth-century Britain influenced the development of Christian Socialism. As social ethicist Gary Dorrien notes, England had no peasant class and had a strong tradition of liberalism, while the anarchist tradition was slight when compared to Continental Europe. Anglicanism catered to the upper class and the universities, emphasizing tradition and formality, but Anglican clergy in general looked at hypercapitalism and individualism with scorn. "These factors," he writes, "helped to make British socialism middle class, idealistic, religion friendly, and communal before it had a Marxist tradition or even a workers' party."[8] Christian Socialism was a way for middle- and upper-class Christians to overcome the hostilities and breaches between the prosperous classes and the working poor in industrial England.

Maurice was influenced by Ludlow, who grew up in France and was familiar with French cooperative socialism. Ludlow and others wanted to organize producer cooperatives, like the labor organizations in France. But members of the group often had divergent opinions on how to reform society. Maurice often objected to practical programs proposed by the group, for fear that this would lead to further divisiveness among the classes, during a period when revolutionary fervor swept through Europe. After Christian Socialism faltered, he focused his attention on education for the working poor and founded with his colleagues the Working Men's College in 1854. Several years earlier, he had established the Queen's College as an educational institution for women at a time when women's educational and job opportunities were limited.[9] While Maurice's cross-class effort on behalf of the workers was appreciated, he did not challenge the structural and systemic problems between the classes, nor did he advocate radical social transformation.

Rowan Williams points out that Maurice did not have a clear grasp of economic matters and showed no sign that he was aware of Marx's work. Maurice was too attuned to social harmony and denied the power patterns that undergirded class conflict.[10] Ludlow, who was more knowledgeable of secular socialism, criticized Maurice as Platonist, because his religious views were often hard to put into practice. Maurice held a hierarchal view of society and claimed that his political commitment was to "monarchy, aristocracy, and socialism."[11] Although he did not support the divine rights of the monarch, he had high regard for the sovereign and saw the Church as an inseparable part of the state. Williams says there is no denying Maurice's influence on later generations, but we should not be blind to the weaknesses of his political thinking. He says Maurice's thought was congenial to the "Victorian Anglican liberal temperament" and characterized by "benevolent paternalism."[12]

Studies on Maurice and the early Christian Socialists seldom place their thoughts in an international frame or scrutinized their positions on the expanding British Empire. In fact, both Maurice and Ludlow showed considerable interest in the culture and history of the people the British had colonized. Ludlow delivered a series of lectures on the history of India at the Working Men's College and published them as *British India*.[13] He had a benign view of the British Empire and its imperial institutions. In 1846 Maurice delivered a set of lectures in King's College London devoted to Islam, Hinduism, Buddhism, and the old Persian faith, which were published as *The Religions of the World and Their Relations to Christianity*.[14] He said that the English needed to know something about Hinduism and Buddhism because of Britain's control of between eighty to ninety million Indians and the Buddhist nation of Ceylon. Not being a specialist in religious traditions, Maurice relied on scholars who had studied the history and religions of the East and shared with them the kind of Orientalist biases that Edward Said criticized. For example, in the chapter on Hinduism, he assumed that Hindu village life was unchanging and stagnant for thousands of years.[15] He showed some regard for the Brahmins's pursuit of inner light and metaphysical truth but chastised popular devotion to the gods as vulgar and idolatrous.[16] He regarded English culture and religion as superior and the English people as possessing true faith and inner strength. He saw the British Empire as an instrument for propagating the gospel and the uplift of humanity, for he said he could not "see how the Hindoo race can ever be permanently raised about its present degradation."[17]

It was clear that Maurice's "paternalistic benevolence" extended not only to the working class in Britain but also to the colonial subjects of the empire. After the Indian mutiny in 1857, in which many British civilians were killed, Maurice's sermon on the National Day of Humiliation on October 7, 1857, did not question Britain's possession of Indian and Muslim lands and instead exhorted his countrymen and women to be forgiving and to witness the truth of humanity as one family under God. He displayed a condescending attitude as he told his countrymen, "You go forth as children of God to claim for Him, brethren for yourself. India asks you to do that, lest she should lose all the new culture you have given her, in the barbarous passions which it has not been able to overcome."[18]

Maurice was a charismatic leader, and his theology and social teachings influenced the later generation of Christian Socialists. The educational and moral emphases of Maurice and his companions and their aim of social fellowship echoed much of the paternalism of the Tory church. As such, their advocacy for religious involvement with social reform could be more acceptable to people in the Church.[19] The Christian Socialist movement was dissolved in the mid-1850s and revived in the late 1870s, largely led by Anglo-Catholics, when an economic recession caused rampant unemployment. Different Christian Socialist organizations in the Church of England and other denominations were formed in the 1880s and 1890s to agitate for social reform and influence the growing labor movement and cooperative societies. The Anglo-Catholic cleric Stewart Headlam (1847–1924), a student of Maurice at Cambridge, was influenced by Maurice's Christian humanism and his idea of universal brotherhood. But he wanted to add a distinct sense of social reform and socialism, gained from working with the young priests at St. Matthew's Bethnal Green in London, who were concerned about the social conditions of the poor. The group formed the Guild of St. Matthew in 1877, and Headlam wanted to combine Christian Socialism, which he took from Maurice and Kingsley, with the sacramental theology of the High Church. Headlam believed that all men were in Christ and there was no distinction between the sacred and the secular because all work on behalf of humanity belonged to God's work. While Maurice and Kingsley wanted to assemble a version of socialism that was compatible with traditional Christianity, Headlam sought to "reinterpret Christianity and to reorientate the Church, to correspond to existing and non-religious radical ideas."[20] Influenced by the Fabians, who espoused state socialism, Headlam was more aware of the need for systematic and political changes, instead of forming cooperative societies of production. The Guild championed the socialization of land and industries, universal suffrage, and a progressive income tax. It saw the disparity between the workers who produced much and consumed little and the classes who produced little and consumed much as against the Christian doctrine of brotherhood. The Guild spread from London to other cities, urging churchmen to work toward the fairer distribution of wealth and giving people a voice in their own government.[21] At its peak, the Guild had a membership of no more than 400 and it remained an elitist organization when its influence subsided in the 1900s.

Another influential group was the Christian Social Union, founded in Oxford by two Anglo-Catholic clergymen Henry Scott Holland (1847–1918) and Charles Gore. Gore was the editor of the widely read *Lux Mundi*, a collection of essays published in 1889 that attempted to bring the Christian tradition into conversation with modern thought and the political and social issues of the day.[22] The Christian Socialist Union was influenced by Maurice and was never committed to socialism in the sense of state ownership of the means of production. Bishop Brooke Foss Westcott served as its first president. The platform of the Union reflected Westcott's goal of applying Christian moral truths and principles to social and economic problems and claiming the Christian Law as the ultimate authority to rule social practice.[23] The work of the Union focused on moral persuasion and education to arouse social awareness in the church and influence cabinet members and bureaucrats for legislative changes. Holland argued that the socialist emphases on corporate responsibility for the welfare of the workers had a moral claim on Christian consciences. Gore's socialism was more like Maurice's, and he actively championed the cooperative movement. Though he supported legislation to improve industrial and social conditions, he did not advocate policies such as the nationalization of industries.[24] Some of the concrete actions taken by the Union included boycotting trades that paid low wages to workers and lobbying for minimum wage for industries where the workers were so scattered and could not easily organize into trade unions. At its peak, the Union had 6,000 members in different branches, including several bishops. But even as the Union sought to improve the welfare of workers, it had no working-class or trade union members, showing its class biases and the limits of its social vision and reach.[25]

In 1906, a third notable group, the Church Socialist League, was formed by Anglo-Catholics led by clerics G. Algernon West, Conrad Noel, and P. E. T. Widdrington. This was the first Anglican society specifically committed to socialism and was the most radical among the three groups. The socialism it pursued was Guild Socialism, which was discussed in the labor movement as an alternative to the wage system. There would be a guild for each industry and members in the guild would have the same status, no matter if they were employers or employees. Various Christian Socialist groups were also formed in other denominations, but it was the Anglo-Catholics who exerted the greatest influence. The British Christian Socialists pursued a wide variety of strategies for social changes, and they were involved in cooperative societies, the Fabian movement, and organizing labor and forming trade unions.[26] A group of leaders in the Methodist tradition, such as Hugh Price Hughes (1847–1902) and Samuel Keeble (1853–1946) embraced socialist ideas, and the Methodists played important roles in the labor movement and the founding of the Labour Party in 1906.[27]

Compared to Maurice's generation, the Christian Socialists of late Victorian England were more aware of the discrepancy between the lofty rhetoric of empire and the concrete exploitative situations. Some of the leaders were anti-imperialists, calling for public control of land, capital, industries, and distribution, as well as the abolition of the privileges of the aristocracy. Radical ideas such as these found their way on the pages of *Christian Socialist*, a paper edited by Anglo-Catholic cleric Charles L. Mason. This generation was more aware of pain, bloodshed, and wars brought about by British colonialism and empire-building. For example, a few young members of the Guild of St. Matthew were more willing to condemn colonialism as it affected the native populations, especially in Africa. The Boer War in South Africa provoked the indignation of Charles Gore and Henry Scott Holland, who criticized the seizure of Boer farmers' lands and the poor conditions of the concentration camps where women and children were placed. They and other British Christian Socialists were influenced by John Hobson's theory of imperialism serving as a tool for capitalism. They saw the problems when the state aligned with capitalist interests and even employed force, if needed, in securing mining interests, expanding the markets for manufactured goods, and suppressing revolts and protests.[28]

But not all Christian Socialists of this generation were against empire and colonial domination. Bishop Westcott represented those who continued to see the expansion of the British empire as an opportunity for the nation and the English church to work for "the brotherhood of Christian nations."[29] He believed the English race was superior and had the obligation to share the gospel with Africans and Asians. The empire was seen as belonging to the destiny of the English race and a progressive enlargement of human fellowship—from the family to the tribe, the kingdom, the nation, and the empire. He had little direct experience of the empire outside Britain and his knowledge of India was superficial, based on his reading and accounts from acquaintances. Yet, he claimed that the colonies in India had voluntarily placed themselves and their resources at the disposal of the "Mother Country." He was confident that the British Empire would not suffer the fate of other empires before it, with their rise and fall, because it was founded on benevolence.[30] Like other late Victorian bishops, he saw God's hand in the growth of the British Empire.

William Temple was influenced by Christian Socialism at Oxford, where it enjoyed its heyday in the early twentieth century. As an undergraduate at Balliol College, Oxford, he was exposed to the condition of the poor in London, which led him to form a lasting friendship with Albert Mansbridge, the founder of the Workers' Educational Association. He joined and taught at the Association and became its president from 1908 to 1924. He was influenced by Holland and Gore, and his fellow student at Balliol, Richard Henry Tawney (1880–1962), who would later write *Religion and the Rise of Capitalism*.[31] Temple joined the Christian Social Union and remained active in it for some years.[32] In 1918, he joined the Labour Party, which he thought could offer the best hope for social reconstruction after World War I, though he resigned after seven years because of his disappointment with the party.[33]

Temple's social thought was influenced by British Idealists, such as T. H. Green and Edward Caird, who in turn were shaped by the German philosophical tradition of the eighteenth and nineteenth centuries.[34] Hegel's understanding of history and society had a particular impact on Temple's thought. Hegel embraced a kind of state-collectivism, emphasizing the role of the state in bringing social freedom and fulfillment to individuals and society. Hegel also believed in continuous progress toward perfection and the providential guidance of world history. Such influences can be seen in Temple's writings, as in *Mens Creatrix*: "We may expect then that the course of history will continue in the future, as in the past, to consist in the conversion of nations, the building of the Christian State, and the incorporation of the Christian States within the fellowship of the Church, until at last Christendom and Humanity are interchangeable terms."[35] With his understanding of the state as a corporate and organic community, Temple was critical of the individualism of the industrialized society and the social condition in England, which he characterized as "a mass of rivalries and hostilities: capital against labour and labour against capital, firm against firm, man against man."[36] He argued that the Christian state would be a community that took care of the spiritual and economic needs of each individual while expecting each individual to assume responsibility toward the whole community.

Temple was one the most influential church leaders in the twentieth century because of his involvement in church and social reforms and his leadership in the ecumenical movement.[37] He was a leader of Life and Liberty, a movement that sought self-government of the Church of England, though he did not support disestablishment. In 1924, he organized the ecumenical Conference on Christian Politics, Economics, and Citizenship, which hoped to guide the British churches toward common political action ranging from education, gender relationships, war, organization of industries, and international relations. During the general strike in 1926, Temple joined an unsuccessful attempt at mediation between the miners and the government. As a senior churchman, Temple also spoke on other social issues and sought to influence government policies. The threat of the World Wars underscored the need for the cooperation of the nations, churches, and human communities. Temple played a significant leadership role in the ecumenical movement. He attended the Jerusalem Missionary Conference in 1928 and was active in the Faith and Order movement. In 1938 he served as the chair of the provisional committee of the World Council of Churches (WCC), then in the process of formation. Church historian John Kent has pointed out that Temple understood the need to unite Christian missions in the ecumenical movement, "but he did not question the missionary duty of Christianity to replace other world religions, and he found no need to go beyond Christianity in a discussion of the concept of 'religion.'"[38] Though Temple worked out from a Christian framework, he was a founder of the Council of Christians and Jews and was outspoken against the treatment of Jews during World War II.[39]

Christianity and the Social Order was Temple's most consequential writing, paving the way for the development of the British welfare state in the post-war years. He argued that the Christian church had the responsibility of interfering in politics and economics because as a fellowship of love, the church could not be blind to social injustice and human suffering. "It is bound to 'interfere' because it is by vocation the agent of God's purpose, outside the scope of which no human interest or activity can fall."[40] Since most of the work of the church in the world is done by Christians fulfilling their responsibilities, the main task of the church is to "inculcate Christian principles and the power of the spirit."[41] Temple developed three social principles. The first is freedom, which recognizes the personhood of each person since each one is a child of God, whom God loves and for whom Christ died. The second is fellowship because no person lives an isolated life but as a member of social units such as the family, school, church, trade union, city, county, and nation. The third is service, which is done when individuals or groups seek the general welfare of society through self-sacrifice or voluntary work.[42] Temple then deduced from these social principles broad practical objectives for the future of British society, including a healthy family and living environment, free education, livable income, representation of labor in industry, paid holidays, and freedom of worship, speech, and assembly. Temple died in 1944 and did not live to see the Labour Party come into power and implement many of his agendas.

Scholars evaluated Temple's social teaching and his involvement in politics in divergent ways. Some hailed him as a prophet, who helped the Church of England to reform and address the social disparities between the classes. Others criticized him for not following through with the social reforms he had proposed and for his consensus-building approach to national and church politics, which was not always successful. Temple's work was international in scope, as evidenced by his leadership in the ecumenical movement, but he had not spoken much on behalf of the vast population that the British colonized. Ellen K. Wondra observes, "Although Temple was a national leader in Great Britain during a crucial period in the history of the British Empire, his work shows little concern with the global reality of the British Empire."[43] His social teaching continues to exert influences in the Anglican Communion and beyond. Writing on the fiftieth anniversary of the publication of *Christianity and the Social Order*,

Stephen Spencer says that it was an unusual volume in that "its author was able to draw from both academic and practical resources, and this may have been one of the reasons for its great success."[44] Archbishop Thabo Makgoba of South Africa finds the social principles developed in the book insightful for addressing apartheid in his country because they were based on the witness of scripture and its interpretation through reason in the light of tradition. As world politics becomes increasingly polarized, Makgoba praises Temple for his example of pursuing dialogue with those who might not agree with him on what constitutes the common good.[45]

The British Christian Socialist tradition is an important part of Anglican moral theology and left an influential legacy. From Maurice to Temple, the Christian Socialists argued for Christian involvement in society to improve the conditions of the poor and eradicate social wrongs. From the earlier attempts to form cooperative societies to Temple's proposals for a welfare society, the Christian Socialists advocated for economic democracy and bridging the gap between the capitalists and laborers. From hindsight, their proposals might not be radical enough to solve structural issues of society, but they did attempt to cross class boundaries to teach, organize, and advocate for the poor. From a postcolonial perspective, we have seen that though some of them spoke against imperialism, others continued to uphold the superiority of the British nation and saw it as having a special role to play in world history as a Christian state. After World War II, as many Asian and African colonies struggled for independence, the church faced new issues and needed to wrestle with a new emerging world order.

The Anglican Tradition and Economic Justice

In the post-war era, European countries had to recover from the ruins of devastation, and the world economy was affected by the war. Meeting several years after the war, the bishops at Lambeth 1948 urged the statesmen of the world "to do their utmost to frame a world policy for the fuller development and more just distribution of the world's economic resources, to meet the needs of men and women in all nations."[46] Various development theories and measures were introduced to alleviate poverty in poor countries and achieve economic growth. These development policies assumed that these poor countries were "undeveloped" or "underdeveloped" and needed to follow Western models of economic development. They were not able to follow a modernization process based on their culture and particular context. As a result, Esther Mombo stated, "Modernization was within the framework of existing economic, political, and military domination and racist attitudes and behavior."[47] Development, she said, became an alienating and humiliating process that did not fit into indigenous legacy. While development improved the livelihoods of certain sectors and moved some people from one class to another, many were left behind and they remained in the underclass, often living in big slum areas inside or near urban cities, such as Nairobi, Lagos, Mumbai, Manila, Mexico City, and Buenos Aires. Moreover, development theories have not adequately addressed the relation between gender and poverty. South African scholar and HIV/AIDS researcher Beverley Haddad wrote, "Development as theory and practice is a gender issue and all our analysis needs to be undertaken from the standpoint that unequal power relations exist between men and women."[48] She argued that poor and marginalized women are discriminated against in macro-social and economic policies resulting in this group bearing the brunt of poverty in society.

Using Marxist social analyses, liberation theologians from Latin America offered the sharpest and searing critique of capitalism and development theories, which resulted in the growing dependency of countries in the Global South on the Global North. Peruvian theologian Gustavo Gutiérrez argued that poverty is a scandalous condition and is against God's will, for God has a preferential option for the poor. Salvation is not just personal and spiritual but has a social dimension, which includes social and political liberation from oppression. The church must commit to a new and radical service for the people and offer itself as a sacrament for the salvation of the world and a sign of liberation of humankind.[49] Base Christian communities were formed in Latin America, mostly among the Catholics, as a grassroots movement to conscientize the people and address communal issues. The Anglican churches in Latin America were relatively small and did not participate much in the movement. Even so, some young

Brazilian Episcopal clergy have been more willing to use the language of liberation theology than others in the Anglican churches in Latin America to articulate political concerns during the authoritarian regimes of the 1960s to the 1990s.[50]

The Cold War divided the world into two different ideological and political camps, with countries in the "Third World" struggling to survive amid the big powers. The old form of colonialism was replaced by neocolonial control, which took the forms of economic, political, and cultural domination and conditional aid. The challenging sociopolitical situations prompted the development of contextual theologies around the world. Taiwanese theological educator Shoki Coe, who coined the term "contextualization" in the 1970s said that this is a way of doing theology that responds "to the Gospel itself as well as to the urgent issues in the historic realities, particularly those of the Third World."[51] M. M. Thomas, a leader in the Asian ecumenical movement, stated that Christian mission is concerned with salvation, "not in any pietistic or individualist isolation, but related to and expressed within the material, social and cultural revolution of our time."[52] Anglican churches around the world had to respond to the sociopolitical development of the newly independent countries, poverty and economic disparity, rapid urbanization, and increasing ethnic and religious strife. Lambeth 1968 addressed the plight of developing countries and the bishops urged for "the careful study of the issues of development including the new economic and political structures which it demands."[53] They supported the efforts of the United Nations agencies to bring about world economic justice and urged churches in industrialized countries to influence their governments to provide more financial support and aid to poorer countries. Meeting after the oil crisis in the 1970s, Lambeth 1978 presented a detailed statement of the world situation and called for "the establishment of a new economic order" to reverse "the process by which the rich become richer and the poor poorer."[54] They implored the churches to pay attention to urbanization and urban mission, nuclear disarmament, the conservation of the environment, the consequences of large-scale development schemes, just distribution of resources, and overindulgent lifestyles.

In the 1980s, neoliberalism championed free-market capitalism, which advocates for the elimination of price controls, the deregulation of capital markets, and the lowering of trade barriers. The neoliberal economic system created greater injustice and disparity because the poor countries could not compete fairly in the so-called free market. The rules devised by affluent governments often advance their own interests at the expense of farmers, laborers, small business owners, and people struggling to survive in the developing world. Again and again, people have risen to protest the free trade agreements and unjust economic policies, such as the Chiapas movement of indigenous peoples and subsistence farmers in Mexico. Anglican church leaders have spoken out against the neoliberal system: for example, Julio E. Murray, bishop of the Episcopal Church of Panama, stated, "Many people in the global South believe they are harmed by global economic policies. . . . Our faith compels us to seek justice, to witness to the presence of God, and to be part of the lives and struggles of the people made weak and vulnerable by structures and cultures."[55]

As neoliberal policies exerted pressure and harmed the economy of poor countries, some resorted to borrowing loans from other governments, international financial institutions, and private capitalist markets to run the government and pay for infrastructure, such as roads, health care, and public services. Some of the loans were used to support the elites in developing countries who allied with Western interests during the Cold War and fattened the purses of dictators. Long-term government debt of all developing countries skyrocketed from $45 billion in 1970 to over $1,459 billion in 2004.[56] The debt crisis affected especially the countries in Sub-Saharan Africa and Latin America. To receive loans, aid, and debt relief, developing countries are required to follow structural adjustment programs imposed by the World Bank and the International Monetary Fund (IMF). Such a process is antidemocratic, for it denies the people and the poor nations the right to determine their own economic and political policies. These countries must cut social spending, privatize public utilities or basic services, reduce inflation, remove price controls, and reduce tariffs and restrictions on foreign trade. As a result, widespread protests against economic liberalization and hardships broke out in the countries affected by the World Bank and IMF programs. In response to the international debt crisis, a global campaign for debt relief and cancellation began in the 1980s and gathered momentum in the 1990s.

Anglican churches have worked for debt relief and joined a broad coalition of churches, ecumenical bodies, and nongovernmental groups to support Jubilee 2000. This international movement in more than forty countries organized protests and mobilized for debt cancellation for the world's poorest countries by the year 2000. Debt relief is appealing to Christians because it is derived from the biblical idea of the year of the Jubilee. The Jubilee year was a year of release from indebtedness and all types of bondages, and all properties would be returned to their original owners (Lev. 25:10, 23–38). Both the Church of England and the Episcopal Church played active roles in Jubilee 2000 and encouraged church members and the public to push for debt cancellation. Within the Anglican Communion, leadership came primarily from the Southern bishops. Meeting in 1997 in Kuala Lumpur, Malaysia, these bishops decried "the crippling effect of international debt" and called for churches in the West to put pressure on their governments and the World Bank and IMF to make the year 2000 a Year of Jubilee.[57] Bishops from the Global South made debt relief a central issue at Lambeth 1998. Speaking at a plenary at the conference, Archbishop Njongonkulu Ndungane of Cape Town urged the bishops to support Jubilee 2000 and said, "It's a vision that releases the poor from the prison of indebtedness and dependent poverty. It's a vision where God's people have all that is necessary to live a human life." He further stressed, "The crisis of international debt that we are debating here today is not just a matter for the poorest countries. Nor is it a matter that only affects sovereign governments. It affects all of us everywhere."[58]

Lambeth 1998 recognized the urgency of the international debt crisis, saying, "Children are dying, and societies are unravelling under the burden of debt." Its resolutions on international debt and economic justice supported substantial debt relief, including the cancellation of unpayable debts of the world's poorest countries and the unilateral initiatives taken by governments to write off some loans. In addition, the resolutions encouraged bringing all creditors together to agree on debt relief and the participation of debtors in the negotiation process.[59] Jubilee 2000 and other similar efforts led successfully to debt cancellation in countries that had qualified under the Heavily Indebted Poor Countries scheme. The political mobilization and demonstrations contributed to a wider context of international demands for global justice. In his book *Dismantling Mammon*, Archbishop Justin Welby writes, "Perhaps the churches' finest hour in dethroning Mammon in recent years has been Church support for Jubilee 2000. . . . Sustained support from Christians and others across the world ultimately led to the cancellation of more than $100 billion of debt owed by thirty-five of the poorest countries."[60]

Even though debt relief and cancellation offer a respite for poor countries, they do not address the root causes of inequity of the neocolonial and neoliberal economy. From a postcolonial viewpoint, unless extractive capitalism and the global economic and financial systems are changed, the debt problem would come back to haunt us again. Anglican church leaders in the Global South had to push back against a system that preys on the world's poor and vulnerable people. Partly as a follow-up to the Lambeth Conference in 1998, the Council of Anglican Provinces of Africa and the World Bank sponsored a conference in Nairobi in March 2000. The conference brought together African Anglican bishops and other church leaders with officials from the World Bank from Africa and abroad. This was the first time that the religious sphere and the World Bank had come together and worked for poverty alleviation in Africa. The Church brought to the discussion the human face of development and the religious imperative of caring for the least among us. In addition to debt relief, both sides agreed to work together on the HIV/AIDS pandemic, the crisis of education, and the lack of health services. They prioritized the most vulnerable in society, including women, children, and youth. Gender inequality was highlighted, as women in rural communities lack access to education, health care, and other opportunities.[61]

Prophetic voices were heard from Anglican leaders from other parts of the Global South. For example, Bishop Murray urged churches to support the AGAPE (Alternative Globalization Addressing People and Earth) process started by the WCC. The AGAPE economy is based on the rejection of debt and financialization and affirming an economy of forgiveness, caring, and justice. It also rejects an economy of consumerism and proposes an "economy of sufficiency," which recognizes limits in all our activities in the economy, in the use of natural resources, in our personal lives, and the exercise of public authorities.[62] Instead of blindly following Western development models, he said, "We need an economy that conserves and celebrates the ways of life and economies practiced by marginalized communities. These ways of life depend on need rather than greed, and respect the integrity of all living beings, which are considered of equal importance." The book *Postcolonial Economies* encourages the reclamation and study of non-Western theories and concepts of economic relations. Murray cited as an example the old tradition of *sumak kawsay*, which means "good living," based on the ancestral and communitarian knowledge and lifestyle of the Quechua people. The concept of "good living" is in contrast to "living good," which places value on consumerism and encourages a hedonistic lifestyle. The ultimate goal of "good living" is to live in harmony with the community, family, nature, and the universe.[63] From a cultural tradition, *sumak kawsay* has grown to become a political project that aims to achieve collective well-being, social responsibility in relation to nature, and a halt to capital accumulation and economic expansion. Both the Ecuadorian and Bolivian governments have adopted it. The principle of *sumak kawsay* teaches us that we belong to the land, and with all other species we are part of an amazing organic web of life. Murray noted, "This principle is present in many communities, such as *Ujama* and *ubuntu*, the African concept of personhood in which the identity of self is understood to be formed interdependently through community."[64]

Anglican churches also addressed economic injustice and practiced solidarity with the poor by supporting the Millennium Development Goals (MDGs). The MDGs were established by the United Nations in 2000, which included the eradication of extreme poverty and hunger, combating HIV/AIDS and malaria, and working for gender equality by the year 2015.[65] In Botswana, Anglican churches have built schools to assist the government in providing primary education and helped educate women to take care of reproductive health. Churches responded to the HIV/AIDS pandemic by establishing numerous daycare centers for children infected by the virus and providing pastoral support and palliative care for people with HIV/AIDS. In addition, the churches emphasize environmental preservation and work with companion dioceses and other churches to form partnerships for global development.[66] Anglican churches in other African countries, such as Angola, the Democratic Republic of Congo, and Malawi, have also taken measures to support the MDGs. In the United States, the Episcopal Church formally endorsed the MDGs in 2003 and voted to make the MDGs a mission priority in 2006. It allocated resources to achieve these goals and asks dioceses and congregations to form ministries to work on these goals. Bishop Frank Griswold, who had served as the presiding bishop of the Episcopal Church, said, "The Millennium Development Goals embody that work of the reconciliation we have been called to do. They are humanity's response, indeed the Church's response, to a world that stands desperately in need of repair and rebuilding."[67]

The Anglican Communion provided opportunities for provinces working on the MDGs and other issues to learn and partner with one another. At the international conference in 2007 in Boksburg near Johannesburg, South Africa, participants reviewed the responses of the Communion to the MDGs and analyzed the impact of the goals on women and children. The conference also offered a platform for African leaders to explore strategies to battle against poverty, HIV/AIDS, and other social ills.[68] One of the MDGs was promoting gender equality and empowering women. Anglican women leaders insisted that the MDGs would not be achieved if women's needs are not met. Helen Wangusa, a former Anglican observer at the United Nations, said, "If gender and women's empowerment are not taken into account, we will not achieve any development, even with our MDGs as a framework."[69] A memorable symbol of the Church's commitment to the MDGs was the Walk of Witness during Lambeth 2008. Hundreds of bishops in their purple cassocks and their spouses walked from Whitehall to Lambeth Palace carrying banners such as "Keep the Promise, Halve Poverty by 2015."

While the MDGs brought Anglican churches together to work for economic and social justice, the goals have not been accomplished and much work needs to be done. Archbishop Makgoba says the Church needs better knowledge about the theories underpinning the global economic order and the challenges of globalization, because the Church faces complex global issues and wrestles with "the interface between economics and theology; profit-making and the prophetic; the market place and mission; self-interest and compassion; market value and Kingdom values; personal wealth and community-building; corruption and integrity; free trade and fair trade." He does not see economics as foreign to theology, because he regards economics as the way we organize ourselves and our resources in response to God's creative love. He dreams that "we will develop new Anglican social teaching on the economy, reflecting a new theology and ecclesiology of generosity, encompassing appropriate liturgies and social outreach, which empower us to speak with a prophetic voice in our local economic contexts."[70] Let us hope that many in the Anglican Communion will share his dream and respond to his call in fresh and innovative ways.

Toward a Sustainable Global Order

The MDGs include ensuring environmental sustainability, which is critical to the future of life on earth. The global order we inherit today is shaped by five hundred years of colonialism, conquest, and genocide, which affected not only humans but also brought lasting changes to the flora, fauna, and natural habitats of the colonized world. The colonizers extracted precious natural resources from the colonies to meet the growing demands and satisfy the insatiable desires of bourgeois life in the metropolitan centers. Environmental historian Alfred Crosby has coined the term "ecological imperialism,"[71] which refers to the dispossession of indigenous lands and the introduction of germs and diseases that decimated the indigenous populations. It also involved the ill-conceived introduction of foreign livestock and plants as well as Western agricultural practices for profit-making. The biological expansion of Europe led to the displacement of native populations and Europe controlling the most important agricultural lands and other resources. Later, with the development of new technology and biological sciences, corporations began to privatize the necessities of life, such as water and the patent control of life forms, in what is called "biocolonization." Big agribusinesses compete to monopolize plants, seeds, and other life forms through patents, licenses, genetic engineering, and other biotechnological methods. Sometimes, they steal or take away biological resources and indigenous knowledge for their own use and gain.

There has been an increased conversation between postcolonial studies and environmental studies, and a subfield, "postcolonial ecocriticism," has been developed. Scholars emphasize the entanglement between human history and environmental history, as Pablo Mukherjee says: "Any field purporting to theorise the global conditions of colonialism/imperialism, decolonisation and neo-colonialism (let us agree to call it 'postcolonial studies') cannot but consider the complex interplay of 'environmental' categories such as water, land, energy, habitat, migration, with political or cultural categories such as state, society, conflict, literature, theatre, visual arts."[72] In recent years, the effects of climate change and global warming have been devastating, as record-breaking heatwaves, terrifying storms and floods, and rising sea levels threatened the livelihood of many people and caused the extinction of numerous species. We have entered the Anthropocene age, in which human activities have significant impacts on the planet's climate and ecosystems. Scientists and the United Nations have warned that "it is now or never" to limit global warming to 1.5 Celsius to avert climate emergencies and catastrophes. Churches and faith communities must take action to transform moral values, change consumerist patterns, advocate policy changes, foster international cooperation, and shape a green culture. In his encyclical *Laudato Si'*, Pope Francis appeals for "a new dialogue about how we are shaping the future of our planet," as environmental crises require "a new and universal solidarity."[73]

Within the Anglican Communion, there was a growing awareness of the environmental crisis, as shown in the resolutions of successive Lambeth Conferences. Lambeth 1978 called attention to the impact of overconsumption, nuclear armament, urbanization, and inappropriate uses of technology on the natural environment. "The resources of our planet are limited; delicate ecological balances can be disturbed by modern technology, or threatened by the toxic effects of human ingenuity."[74] A decade later, the Lambeth Conference encouraged the provinces to participate in the "Justice, Peace, and Integrity of Creation" program of the WCC. It also addressed specifically the concerns of churches in the South Pacific Islands and supported their opposition to the testing of nuclear weapons, the dumping of nuclear waste, and the establishment of military bases on their lands and seas.[75] By 1998, the environmental crisis had become more severe, and the Lambeth Conference issued a comprehensive call to churches, ecumenical partners, faith communities, governments, and transnational companies "to work for sustainable society in a sustainable world; to recognise the dignity and rights of all people and the sanctity of all life, especially the rights of future generations; to ensure the responsible use and re-cycling of natural resources; [and] to bring about economic reforms which will establish a just and fair trading system both for people and for the environment."[76] The 2022 Lambeth Conference devoted a day to discuss the environment and sustainable development. Elizabeth Wathuti, a Kenyan environment and climate activist and founder of the Green Generation Initiative, said at the Conference, "Faith leaders and faith communities have a role to play when it comes to helping us to tackle the climate crisis with urgency. . . . [W]e are facing the greatest challenge of humanity right now, and unless we take urgent action, then the world and this planet [are] going to be uninhabitable and unlivable for most people, especially those who have done the least to cause the crisis."[77]

Anglican church leaders and organizations have issued statements on climate crisis and called for action. In June 2015, the Ecumenical Patriarch Bartholomew, leader of the Eastern Orthodox Church, and Archbishop Justin Welby jointly wrote in the *New York Times,* "Our response to climate change—both in terms of mitigation and adaptation—will reduce human suffering, while preserving the diversity and beauty of God's creation for our children."[78] The Anglican Communion Environmental Network (ACEN) has organized programs and coordinated efforts "to strive to safeguard the integrity of creation, and sustain and renew the life of the earth"—one of the five marks of mission of the Anglican Communion. It has worked with the Anglican Indigenous Network to bring the perspectives from indigenous communities from Aotearoa, Polynesia, Amazonia,

Africa, and the Arctic on planetary environmental emergency to the attention of the Communion. The chair of the ACEN Archbishop Makgoba hosted a meeting for seventeen Anglican Bishops for Climate Justice, often dubbed the eco-bishops, near Cape Town in 2015. These bishops came from places impacted by climate change, many in drought-stricken or coastal regions and cities vulnerable to rising sea levels. The report from the meeting "The World Is Our Host: A Call for Urgent Action for Climate Justice" emphasizes the link between climate justice and social justice because climate change affects poor communities disproportionately. It also clearly states that climate justice and environmental degradation have a spiritual dimension and the Church needs to act.

> We believe that the problem is spiritual as well as economic, scientific and political, because the roadblock to effective action relates to basic existential issues of how human life is framed and valued: including the competing moral claims of present and future generations, human versus non-human interests, and how the lifestyle of wealthy countries is to be balanced against the basic needs of the developing world. For this reason the Church must urgently find its collective moral voice.[79]

Dioceses, local churches, and laypeople in the Anglican churches have taken initiatives to respond to the environmental crisis in their particular contexts. Churches in the Global North address consumerism, recycling, and renewable energy to curb CO2 emissions. For example, the Episcopal Power and Light project was formed to encourage churches to use renewable energy, create emission-free churches, and educate parishioners to become energy-conscious. This work has since been expanded to become the Interfaith Power and Light project, which encourages "putting faith into action for a safe climate."[80] In the Global South, churches work with NGOs and international partners to bring a spotlight to the ways climate change has destroyed their communities and press for relief. For example, the priests in the Anglican Church of Melanesia in the South Pacific had to provide support and pastoral care when king tides encroached the shorelines of the Solomon Islands and the floods in Honiara in 2014 displaced 10,000 people and killed 22. As the church undertook the work of climate change mitigation because its members were at risk, Archbishop of Melanesia George Takeli appealed for help through the Anglican networks.[81]

An increasing number of theologians and ethicists have responded to the planetary crisis by reexamining the relationships between humans, nature, and God. Some of the Anglican theologians have looked to the Anglican tradition for insights to contribute to Christian ecological theology that can provide the basis for an earth ethic. Martha Kirkpatrick, an Episcopal priest and the Diocese of Maine's Missioner for Environmental Stewardship, focuses on the doctrine of Incarnation, which is central to Christian belief and a matter of emphasis in Anglican theology. She writes, "Classical incarnational theology and its understandings of the nature of the relationship between the spiritual and material world provide an essential foundation for aligning ourselves to God and creation, as the Incarnation explicates our covenantal and sacramental relationship to God and to all life."[82] Drawing from the covenant with Noah, the book of Isaiah, and the story of Job, Kirkpatrick emphasizes a close linkage between humans and the rest of creation in the Bible. "The natural world suffers as humans suffer, and is reborn and renewed as humans experience redemption" (e.g., Isa. 24:4–6a).[83] God so loved the world that God decided to enter into creation, and in Jesus Christ, the divine nature and the human nature became one. Jesus became human flesh and symbolized the immanence and full presence of God in the material world. "The Incarnation affirms the flesh, and with it all materiality. This means the vocation of Jesus Christ is to serve the whole of creation, not just humans."[84] In this incarnational ecology, the transcendence and immanence of God are not separated, neither are creation and redemption. This understanding of Jesus does not lead to an anthropocentric or individualistic orientation of Christian faith hostile to a loving relationship with the earth. Instead, God's incarnation points to the reconciliation and union of God with creation and our responsibility to transform and heal the earth. Kirkpatrick says, "Reclaiming our understanding of the Incarnation as set forth by the ecumenical councils calls us to recognize our oneness with creation, and to participate in the divine project of bringing God's kingdom to earth—to an earth renewed.

The new kingdom is not a spiritualized one, but rather heaven on earth, recapitulating all of creation."[85]

While it is helpful to reclaim incarnational theology to address our environmental crisis, some Anglican theologians from the Global South expand our theological repertory by bringing their cultures into critical dialogue with Christian theology. Kapya John Kaoma, an Anglican priest, scholar, and human rights activist originally from Zambia, points to the ecological themes in African worldviews, such as the creation myths, the understanding of land as commons or community trust, the principle of interconnectedness, and the African notions of time and space.[86] He focuses on the African concept of *ubuntu*, which "emphasizes right relationships in the universe. It also recognizes that we are all inextricably bound up with each other's being."[87] The ethics of *ubuntu* has the potential to address corruption, environmental degradation, and genocide and transform social and political conditions and global relations. Archbishop Desmond Tutu applied the *ubuntu* principle when he established the Truth and Reconciliation Commission, and he also saw the harmonious relationships of humans with nonhuman members of the cosmos as crucial to *ubuntu*.[88] Drawing from Africans' reverence to the "elders" and "ancestors," Kaoma develops a model of Christ as the ecological ancestor. He argues that the biblical world also held ancestors in great esteem. Abraham, Sarah, and Hagar; Isaac and Rachel; and Jacob, Rebecca, and Leah were regarded as founders of the tribe and nation. Honoring the traditions of ancestors can also be found in Jesus's genealogy, which linked the past, present, and future generations. Christ is not just "our ancestor" for humans, but the ecological ancestor of all creation, as John's Gospel states, "All things came into being through him, and without him not one thing came into being" (John 1:3). As Christ is the firstborn of all creation, we were created to be in communion with nature and not dominion.[89] Kaoma underscores that African culture and philosophy have much to offer to the development of Christian ecological ethics, just as Greek and Western philosophical concepts had contributed to theological construction.

This chapter traces the responses of the Anglican churches to the changing world order from the mid-nineteenth century to the present day. Whereas the mid-nineteenth-century Christian Socialists were still confident in the "benevolent" British Empire, Anglican thinkers at the end of the century cast doubt on colonialism and the brutality of imperialistic expansion. With the decline of the British Empire and the dissolution of colonies in the twentieth century, the Anglican Communion had to grapple with the emerging world order defined by neocolonialism and financial control. Theologian Kathryn Tanner has encouraged us to draw from our theological resources to address the devastating impact of the current finance-dominated capitalist system.[90] In order to do so, voices of Anglican leaders from the Global South are indispensable, as they have criticized Western models of development and articulated critical social and ethical principles such as *sumak kawsay* and *ubuntu*, rooted in indigenous Quechua tradition and African cultures, to stimulate alternative thinking about the common good and our responsibility to future generations. In July 2023, the planet saw its hottest days on record and extreme weather worldwide endangered the survival of vulnerable populations and species. As we face global environmental emergency which threatens the habitability of the planet, Anglican social teaching can be appropriated critically through a postcolonial lens, and Anglican networks, as evident in the past, can provide the linkages for collective action and solidarity.

Notes

1. William Temple, *Christianity and the Social Order* (1942; repr., New York: Seabury, 1976).
2. "World's Richest 1% Have More Than Twice as Much Wealth as 6.9 Billion People, Says Oxfam," Oxfam Canada, January 19, 2020, https://www.oxfam.ca/news/worlds-richest-1-have-more-than-twice-as-much-wealth-as-6-9-billion-people-says-oxfam.
3. For example, S. Charusheela and Eiman Zein-Elabdin, eds., *Postcolonialism Meets Economics* (New York: Routledge, 2004); Revathi Krishnaswamy and John C. Hawley, eds., *The Postcolonial and the Global* (Minneapolis: University of Minnesota Press, 2008);); and Olivia U. Rutazibwa and Robbie Shilliam, eds., *Routledge Handbook of Postcolonial Politics* (New York: Routledge, 2018).
4. Jane Pollard, Cheryl McEwan, and Alex Hughes, eds., *Postcolonial Economies* (London: Zed Books, 2011).
5. Frederick Denison Maurice, *The Kingdom of Christ, or, Hints on the Principles, Ordinances, and Constitution of the Catholic Church in Letters to a Member of the Society of Friends*, vol. 1, 2nd ed. (1842, repr., London: James Clark, 1959), 254–55.
6. Jeremy Morris, *F. D. Maurice and the Crisis of Christian Authority* (New York: Oxford University Press, 2005), 148–49.

7. Maurice wrote this in *The Christian Socialist* (July 25, 1851), quoted in Ronald H. Preston, "The Legacy of the Christian Socialist Movement in England," in *Religion, Economics and Social Thought*, ed. Walter Block and Irving Hexham (Vancouver, BC: Frazer Institute, 1986), 183.
8. Gary Dorrien, "Economic Democracy as Political Theology: The British Anglican Socialist Tradition," *Anglican Theological Review* 102, no. 4 (2020): 541.
9. Ellen K. Wondra, "Introduction," in Frederick D. Maurice, *Reconstructing Christian Ethics*, ed. Ellen K. Wondra (Louisville, KY: Westminster John Knox Press, 1995), xi–xii.
10. Rowan D. Williams. "Liberation Theology and the Anglican Tradition," in Rowan D. Williams and David Nicholls, *Politics and Theological Identity: Two Anglican Essays* (London: Jubilee Group, 1984), 19.
11. Letter to J. M. Ludlow, quoted by W. Merlin Davies, *An Introduction to F. D. Maurice's Theology* (London: SPCK, 1964), 123.
12. Williams, "Liberation Theology and the Anglican Tradition," 19.
13. John M. Ludlow, *British India: Its Races and History Considered with Reference to the Mutinies of 1857* (London: Macmillan, 1958).
14. Frederick Denison Maurice, *The Religions of the World and their Relations to Christianity*, 6th ed. (London: Macmillan, 1886).
15. Maurice, *Religions of the World*, 38–39.
16. Maurice, *Religions of the World*, 44–45.
17. Maurice, *Religions of the World*, 63.
18. Frederick Denison Maurice, *Sermons Preached at Lincoln's Inn Chapel*, vol. 2 (London: Macmillan, 1891), 218. Alison Milbank brought my attention to this sermon, see "Maurice as a Resource for the Church Today," in *Theology Reforming Society: Revisiting Anglican Social Theology*, ed. Stephen Spencer (London: SCM, 2017), 29.
19. Edward Norman, *The Victorian Christian Socialists* (Cambridge: Cambridge University Press, 1987), 8–9.
20. Norman, *Victorian Christian Socialists*, 107.
21. Henry Pelling, *The Origins of the Labour Party, 1880–1900* (Oxford: Clarendon Press, 1954), 134.
22. Charles Gore, ed., *Lux Mundi: A Series of Studies in the Religion of the Incarnation* (London: John Murray, 1889).
23. Norman, *Victorian Christian Socialists*, 173.
24. Paul Avis, "Anglican Social Thought Encounters Modernity: Brooke Foss Westcott, Henry Scott Holland and Charles Gore," in Spencer, *Theology Reforming Society*, 77.
25. Preston, "Legacy of the Christian Socialist Movement in England," 186.
26. Dorrien, "Economic Democracy as Political Theology," 544.
27. Nigel Scotland, "Methodist and the English Labour Movement 1800–1906," *Anvil* 14, no. 1 (1997): 44–45.
28. Philip Lockley, "Social Anglicanism and Empire: C. F. Andrew's Christian Socialism," *Studies in Church History* 54 (2018): 420.
29. Brooke Foss Westcott, "The Call of the English Nation and of the English Church," in *Christian Aspects of Life* (London: Macmillan, 1897), 147, quoted in Lockley, "Social Anglicanism and Empire," 419.
30. Avis, "Anglican Social Thought Encounters Modernity," 58–59.

31. R. H. Tawney, *Religion and the Rise of Capitalism* (New York: Harcourt, Brace, 1926).
32. John Kent, *William Temple: Church, State, and Society in Britain, 1880–1950* (Cambridge: Cambridge University Press, 1992), 12.
33. Stephen Spencer, *William Temple: A Call to Prophesy* (London: SPCK, 2001), 62.
34. Stephen Spencer, "History and Society in William Temple's Thought," *Studies in Christian Ethics* 5, no. 2 (1992): 61–73.
35. William Temple, *Mens Creatrix: An Essay* (London: Macmillan, 1917), 332.
36. William Temple, *The Kingdom of God* (London: Macmillan, 1914), 78.
37. Stephen Spencer has written on various aspects of Temple's leadership, see *Archbishop William Temple: A Study in Servant Leadership* (London: SCM Press 2022).
38. Kent, *William Temple*, 54.
39. I thank Stephen Spencer for pointing this to me.
40. Temple, *Christianity and the Social Order*, 38.
41. Temple, *Christianity and the Social Order*, 45.
42. Temple, *Christianity and the Social Order*, 67–77.
43. Ellen K. Wondra, "William Temple," in *Empire and the Christian Tradition: New Readings of Classical Theologians*, ed. Kwok Pui-lan, Dom H. Compier, and Joerg Rieger (Minneapolis: Fortress Press, 2007), 324.
44. Stephen Spencer, "William Temple's *Christianity and the Social Order* After Fifty Years," *Theology* 95, no. 763 (1992): 33.
45. Thabo Makgoba, "Politics," in *The Oxford Handbook of Anglican Studies*, ed. Mark D. Chapman, Sathianathan Clarke, and Martyn Percy (Oxford: Oxford University Press, 2016), 376, 382–83.
46. Lambeth Conference 1948, Resolution 14, Anglican Communion, https://www.anglicancommunion.org/resources/document-library/lambeth-conference/1948/resolution-14-the-church-and-the-modern-world-the-church-and-war.aspx.
47. Esther Mombo, "The Church and Poverty Alleviation in Africa," in *Anglican Women on Church and Mission*, ed. Kwok Pui-Lan, Judith Berling, and Jenny Plane Te Paa (New York: Morehouse Publishing, 2013), 138.
48. Beverley Haddad, "Theologising Development: A Gendered Analysis of Poverty, Survival and Faith," *Journal of Theology for Southern Africa* 110 (2001): 6.
49. Gustavo Gutiérrez, *A Theology of Liberation: History, Politics, and Salvation*, trans. Caridad Inda and John Eagleson (Maryknoll, NY: Orbis Books, 1973).
50. Kevin Ward, *A History of Global Anglicanism* (Cambridge: Cambridge University Press, 2006), 107.
51. Shoki Coe, "In Search of Renewal in Theological Education," *Theological Education* 9, no. 4 (1973): 243.
52. M. M. Thomas, "The Meaning of Salvation Today: A Personal Statement," *International Review of Mission* 62, no. 245 (1973): 162.
53. Lambeth Conference 1968, Resolution 21, Anglican Communion, https://www.anglicancommunion.org/resources/document-library/lambeth-conference/1968/resolution-21-developing-countries.aspx.
54. Lambeth Conference 1978, Resolution 2, Anglican Communion, https://www.anglicancommunion.org/resources/document-library/lambeth-conference/1978/resolution-2-a-response?author=Lambeth+Conference&subject=Economic+justice.

55. Julio E. Murray, "The AGAPE Economy: The Church's Call to Action," *Anglican Theological Review* 98, no. 1 (2016): 126.
56. Timothy Jones, "Waiting for Jubilee: The Campaign for Debt Cancellation," in *British Foreign Policy and the Anglican Church: Christian Engagement with the Contemporary World*, ed. Timothy Blewett, Adrian Hyde-Price, and Wyn Rees (Burlington, VT: Ashgate, 2008), 120.
57. See John Hammock and Anuradha Harinarayan, "Debt Relief: Giving Poor Countries a Second Chance," in *Beyond Colonial Anglicanism: The Anglican Communion in the Twenty-First Century*, ed. Ian T. Douglas and Kwok Pui-lan (New York: Church Publishing, 2001), 181.
58. David Skidmore, "Lambeth Plenary Focuses on Issue of International Debt," Anglican Communion News Service, July 26, 1998, https://www.anglicannews.org/news/1998/07/lambeth-plenary-focuses-on-issue-of-international-debt.aspx.
59. Lambeth Conference 1998, Resolution I.15, Anglican Communion, https://www.anglicancommunion.org/media/76650/1998.pdf.
60. Justin Welby, *Dethroning Mammon: Making Money Serve Grace* (London: Bloomsbury, 2016), 154.
61. Mombo, "The Church and Poverty Alleviation in Africa," in Kwok et al., *Anglican Women on Church and Mission*, 145–46.
62. Murray, "AGAPE Economy," 127.
63. Murray, "AGAPE Economy," 128.
64. Murray, "AGAPE Economy," 128.
65. "Millennium Development Goals and Beyond 2015," United Nations, https://www.un.org/millenniumgoals/bkgd.shtml.
66. Musonda Trevor Selwyn Mwamba, "The Lambeth Conference 2008 and the Millennium Development Goals: A Botswana Perspective," *Journal of Anglican Studies* 7, no. 2 (2009): 229–42.
67. Frank T. Griswold, "A Theological Reflection on the Millennium Development Goals," Episcopal Church, May 21, 2012, https://www.episcopalchurch.org/pbfrankgriswold/a-theological-reflection-on-the-millennium-development-goals.
68. "Anglicans Worldwide Prepare Strategies to Achieve the Millennium Development Goals," Anglican Communion News Service, October 12, 2007, https://www.anglicannews.org/news/2006/10/anglicans-worldwide-prepare-strategies-to-achieve-the-millennium-development-goals.aspx.
69. "Women's Needs Must Be Met to Meet Millennium Goals," Anglican Communion News Service, July 23, 2008, https://www.anglicannews.org/news/2008/07/womens-needs-must-be-met-to-meet-millennium-goals.aspx.
70. Archbishop Thabo Makgoba, "We Need New Social Teaching on an Economy Rooted in Love," Anglican Communion News Service, March 16, 2017, https://www.anglicannews.org/blogs/2017/03/we-need-new-social-teaching-on-an-economy-rooted-in-love.aspx.
71. Alfred Crosby, *Ecological Imperialism: The Biological Expansion of Europe, 900–1900*, 2nd ed. (Cambridge: Cambridge University Press, 2015).
72. Pablo Mukherjee, "Surfing the Second Waves: Amitav Ghosh's Tide Country," *New Formations* 59 (2006): 144.
73. Pope Francis, "Encyclical Letter *Laudato Si'* of the Holy Father Francis on Care for Our Common Home," The Vatican, May 24, 2015, #14, http://www.vatican.va/content/francesco/en/encyclicals/documents/papa-francesco_20150524_enciclica-laudato-si.html.

74. Lambeth Conference 1978, Resolution 1, Anglican Communion, https://www.anglicancommunion.org/media/127746/1978.pdf.
75. Lambeth Conference 1988, Resolution 35 and 40, Anglican Communion, https://www.anglicancommunion.org/media/127749/1988.pdf.
76. Lambeth Conference 1998, Resolution I.9. Anglican Communion, https://www.anglicancommunion.org/media/76650/1998.pdf.
77. "Highlights from Day 8 of the Lambeth Conference," Lambeth Conference, https://www.lambethconference.org/highlight_films/day-8.
78. Bartholomew and Justin Welby, "Climate Change and Moral Responsibility," *New York Times*, June 19, 2015, https://www.nytimes.com/2015/06/20/opinion/climate-change-and-moral-responsibility.html.
79. "The World Is Our Host: A Call for Urgent Action for Climate Justice," Anglican Communion, Good Friday 2015, https://acen.anglicancommunion.org/media/148818/The-World-is-our-Host-FINAL-TEXT.pdf. I thank Megan Swett for drawing my attention to this meeting.
80. Interfaith Power and Light website, https://www.interfaithpowerandlight.org.
81. Adam Bobbette, "Priests on the Shore: Climate Change and the Anglican Church of Melanesia," *GeoHumanities* 5, no. 2 (2019): 554–69.
82. Martha Kirkpatrick, "For God So Loved the World: An Incarnational Ecology," *Anglican Theological Review* 91, no. 2 (2009): 193.
83. Kirkpatrick, "For God So Loved the World," 200.
84. Kirkpatrick, "For God So Loved the World," 206.
85. Kirkpatrick, "For God So Loved the World," 210.
86. Kapya John Kaoma, *God's Family, God's Earth: Christian Ecological Ethics of Ubuntu* (Zomba, Malawi: Kachere Series, 2013), 60–90.
87. Kaoma, *God's Family, God's Earth*, 102.
88. Kaoma, *God's Family, God's Earth*, 103.
89. Kaoma, *God's Family, God's Earth*, 174–80.
90. Kathryn Tanner, *Christianity and the New Spirit of Capitalism* (New Haven, CT: Yale University Press, 2019).

CHAPTER

4

Contextualization of Worship

Since **Anglican churches** do not have a confessional statement or a common set of agreed theological doctrines, many turn to the Book of Common Prayer as a unifying element across geographical distances and cultural diversity. Anglicans are fond of saying *lex orandi, lex credendi* (the law of prayer is the law of belief) and the BCP becomes a symbol of unity and *koinonia* (communion) of member churches. Today, when we visit Anglican churches in other countries, even if we do not know the language, we can more or less follow the sequence of the liturgy. The Anglican liturgy, originally intended for the church in one nation, has been widely adopted mainly due to the British colonial legacy. Given the importance of liturgy and the BCP in Anglican churches, postcolonial scrutiny of its language and values, as well as the politics of translation and revision is much needed.

The first BCP in 1549 served both theological and political purposes. It sought to put theological reflections from the Reformation into praying words and emphasize the use of the vernacular. The Prayer Book was meant to establish a "new, universal relationship between every worshipper and the single, authoritative service book for the whole nation."[1] A set liturgy promoted uniformity and a single form of prayer for the whole church helped prevent schism and division. Archbishop Thomas Cranmer, the architect of the first Prayer Book, made full use of material from traditional English services, while adding contemporary sources, including a wide range of Lutheran texts, and other liturgies.[2] It was expressed in the culture of its time, using Tudor English, which set a precedent for future translation into local languages. Reflecting the cultural and political ethos of English society, the Prayer Book employed monarchical language to speak to and about God, for example, "thy divine Majesty."[3] From the beginning, the BCP had a serious political undertone, as its use was enforced by the authority of Parliament. Papal authority was transferred to the king, seen as a "godly prince" who ordered the society and the lives of the subjects. The bishops and convocations were subservient to the monarch, and the new liturgy inculcated obedience as the proper response of the people.[4]

Theologian Charles Hefling notes that since the first BCP, "the Church of England's 'established' status has involved its liturgy in domestic, colonial, imperial, and post-imperial politics."[5] The introduction of the Prayer Book to Ireland and Scotland was not without struggle because of the ecclesiastical differences and resistance to English influences. In Ireland, the English government sought to impose its authority over the island and Anglicize the people. The first BCP was used at Christ Church Cathedral in Dublin in 1551. The provision was that the BCP would be read in English where people understood English. But the instructions to have the services read in the Irish language were not followed in areas where people only spoke Irish, which was the majority of the country. During the reign of Elizabeth I, the third and slightly revised BCP was imposed on the Church of Ireland by the Act of Uniformity passed by the Irish Parliament in 1560. The book was in English, though attempts at translation into Irish were made in subsequent years. Many Irish people resisted English domination, and wars and rebellions broke out during Queen Elizabeth I's reign. The rebellion against English rule and the upheaval during the English Civil War as it impacted Ireland led to the banning of the use of BCP in 1645. After Charles II's restoration and his steering of the country through the conflicts between Anglicans, Catholics, and Dissenters, the BCP could be used again. The BCP of 1662 formed the basis of worship of the Church in Ireland until disestablishment took effect in 1871.[6]

The first complete BCP intended for use outside England was the Scottish Prayer Book. Because the English monarch's authority did not extend to Scotland, Queen Elizabeth I could not enforce Prayer Book uniformity there. The use of the BCP was spotty and it was mainly adopted by the Scottish lords. Later, King Charles I with Archbishop of Canterbury William Laud sought to introduce religious practices in use in England to Scotland, which had a strong Presbyterian tradition. The Scots did not want episcopacy and supported a Presbyterian church governed by ministers and elders. The Scottish Prayer Book made certain compromises and included alterations to the Communion service, which was a bone of fierce contention. Even so, when the Scottish Prayer Book was introduced in 1637 at St. Giles Cathedral in Edinburgh, a riot broke out and subsequent political upheavals occurred across Scotland. Protesters opposed episcopacy and episcopal imposition of any service book and innovative liturgies, as much as they opposed the book itself. A more commonly used and definitive Scottish Prayer Book came about in 1764 only after a gradual process of reception and trial use, but the majority Church of Scotland was resolutely Presbyterian and never accepted the BCP.[7]

As the Church of England established missions and churches in the colonies, churches needed to adapt the BCP to the new contexts. In the early stage of the colonial setting, the church would use an informal style of worship because of the limited number of clergy. As the colonial order took hold, churches developed structures and forms of worship according to the BCP of 1662. The first example of the reliance on the BCP outside the British Isles was in Jamestown, Virginia, and other churches in the West Indies and Africa followed. As churches continued to grow, they had to adapt the BCP to local congregational life and mission. William L. Sachs writes, "The Book of Common Prayer embodied the tension Anglicans experience between continuity and change. On the one hand, the Prayer Book offered secure grounding for those who prized the church's English heritage; on the other, it served as a template for novel patterns of worship suitable for a church in the mission field."[8] Today, as we discuss the need to challenge English hegemony in a postcolonial Anglican Communion, what is the place of BCP in worship? Should a prayer book that was so bound to the history and politics of a particular nation continue to define the worship and spirituality of people of diverse linguistic, cultural, and political backgrounds? What is the politics behind the translation of the BCP and the issuing of new Prayer Books, as we have seen in the provinces of Aotearoa

New Zealand, Kenya, Brazil, and Southern Africa? Besides the liturgical text, what other dimensions in worship do we need to change and reform? Before we examine these questions more closely, I will discuss the introduction of postcolonial theory to the study of Anglican worship.

Postcolonial Studies and Anglican Worship

In *Christian Worship: Postcolonial Perspectives*, Reformed scholar Michael J. Jagessar and Anglican liturgical scholar Stephen Burns write, "From a postcolonial perspective, there is much to critique in the study of liturgy and the celebration of Christian worship."[9] The task is challenging because it requires us to "negotiate both openness to the tradition and a commitment to subject it to questions in the light of colonial, postcolonial and contemporary concerns."[10] While tradition provides a rich depository of knowledge and wisdom to prevent us from being captive to contemporary perspectives, we also need to reconsider our assumptions about tradition, search for marginalized traditions, and evaluate whether the prevailing tradition needs to be relativized.

Postcolonial theory can be applied to draw attention to and question the colonial and imperial influences in Christian worship, liturgical texts, architecture, symbols, art, and music, and to offer reconstructive readings of these texts and liturgical interpretation. In this process, Jagessar and Burns write, questions such as these become pertinent:

> Do the discourse, texts, symbols and imageries perpetuate bondage and notions of empire? How do they represent Black peoples, ethnic minorities, the Other, gender and sexuality? What do the symbols, the language and the shape of our liturgical/worship spaces, communicate *vis à vis* the agenda of empire/colonialism and the politics of location? What do they communicate in terms of inclusivity of recent migrants who have to re-negotiate sacred spaces?[11]

Since the BCP serves as a "grammar" to understand the language and religious practices of Anglicanism, it is important to analyze the cultural, linguistic, and sociopolitical world created by it. The first BCP was known as the First Prayer Book of Edward VI (1549), while subsequent revisions had close connections with the accession of a new monarch to the throne: the Elizabethan Prayer Book (1559), the Jacobean Prayer Book (1604), and the revision of 1662 when Charles II restored the monarchy. The images of king and empire are found frequently in the liturgy, canticles, and hymns. God is imaged as "the King eternal" (Collect for the Renewal of Life), a "great King above all gods" (Venite), and the "heavenly King" (Gloria in Excelsis).[12] Cultural imperialism is often unchecked: "Grant that people everywhere may seek after you and find you, bring the nations into your fold" (Collect for the Mission of the Church) and the hymn "At the name of Jesus every knee shall bow."[13]

Feminist scholars, such as Gail Ramshaw, have challenged the use of the images of the "king" and "the kingdom of God" in worship. She suggests the alternatives of "sovereign" and "monarch," because these words are nongender specific. Instead of kingship, she offers "reign," dominion," and "commonwealth" as alternatives to retranslate "kingdom."[14] In her attempt to produce an inclusive-language version of the lectionary, she opts for the image of the "dominion of God."[15] But the language of dominion and the commonwealth of God can be easily used to justify earthly kingship and colonial control. While white feminist scholars prefer gender-inclusive language, they have not concomitantly considered the colonial connotations. Even though the images of reign or dominion may be non-gendered, "they still smack of the language of 'empire.'"[16]

The issue of inclusive language has created much controversy in the church. The masculine pronouns for God and the use of "men" as a generic term for "human" in English usage are especially problematic. The Anglican Communion needs to pay attention to the biases of the English language because the BCP of 1662, as a part of the colonial legacy, continues to influence worship in many provinces of the Communion. Even when the BCP was translated into indigenous languages, which may not have the problems of gendered pronouns, the masculine metaphors and images remained. Sometimes, these masculine images were further reinforced by androcentric biases in indigenous languages and concepts of the divine. Although there have been liturgical renewals to adopt inclusive language, many of these attempts were initiated by women of European descent, without the participation of women in other contexts.

The colonization process was closely related to the assumption of the superiority of the white race. The Episcopal Church's 1979 BCP is full of the imageries of light and darkness, some of which can be traced back to the biblical tradition. God is imagined as the eternal light chasing away the darkness, which is taken to be the symbol of danger, ignorance, or death: "Be our light in the darkness, O Lord" (Collect for Aid against Perils), "O send out thy light and thy truth" (Introductory sentence, Morning Prayer I), "O God, the King eternal, whose light divides the day from night and turns the shadow of death into the morning" (Collect for Renewal of Life).[17] The glorification of light and the denigration of darkness in the Bible and the BCP can be used to marginalize dark-skinned people and create false racial stereotypes. The use of light imagery is pervasive in the Church of England's *Common Worship* from Advent through to Candlemas.[18] In white-dominated societies, people might erroneously associate light with whiteness and darkness with Blackness. Mukti Barton, an Indian Bengali British Anglican biblical scholar who served as bishop's adviser for Black and Asian Ministries in the Diocese of Birmingham, argues, "Racism is perpetuated when the colour Black is used in negative, and White in positive, ways."[19] She also notes that in some languages, such as her own Bengali, Blackness and darkness are not synonymous, whereas the overlapping of the two terms is quite ambiguous in the English language.[20]

The above discussion shows that it is not enough for the new dioceses to translate the BCP into local languages, without a radical examination of the book's cultural and linguistic world. In translating the BCP, judgment needs to be made as to whether to keep or reject certain cultural assumptions in the linguistic world of the original text. Otherwise, the unequal power relationships embedded in the text of a bygone era will be reinscribed in the translation process. Translation is not a simple and straightforward process but requires creativity and making choices of words, idioms, and concepts. The analysis of "translation" in postcolonial theory is helpful to look at this complicated process. Translation, for Stuart Hall, is more than finding a linguistic equivalent, but "a continuous process of re-articulation and re-contextualization, without any notion of a primary origin."[21] When the BCP enters a new cultural space, its terms and the world it represents unavoidably change, and for the liturgy to be living, it must be adapted to the local context.

In the past, prayer book uniformity was a means for exerting political control and for consolidating Anglican identity and unity. The second Lambeth Conference of 1878 stated that "the Book of Common Prayer, retained as it is, with some modifications, by all our Churches, has been one principal bond of union among them," and "excessive diversity of ritual" would endanger communion in worship.[22] The resolutions also spelled out the provision and authorization of the BCP in the British colonies and countries not under English or American rule.[23] The emphasis on BCP uniformity could also be found in subsequent Lambeth Conferences until 1958. However, after studying the history of the adoption of the BCP in the British Isles and other diverse contexts, liturgical scholar Shawn Strout argues that the historical evidence shows that prayer book uniformity is a myth rather than reality. "Complete prayer book uniformity was never achieved even with stringent legal authority."[24] He further cautions, "Anglicans must be careful that the desire for prayer book uniformity is not just a desire to preserve Anglican identity but also Anglo identity and culture. The impact of British and American colonialism on prayer book uniformity and Anglican identity cannot be underestimated."[25]

Anglican worship is far more than the liturgical texts found on the pages of the BCP. Bishop Colin Buchanan notes that missionaries introduced the BCP together with an all-pervasive Anglican subculture, such as "robes (and clericalism), ceremonial, architecture, music (and lyrics), even church-bells, hassocks, brass eagles at lecterns, collection-bags, murals, candlesticks, choirboys smiling seraphically in ruffs, and a thousand more besides."[26] As a result, the styles of Anglican worship in the former British colonies and other churches in the Global South retain elements of English Victorian worship foreign to their indigenous cultures. The late bishop of São Paulo and primate of the *Igreja Episcopal Anglicana do Brasil* Glauco S. de Lima said, "Beyond the very order and linguistic sources of our worship, even our clothing bears witness to a colonial origin. In the vestments and trimmings of the clergy, for example, on the bishop's surplice, the sleeves finish up at the cuffs in the same way as those of the noblemen in the British court."[27]

With the independence of the colonies came a stronger push for cultural autonomy and the wish for revising the BCP. After the Indian independence, the churches that merged to form the Church of South India produced *The Book of Common Worship* in 1950. BCP revisions were underway in the Church of India, Pakistan, Burma, and Ceylon[28] as well as in the churches in West Indies, Canada, and Japan, etc. These changes prompted the Lambeth Conference of 1958 to give serious consideration to liturgical revisions for the first time.[29] The Conference acknowledged that revisions of the BCP were being done and called attention to "those features in the Books of Common Prayers which are essential to the safeguarding of our unity," such as the use of scripture and creeds, baptism, confirmation, communion, and the ordinal.[30]

The revisions of the BCP and the liturgical renewal movement in the twentieth century, which emphasized more lay participation in worship and greater freedom to innovate, called for more creativity and flexibility in worship. The bishops at Lambeth 1978 said, "In the past, the Book of Common Prayer was an important unifying factor in Anglican worship," and added, "We believe . . . unity in structure can rightly co-exist with flexibility in context and variety in cultural expressions for the Holy Spirit is both a spirit of order and an unpredictable wind."[31] Prior to Lambeth 1988, the International Anglican Liturgical Consultation (IALC), which began in 1985, held its second meeting in Brixen, North Italy, in 1987. Elisha Mbonigaba, who was a lecturer in liturgy at Bishop Tucker Theological College in Uganda, presented a paper on "Indigenization of Liturgy," which set the stage for the important conversation in the Communion on what is now usually called "inculturation."[32]

At Lambeth 1988, the inculturation of liturgy was discussed and the resolutions mentioned this for the first time.

> The Church has to worship incarnationally, separated from the world by the offence of the Cross, but not by any alien character of its culture. We affirm expressions of true local creativity within the life of the worshipping

> local community which well up from within the people in response to the stirrings of the Spirit. Thus we commend and encourage authentic local inculturation of the liturgy, and fear lest in some parts of the Anglican Communion we have been all too hesitant about it.[33]

Following the Lambeth Conference, the IALC focused on the inculturation of liturgy for its third meeting in York, England, in 1989. Victor R. Atta-Bafoe from Ghana and Philip Tovey from England differentiated between adaptation, which is the adjustment of the Prayer Book to a new context, and inculturation. They defined inculturation as "the incarnation of the Christian life and message in a particular cultural context in such a way that not only do local Christians find expression for their faith through elements proper to their culture, but also that faith and worship animate, direct and unify the culture. Inculturation in this sense is the dialogue of gospel and culture."[34] The York Statement, "'Down to Earth Worship': Liturgical Inculturation and the Anglican Communion," acknowledged the connection between colonialism and worship:

> Inculturation must therefore affect the whole ethos of corporate worship, not only the texts but also, for example, the use of buildings, furniture, art, music and ceremonial. From one aspect it means cultural de-colonization of worship, from another it requires recognition of the special needs of an ethnic or other minority, which may be culturally distinct from the prevailing ethos of the Province.[35]

The inculturation of liturgy was a particular concern for Anglican churches in Africa. Mbonigaba's influential writings on this issue showed a sharp postcolonial consciousness. He noted that Western anthropologists and missionaries dismissed African culture and traditional religion as primitive, pagan, animist, savage, totemist, and fetishist. The CMS missionaries introduced Anglicanism and Western lifestyle in their attempt to "civilize" African countries with different political, cultural, social, and religious contexts. "They tried to reach the intellectual and ethical levels of African consciousness without ever appealing to the deeper emotional sphere that could only be expressed through symbols, myths, rituals and exuberant music.

They tried to make converts speak and behave like the white man."[36] He lamented that most of the African Anglican churches used liturgies modeled after the 1662 BCP, the American 1928 BCP, or the English Alternative Service Book. "Anglicanism in the western English sense was adopted as part and parcel of the Christian faith" and African churches clung to those archaic traditions that the Church of England rejected a long time ago.[37] African churches and other Third World provinces were afraid to lose their identity and were slow in developing indigenous liturgies.

Mbonigaba contended that liturgical inculturation in Africa needs to acknowledge the rich African heritage embedded in rituals, symbolic language, prayers, body language, movement, music, and rites of passage. He compared English religious expression and worshipping style as reflected in the 1662 BCP with that of Africans. Worship according to the BCP, he said, is intellectual and meditational, and congregants remain passive without much interaction. In contrast, African religious life involves fostering community through body language, gesture, and movement, such as "dancing, rhythm swaying, rhythm tapping, drumming, clapping, ululation, embracing, and other genuine, authentic symbolic gestural language."[38] Instead of using written prayers, Africans offer spontaneous, extempore prayers, pouring out their hearts to God and expressing feelings, anxieties, pain, joy, and aspirations. He argued that indigenous liturgy would be more relevant if the richness of African prayers can be used, rather than adapting medieval or Reformation prayers or even Western prayers in modern liturgies. The Kanamai Statement, which came out from a 1993 consultation on "African Culture and Anglican Liturgy," held by the Council of Anglican Provinces in Africa in Kanamai, Kenya, stated, "The liturgy needs to be open to opportunities for the expression of joy and suffering, of death and hope, affirming people's deepest affections."[39] To make the Eucharist incarnational in local cultures, Mbonigaba said African food and drink can be used in lieu of bread and wine, which can be expensive in some contexts. He argues that the indigenization of liturgy and worship must celebrate and express African beauty and joy, paying attention to liturgical space, furnishings, and vessels, etc. For example, instead of an imported gold or silver chalice and paten, local earthenware or wooden cups and beautiful baskets can be used. He urged African churches to explore and experiment with worship styles that embody African spirituality and address the needs of the people.[40]

Inculturation is an important step in decolonizing worship and recovering the richness and beauty of indigenous cultures. Yet, caution must be taken in the inculturation process. First, inculturation does not imply nativism or an uncritical appropriation of past cultures and traditions. Mbonigaba reminded us, "Indigenization does not mean to resurrect the negative past, but to acknowledge the positive cultural values and the present realities of social, economic, political and religious factors that influence and condition our life; culture is not static but dynamic."[41] This critical discernment is important because some of the traditional elements and rituals can be patriarchal and exclusive of women. Second, culture is not monolithic, and many countries are multicultural and multilingual with particular local traditions. It is important to honor and respect the experience of ethnic minorities, as the York Statement said. Third, Jagessar and Burns encourage us to go one step further to evaluate the goal of inculturation and gauge whether this process will reinforce or dislodge the dominant paradigm and whether cultural and ideological assumptions are reinscribed in the acculturation or translation process. They write, a postcolonial perspective "will also be critical of and question the very notion of inculturation, how it is employed and whether it is another form of hegemonic control, empire building and colonization."[42] These are important questions to consider, and I will investigate the dynamics and politics of inculturation by analyzing Prayer Book revisions in Aotearoa New Zealand, Kenya, and Brazil.[43]

Revisions of the Book of Common Prayer

Luiz Coelho, an Anglican priest who served on the team to revise the BCP for the *Igrega Episcopal Anglicana do Brasil*, outlines four phases of Prayer Book revisions from the sixteenth century to the present.[44] The first phase involved the evolution of the Prayer Book before the nineteenth century, which included the Reformation books (1549, 1552, and 1559), the 1662 BCP, the 1637 Scottish Prayer Book, and local books derived from these.

These Prayer Books were informed by theology from the Protestant Reformation. The American 1789 BCP, based on the 1662 BCP and the 1764 Scottish Liturgy, and the translation of the American Prayer Book into Portuguese in 1860 belonged to the first generation. The second phase was influenced by the nineteenth-century Catholic revival and Prayer Book revisions included adaptations to Anglo-Catholic practices, such as the reintroduction of the prayers for the dead. The American 1892 and 1928 BCPs and their translations belonged to this category. The liturgical movement that began in the second half of the twentieth shaped the third phase of revisions. There was a greater emphasis on the role of all baptized, active lay participation in worship, modernization of the language, reinstitution of weekly Eucharist, a three-year lectionary, and more choices of prayers. The concept of "Common Prayer" evolved in the Communion, and local BCPs were not required to strictly conform to previous usage. The American 1979 BCP and its Brazilian offshoot of 1984 are examples of this third phase.

Coelho argues that the inculturation in the third phase did not go deep enough as local variations and native elements were not adopted. Prayer Book revisions tended to retain the translation of archaic languages, which did not reflect the language of the people. The problems of inclusive language in romance languages and issues of sexism and heterosexism were not addressed. Coelho opts for a decolonial approach such that worship will no longer reflect assumptions of colonial design and language. The fourth phase began in the late 1990s, which went beyond traditional models of inculturation, and the revisions were more creative and innovative. The goal was to produce "liturgy that is fully embraced by all the baptized and that is adaptable to a variety of local contexts while keeping up with the essence of Anglican prayer book theology and practice."[45]

The Prayer Book, like the Bible, is a traveling book, that has been brought to different cultures and societies largely because of colonialism. Postcolonial biblical critic Musa W. Dube from Botswana has argued that "the biblical story is an unfinished story: it invites its own continuation in history."[46] The same can be said of the Prayer Book. As the missionaries introduced the Prayer Book, colonial elements were inscribed in the liturgy. A postcolonial approach needs to challenge and deinscribe these elements and rearticulate and reinscribe new liturgical expressions that reflect the religious life of local peoples and their relationship with God.[47] In this way, the Prayer Book can be appropriated, translated, and read anew, as expression of "living liturgy" among worshipping communities in the Communion.[48]

I will discuss Prayer Book revisions in three different contexts that address postcolonial concerns and use material from local contexts. *A New Zealand Prayer Book = He Karakia Mihinare O Aotearoa*, published in 1989, can be seen as an example of postcolonial liturgy. Twenty-five years in the making, the Prayer Book is unique in the Anglican Communion for its liberal use of the Maori language and the inclusion of regional languages of English, Fijian, Tongan, and Samoan. The multiplicity of voices reflects the hybridized nature of the Prayer Book, which seeks to signal the bicultural commitment of the church and give liturgical expression to what it is to be a postcolonial people of God.[49] For Anglicans of European descent (Pakehas), the Prayer Book also "helped to reinvigorate a sense of their own cultural development, distinct from that of Britain."[50] Jenny Te Paa writes, "As the Anglican Church in Aotearoa, New Zealand, and Polynesia continues to come of age as a post-colonial church committed to honoring ethnic diversity, *A New Zealand Prayer Book* offers in its deep structure a globally unique and influential template."[51]

The *New Zealand Prayer Book* is diglot and is meant for people with two worldviews, languages, and cultural expressions. While the predominance of the Prayer Book is in the English language of the colonial settlers, there is the Maori language throughout the baptismal and Eucharistic liturgies, as well as diglot versions of a Eucharistic service and other liturgies. The adequate translation of the liturgies into the Maori language requires utmost care and sensitivity. The old Maori Prayer Book first published in 1839, referred to as *Te Rawiri*, provided the orders of services for the sacraments, ordination, and all other Anglican services. It was based on the 1662 BCP and translated by CMS missionaries William Puckey and William Williams.[52] Maori church historian Hirini Kaa says, "Translation became a challenging process of cultural exchange, in which theological concepts were sifted through cultural and political filters until they became, as [Kuni] Jenkins says, 'words between us.'"[53] *Te Rawiri* was a cultural hybrid which used Maori language and symbolisms to translate the BCP and combined with the conventional theology of CMS missionaries.

The translation team of the new 1989 Prayer Book wanted to ensure that the language reflected the Maori worldview. Te Paa observes, "The resulting translations are extraordinarily evocative of the Maori understandings of God's indescribably immaculate creation and of relationships with the living and the dead; of Maori traditions that honour the inherent goodness of all God's people; of Maori expressions of adoration and thanksgiving for the gift of faith; and of Maori gratitude for God's never-ending promise of life everlasting."[54] For example, in the Eucharist Liturgy of Thanksgiving and Praise, the English version says, "We shall all be one in Christ, one in our life together," while the Maori version can be roughly translated as "Christ is the ridgepole of our meeting house to which we tie our *waka* (oceangoing canoe)."[55] Te Paa says Maori speakers consider their translation of the Prayer Book "delightfully subversive" because of its liberal and expansive ways of using Maori allusions, imageries, and language, instead of a literal one-way translation.[56] In addition to the translation of the liturgy, the Prayer Book contains a Eucharist liturgy in Maori alone and Eucharistic prayers translated into Fijian and Tongan.[57] The Prayer Book is beautifully designed and produced and includes Maori art on its pages.

The bold attempt of producing *A New Zealand Prayer Book* contributed to the process of revisioning the identity and mission of the church. Three years after the publication of the Prayer Book, the Anglican Church in Aoteraoa New Zealand produced a new constitution and reformed itself with three distinct cultural strands: *tikgnga Maori*, *tikanga Pakeha* (non-Maori of European origins), and *tikanga Pasifika* (local adaptation of the word Pacific). Each cultural strand has the same rights and authority.[58] Although the church in Aotearoa New Zealand has yet to realize the ideal of true partnership and resource-sharing,[59] it has demonstrated to the Communion how churches can reckon with their colonial past and imagine a new possible future.

Just as it took many years to produce *A New Zealand Prayer Book*, liturgical renewal in the Church of the Province of Kenya (now called the Anglican Church of Kenya) evolved over decades. After Kenya became independent in 1963, the Church became an autonomous province in 1970. It authorized a modern translation of the Prayer Book, which was published as *Modern English Services* in 1975. The order and theology of this book largely followed that of the 1662 BCP, though the Elizabethan English was changed, and prayers were shortened and revised to reflect Kenya's political independence. Further commitment to liturgical renewal in the 1980s led to the publication of *A Kenyan Service of Holy Communion* in 1989 and the booklet *Modern Services* in 1991, which contains trial versions of different services. With the support and encouragement of Archbishop David Gitari, who had been involved in liturgical inculturation in Africa, the completed *Our Modern Services* was officially released in 2002.[60]

A Kenyan Service of Holy Communion grew out of developments in African Christian theology and liturgical research. The preface says, "It is both thoroughly Biblical and authentically African, both faithful to the Anglican tradition and refreshingly creative."[61] It was used for the opening Eucharist of the 1998 Lambeth Conference. *Our Modern Services* includes significant innovations honoring the African religious and cultural contexts and adopting local elements. Most of the services are structured around short and rhythmic phrases and this quick rhythm encourages the participation of the congregation. Since Africans have deep respect for their ancestors, the Holy Communion service mentions the ancestors frequently. For example, in the introduction to the Sanctus, the minister prays, "Therefore with angels, archangels, faithful ancestors and all in heaven"[62] instead of the more familiar "Therefore with Angels and Archangels, and with all the company of heaven."[63] The invitation to the table adapts the African communal belief "I am because we are." Following the Lord's Prayer and before the *Agnus Dei*, the following is included:

> *Minister:* Christ is alive forever.
> *People:* **We are because he is.**[64]

Our Modern Services includes services that address the needs of the Kenyan Church, such as a service for the commissioning of evangelists, because of the Church's emphasis on evangelism and mission. It also has a Litany for the Preservation of the Environment. The intercessory prayers include the collects for the protection of the environment and for rain, for the hungry and unemployed, and for those infected with or dying from HIV/AIDS. In addition to revising the Prayer Book, there has been conversation about using indigenous elements for Holy Eucharist instead of bread and imported wine,[65] and indigenous appropriation of confirmation practice, with adaptations from African rites of passage, to recognize people's dual identity as both Christian and African.[66]

Even though some of the Anglican churches in Africa have made progress in the inculturation of liturgy, questions remain. Esther Mombo writes, "There is an obvious gap between what theologians write about liturgy, and what Christians do in their various contexts."[67] Mombo notes that people, especially women, love music, and they worship outdoors or under the trees to express their joy and pain. In places where the congregants are illiterate, the written words may be a barrier and the pastor or evangelist needs to interpret the words in their context.[68] Those who have the service book and know how to use it are the leaders, and this reinforces hierarchical church structure and clericalism. One of the biggest challenges to Anglican liturgy is Pentecostal worship, which allows more freedom and spontaneous participation. It is no wonder that some people attend more than one service on a Sunday, one of them conducted according to the Anglican Prayer Book, the other Pentecostal.

Liturgical reform has been debated for some time in *Igreja Episcopal Anglicana do Brasil* between those who adhered to the tradition and those who wanted to see changes. Writing in 2000, Brazilian philosopher and priest Jaci Maraschin lamented that the mainline Protestant churches in Brazil, including the Anglican, still held strongly to their inherited traditions. The Episcopal Anglican Church of Brazil, he argued, needs to stretch Anglican worship beyond the BCP and boldly revise or even create their liturgical practices under the guidance of the Spirit. These new liturgical practices must be based on a contextualized theology and incorporate the Dionysian elements of the Brazilian culture, such as dance, gestures, color, and song. If the Brazilian Anglican church transcends the limits of the BCP, the church will enter into new ecumenical dialogue with Christians in other denominations and equip itself to carry out God's mission reflecting the joy, pleasure, and beauty of Brazilian culture.[69]

The Brazilian Anglican church has since taken bold steps and published a new version of the Prayer Book, entitled *Livro da Oracao Commun* in 2015. The church's 1984 BCP was basically a translation of the 1979 BCP of the Episcopal Church and did not reflect local cultures and theologies. In contrast, the new version makes adaptations to meet the spiritual needs and pastoral concerns of the people. The new BCP is influenced by the liturgical movement and ecumenical and inter-Anglican conversations. Luiz Coelho says the new version is not simply a translation of foreign sources. For example, "Most Eucharistic prayers and litanies are new and touch issues akin to contemporary Brazilian needs, such as inequality, economic justice and creation care, without obliterating other theological points that comprise our tradition, and remind us of the faith that was transmitted from generation to generation."[70] According to Coelho, the new BCP has several important features. It reflects an expansive view of God and adopts an inclusive ecclesiology, which seeks to overcome the tradition of sexism and homophobia in the church. The Prayer Book uses gender-inclusive language and some of the collects for social justice tackle the sins of homophobia, sexism, and domestic violence. The new BCP takes seriously the idea that liturgy is the work of the people and is designed in a way to accommodate the needs of less educated people. Instead of passive onlookers, worshippers are encouraged to be actively involved, and some of the new Eucharistic prayers are devised as responsorial, litany-style prayers. The new BCP also adapts some of the liturgies, such as funeral rites and healing Masses, to local traditions and includes seasonal prayers for various occasions drafted by local congregations. A series of local saints were added to the Calendar of Saints, which includes a larger number of women and an attempt to include minorities.

Music, Preaching, and Space

Music plays an important part in Anglican worship. The hymns inculcate Christian values, shape the identity of the people, and convey thoughts and feelings. Congregational singing is an integral part of corporate worship and a collective meaning-making process. Missionaries introduced not only the Bible and the Prayer Book but also their hymnody and musical forms. In *Imperialism and Music: Britain 1876–1953*, Jeffrey Richards shows how the Victorian hymns were imperialistic and many Christian songs are imbued with themes of empire and Christian militarism.[71] These hymns were part and parcel of the "civilizing mission" to produce loyal, faithful, and subservient religious and political subjects. Translated into indigenous languages, these hymns of a bygone era are still sung in churches in many parts of the Global South as part of colonial Christianity. Therefore, we need to use a postcolonial optic to scrutinize the language of the hymns and the ways that hymns and music are used in worship.

Historian Renie Chow Choy notes that many hymns transported to the colonies via Anglican hymnals, such as *Hymns Ancient and Modern* and other denominational hymnals, invoke imperial imagery, such as "'All Glory, Laud and Honour"; "O Worship the King, All Glorious Above"; and "Praise, My Soul, the King of Heaven." She writes, "The transportation of hymns to the colonies asserted a clear sense of English superiority."[72] Yet, many of these hymns are sung in translation and cherished by non-English Christians around the world. Lim Swee Hong, a composer and professor of sacred music, contends that it is simplistic and sometimes not practical to ask congregations to stop using Western hymns and music. He writes, "Postcolonial liturgical celebration as reflected in the practice of music is not simply about the eradication of western idioms or nuances because they are vestiges of empire. It is also not simply about showcasing indigenous expressions because these challenge colonial power structure."[73] In our interconnected world in which music blends and mixes, it is naïve to suppose that "indigenous" music is the only appropriate form of subaltern expression. Lim argues that we need to pay attention to the dynamics of the specific social and cultural context and the background of the faith communities. He notes that many congregations in Asia are passionate about imitating and continuing their Western Christian heritage and using Western musical expressions instead of adapting local cultures and idioms. This is the result of past Western influences and the assertion of a distinct Christian identity, especially in places where Christianity is a minority religion.[74] Lim says this is an unavoidable step and he hopes that this will change when more Asians are trained in church music and liturgy.

In Anglican churches in Africa, the use of African traditional music is considered vital in resisting the colonial heritage and in the inculturation of liturgy. Missionaries initially banned African instruments because they were considered pagan or associated with pagan rituals, and the styles of playing these instruments were not suitable for the Christian music introduced. The African instruments were publicly condemned and excluded. The earliest instruments introduced were organ for high churches, accordions, drums (side drums as in Salvation Army practice or African drums appropriated as signals or metric markers), and some percussion. Beginning in the 1950s, guitars became very popular and nowadays synthesizers, keyboards, and soundtracks are very commonplace in gospel music and younger generation urban churches.[75] To support the inculturation of music, the Kanamai Statement says: "We encourage the use of local words and music to make worship more joyful and authentically African. Attention needs to be given to creative writing and composition. Music should not appear to decorate the liturgy but should be regarded as being integral."[76] John Mbiti, a Kenyan Anglican and a pioneer in African philosophy, says that singing helps to pass religious knowledge from one group to another and is instrumental in strengthening corporateness and solidarity.[77] In rural communities, in which oral tradition and communication are important, singing traditional hymns is an authentic way of teaching and preserving the Christian faith. African traditional music is polyrhythmic, with rhythmic synchronization between text-rhythm, melody-rhythm, and clapping rhythm. Mbonigaba underscores the significance of using African music in worship and says, "We should not be ashamed to use our traditional music and the traditional musical instruments, and dancing."[78] In the Anglican Church of Kenya, the revision of the Prayer Book was accompanied by the release of the Kikuyu hymn book *Nyimbo Cia Gucanjamura Ngoro* in 1995. Hymns for different occasions were created and the hymn book represented a grassroots effort of inculturation or worship drawing on secular and local musical forms.[79]

While Asian and African churches discuss how to adopt local music in worship, Western churches have tried to include "world church music" in their hymnals and worship experience. On the one hand, this may show their willingness to learn from and be enriched by musical offerings from other cultures. On the other hand, this may be another form of cultural misappropriation or even theft if this is not done in a respectful way. There is the question of Western churches or institutions copyrighting materials that have emerged from other cultures.[80] This may fall into the pattern of Western consumerist culture, which exploits the labor of other peoples and allows the rich to sample and enjoy goods and services from all over the world. When Asian or African songs are sung in Western congregations, they are often so off-beat or out of the original style that they can hardly be recognizable in their local contexts. We cannot use music and songs from other cultures simply to show our "cultural sensitivity" or "inclusivity," without genuine learning and working in solidarity with those who gift us with their songs.

In addition to hymns and music, preaching occupies an important place in worship. Postcolonial theory has been introduced to the field of homiletics, yet Anglican scholars have not paid sufficient attention to it. In the past several decades, the discussion on preaching has shifted from the preacher as the messenger delivering divine truth to one that celebrates mutuality and solidarity between the preacher and the congregation. I have defined postcolonial preaching as "a locally rooted and globally conscious performance that seeks to create a Third Space so that the faith community can imagine new ways of being in the world and encountering God's salvific action for the oppressed and marginalized."[81] Preaching is a performance because it uses speech-act to convey messages and elicit certain feelings and responses. As for any performance, we cannot focus on the performer without considering the context and rich convergence of the performer, situation, setting, audience, and society. Preaching needs to adapt to the specific sociocultural context, while at the same time being mindful of how global situations impinge on the local. The goal of preaching is not to reinforce the status quo or provide religious sanction for the rich and powerful; rather it is to create what Homi Bhabha calls a "Third Space."[82] The Third

Space is a transitional space in which hybrid identifications are possible and social transformations can happen. In this in-between space, where different cultures intersect and collide, new identities are formed, negotiated, and are constantly in a state of becoming. The exploration of the Third Space might avoid the politics of polarity and enable new possibilities to emerge. Postcolonial preaching creates a Third Space by proclaiming God's Good News and inviting us to imagine new ways of being the people of God and fresh opportunities for working with God to mend the broken world and creation.

Postcolonial study of homiletics in the Anglican tradition builds on various studies of the sermons preached in Britain or the colonies during the colonial period to show how colonial imagination has been formed and taken effect. Rowan Strong has analyzed the annual sermons of the Society of Propagation of the Gospel delivered in London in the early eighteenth century. He argues that these sermons represented a public theology that "gave rise to an Anglican vision of imperialism" by envisioning the new overseas empire acquired by the English.[83] "In this discourse the Church of England began to fashion the identities of colonial populations of Indigenous peoples, white colonists, and Black slaves" through a theological understanding.[84] Postcolonial biblical critic R. S. Sugirtharajah studies the use of biblical texts by Victorian preachers during the Indian rebellion of 1857. His analysis of the sermons preached at the National Day of Humiliation points to the conscription of the Bible in shaping the British as the new Israel, the allusion to the British's suffering as like Job, the confidence of divine punishment of the culprits, and negative stereotypes of Indians as corrupt and ungrateful. Sugirtharajah observes that these sermons showed a "remarkable collusion of biblical text, homiletics and Christian piety, while revealing racial attitudes and lopsided interpretation at work within the Christian discourse of the nineteenth century."[85] Scholars have also studied sermons preached in the far-flung corners of the empire. Jennifer Benjamin Brooks examines the preaching of British Protestant foreign missions to the British colonies of the Caribbean during the period from 1770 to 1886. She shows that preaching at the time was undergirded by a white supremacist racial agenda, which denied the full humanity of indigenous people and people of color, especially the African slaves and their descendants.[86]

Given this lengthy colonial legacy that has shaped Anglican theology and proclamation, preaching with a postcolonial imagination is not an easy task. This requires the recognition of the relationship between the church and empire, naming the disastrous effects of colonialism and imperialism, and challenging colonial myths and discourses. Sarah Travis says, "Preaching has the opportunity to construct a space in which understanding might flourish."[87] If done appropriately, sermons can play a role in bringing about reconciliation between people torn apart by colonial or imperial violence. It is because "preaching proclaims a new reality based in God's own nature and God's intention for human life and community. The future is not simply the outgrowth of the past. A postcolonial imagination enables both preachers and listeners to envision a world free from colonizing discourse."[88]

Postcolonial preaching shares similarities with Black preaching because unmasking racial hegemony is integral to debunking colonialism. In his study of Black Anglican preaching, Harold T. Lewis observes that the sermons and pronouncements of Black Anglican preachers show what W. E. B. Du Bois has called "double consciousness."[89] The sermons often draw on racial themes, as the preachers seek to relate the gospel to the challenges, experiences, and struggles of Black people. They indict the discrimination of the white society and unjust social policies which disfranchise and marginalize Black people. The womanist preachers, among them, bear witness to female leadership and calling through their powerful words and deeds. Lewis also comments on the particular style of Black preaching: "I was particularly mindful of the preachers' straightforwardness, their unabashed and unswerving attention to the message of the gospel, and a commitment to its being not merely recounted, but proclaimed."[90] It was preaching with a purpose and the utterances from the pulpit were unapologetic and there was a sense of self-confidence in the delivery.

Since most Anglican churches follow a lectionary and preaching is often based on the texts assigned, it is important to learn from the insights of postcolonial biblical studies. Emerging in the mid-1990s, postcolonial criticism has grown and developed into a subfield in biblical studies.

Sugirtharajah writes, "What postcolonial biblical studies does is to focus on the whole issue of expansion, domination, and imperialism as central forces in defining both the biblical narratives and biblical interpretation."[91] He has published many volumes on postcolonial biblical interpretation and postcolonial commentary on the Bible. Of particular interest is his discussion of the political and ideological function of the King James Bible in 1611.[92] Cuban American scholar Fernando F. Segovia is another significant figure in postcolonial biblical studies, and he says that postcolonial criticism has a "focus on geopolitics, and, more specifically, on the differential relations of power (domination and submission) at work within imperial-colonial frameworks."[93] In her postcolonial feminist reading of the Bible, Musa W. Dube challenges metropolitan readings, analyzes the relationship between gender and imperialism, interrogates the travel motifs in the Bible, and uncovers the ways that ordinary African female readers interpret the Bible.[94] These postcolonial biblical critics help us decolonize biblical studies, challenge the legacy of biblical interpretation in Anglicanism, and search for clues for prophetic preaching.

Worship is a wholistic and embodied experience, which is shaped not only by the oral/aural aspects but also by the physical space, architecture, art, and design. Anglican churches in England were built reflecting the liturgical and theological understanding of the time, and considered the acoustic and visual effects that the setting of liturgy created.[95] When the English church's architectural designs were transplanted to the colonies, they refashioned the landscape and reinforced the power of the empire. During the Gothic revival in England and Ireland in the nineteenth century, the British thought that the Gothic style achieved the best expression there. The Gothic style was embraced by Anglicans, Catholics, and other denominations, and they began building churches "with gothic arches, flying buttresses, stained-glass windows, turrets, battlements and spires, and this was also reflected in the colonies."[96] In Australia, both the Anglicans and Catholics favored the Gothic style, though people of English descent were particularly enthusiastic about it. The Nonconformists in general preferred the Classical style. The adaptation to the Australian vernacular was slow, leading Hilary M. Carey to argue that "the Gothic style can therefore be regarded as a benign vehicle for English religious imperialism in the Australian colonies."[97]

In other colonies, the introduction of English church architecture created incongruity with the local cultural and social environment. After Hong Kong became a British colony, the British built the St. John's Cathedral in English Gothic style without adapting to Chinese local culture. Completed in 1849, the Cathedral was a meeting place for the colony's political and social elites, thus strengthening the colonial social order. The British Royal Coat of Arms was attached to the front pew. The Cathedral's architectural style was foreign to the Chinese residents because traditional Chinese temples and architecture emphasized breadth and not height. The Cathedral's soaring tower and pointed arches reinforced the notion that Christianity was a strange and imposing religion. During the early decades of the twentieth century, the number of Chinese converts grew and the Chinese clergy increased in number and influence. In 1937, St. Mary's Church was built in a Chinese Renaissance style, so that it would no longer look foreign to the local people. The style appealed to the local elites, who saw this as asserting their ethnic identity in a British colony. Interior decorations and furnishings adopted symbols from Daoist, Buddhist, and Chinese popular religion.[98] The church in which I grew up in Hong Kong, Holy Trinity Church—which has now become a cathedral—was also built in Chinese architectural style in the same period. Inside, it has Christian symbols such as the cross and the vine, and also Chinese symbols with the cloud-and-thunder motif, symbolizing life-giving and abundant harvest that rain would bring to the people in agrarian society. Bishop Ronald Owen Hall, who served as bishop at the time, embraced the contextualization of Christianity and he would later ordain Li Tim-Oi to be the first woman priest in the Anglican Communion.

Similar attempts of using indigenous architectural designs and religious symbols and motifs can be found in other parts of the Anglican Communion. In India, Bishop Vedanayagam Samuel Azariah (1874–1945) oversaw the construction of the Cathedral Church of the Epiphany in Dornakal, which was consecrated in 1939. As the first Indian bishop consecrated in the Anglican Communion in 1912, he was a pioneer of ecumenism in

India. The Cathedral Church was noteworthy because it used elements of the Hindu, Buddhist, Muslim, and Christian traditions. It had "twelve pillars representing the twelve apostles of Christ and that each incorporated the imagery of the lotus flower, representing purity in both Hindu and Buddhist traditions; the datura, representing death in Hindu understanding; and the shoot of the banana tree, representing new life."[99] In Aotearoa New Zealand, Frederick Bennett (1871–1950) proposed to include Maori decorative arts, such as carvings and embroidery with their distinctive colors and symbolisms, in church buildings, so that Maori Anglicans could retain the spirituality of their ancestors. He has led the construction of St. Faith's Church at Ōhinemutu in Rotorua at the turn of the century and the church was a prime example of weaving Maori understanding into an Anglican church.[100]

In addition to architecture, the use of liturgical space needs to be considered. In African worship, which embraces singing, clapping, and body movement, we need to think of the configuration of church space that will facilitate this. The location of the altar and the ways that congregants share the communion at the table need to be rethought. In many churches, the pulpit occupies an important space and is elevated and separated from the congregation, signifying the importance of the preaching of the word. But this arrangement separates the preacher from the congregation and often reinforces clericalism. As postcolonial preaching is not didactic and may use different styles, such as dialogue, call and response, and dramatic expression, the use and arrangement of the pulpit can be more creatively adapted to the local situation.

Ritual is an enactment of what we believe, and worship is the embodiment of Anglican identity, theology, and mission. Don S. Armentrout and Robert Boak Slocum say that "liturgy expresses the church's identity and mission, including the church's calling to invite others and to serve with concern for the needs of the world."[101] A postcolonial approach to worship challenges the cultural hegemony of the Prayer Book defined by the English language, idioms, and customs. With the Prayer Book as the foundation, different provinces continue to create "living liturgies" with increased emphasis on culture and context and to respond to the changing sociopolitical circumstances.[102] As cultural hybrids, these new Prayer Books combine elements of the BCP and local prayers, idioms, and expressions to meet the spiritual needs of God's people. The use of indigenous music and prayers has enriched the worshipping experience and helped Anglicans encounter God in a deeper way. Archbishop Desmond Tutu has edited *An African Prayer Book*, which contains prayers, songs, litanies, acts of adoration, thanksgiving, supplication, and so forth. He says prayers remind us that we are children of God and loved by God. "And so, as we keep still in the presence of God, we luxuriate in this knowledge: that we are loved, that all we are, all we have is a gift, freely and generously bestowed."[103] Worship in a postcolonial way allows us to live more fully into the church's baptismal ecclesiology and have a foretaste that every language, culture, and people will be equally pleasing to God and welcome in God's bounteous love.

Notes

1. Kenneth Stevenson, "Worship by the Book," in *The Oxford Guide to the Book of Common Prayer: A Worldwide Survey*, ed. Charles Hefling and Cynthia Shattuck (Oxford: Oxford University Press, 2006), 9.
2. Gordon Jeanes, "Cranmer and the Common Prayer," in Hefling and Shattuck, *Oxford Guide to the Book of Common Prayer*, 28.
3. Ruth A. Meyers, "Diversity and Common Worship," in *In Spirit and Truth: A Vision of Episcopal Worship*, ed. Stephanie Budwey et al. (New York: Church Publishing, 2020), 54.
4. Jeanes, "Cranmer and the Common Prayer," 29.
5. Charles Hefling, "Introduction: Anglicans and Common Prayer," in Hefling and Shattuck, *Oxford Guide to the Book of Common Prayer*, 2.
6. Brian Mayne, "Ireland," in Hefling and Shattuck, *Oxford Guide to the Book of Common Prayer*, 202–3.
7. Charles Hefling, "Scotland: Episcopalians and Nonjurors," in Hefling and Shattuck, *Oxford Guide to the Book of Common Prayer*, 166–69.
8. William L. Sachs, "Plantations, Missions, and Colonies," in Hefling and Shattuck, *Oxford Guide to the Book of Common Prayer*, 154.
9. Michael N. Jagessar and Stephen Burns, *Christian Worship: Postcolonial Perspectives* (London: Routledge, 2011), 5.
10. Jagessar and Burns, *Christian Worship*, 5.
11. Jagessar and Burns, *Christian Worship*, 27.
12. Quotations are from *The Book of Common Prayer and Administration of the Sacraments and Other Rites and Ceremonies of the Church According to the Use of The Episcopal Church* (New York: Church Hymnal Corporation, 1979), 56, 82, 356.
13. *Book of Common Prayer*, 257, and *The Hymnal 1982* (New York: Church Hymnal Corporation, 1982), no. 435.

14. Gail Ramshaw, *Liturgical Language: Keeping It Metaphoric, Making It Inclusive* (Collegeville, MN: Liturgical Press, 1996), 29.
15. See the three-volume *Readings for the Assembly*, cycles A, B, and C, ed. Gail Ramshaw and Gordon Lathrop (Minneapolis: Fortress Press, 1995–97).
16. Jagessar and Burns, *Christian Worship*, 43.
17. *Book of Common Prayer*, 123, 40, 56.
18. Jagessar and Burns, *Christian Worship*, 42.
19. Mukti Barton, "I Am Black and Beautiful," *Black Theology* 2, no. 2 (2004): 167.
20. I benefited from the discussion of the racial overtones of light and darkness and inclusive language in liturgical texts in Jagessar and Burns, *Christian Worship*, 37–44.
21. David Morley and Kuan-Hsing Chen, eds., *Stuart Hall: Critical Dialogues in Cultural Studies* (London: Routledge, 1996), 393.
22. Lambeth Conference 1878, Resolution 7, Anglican Communion, https://www.anglicancommunion.org/media/127719/1878.pdf.
23. Lambeth Conference 1878, Resolution 10, Anglican Communion, https://www.anglicancommunion.org/media/127719/1878.pdf.
24. Shawn Strout, "Prayer Book Uniformity: Myth or Icon?" *Anglican Theological Review* 105, no. 1 (2023): 31.
25. Strout, "Prayer Book Uniformity," 38.
26. Colin Buchanan, "Issues of Liturgical Inculturation," in *Anglican Liturgical Inculturation in Africa: The Kanamai Statement "African Culture and Anglican Liturgy,"* ed. David Gitari, Alcuin/GROW Liturgical Study 28 (Bramcote, UK: Grove Books, 1994), 15–16.
27. Glauco S. de Lima, "Preface," in *Beyond Colonial Anglicanism: The Anglican Communion in the Twenty-First Century*, ed. Ian T. Douglas and Kwok Pui-lan (New York: Church Publishing, 2001), 3.
28. M. E. Gibbs, *The Anglican Church in India 1600–1970* (Delhi: ISPCK, 1972), 398–400. The Church of India, Burma, and Ceylon was an autonomous province in British India. After Pakistan was formed, it became the Church of India, Pakistan, Burma, and Ceylon.
29. Buchanan, "Issues of Liturgical Inculturation," 17.
30. Lambeth Conference 1958, Resolution 74, Anglican Communion, https://www.anglicancommunion.org/resources/document-library/lambeth-conference/1958/resolution-74-the-book-of-common-prayer-prayer-book-revision.aspx.
31. Lambeth Conference, *The Report of the Lambeth Conference 1978* (London: CIO Publishing, 1978), 94–95.
32. Elisha Mbonigabe, "Indigenization of the Liturgy," in *A Kingdom of Priests: Liturgical Formation of the People of God*, ed. Thomas J. Talley, Alcuin/GROW Liturgical Study 5 (Bramcote, UK: Grove Books, 1988), 39–47. See also Paul Gibson, "International Anglican Liturgical Consultations: A Review," *Studia Liturgica* 29, no. 2 (1999): 238.
33. Lambeth Conference, *The Truth Shall Make You Free: The Lambeth Conference 1988* (London: Church Publishing, 1988), 67.
34. Victor R. Atta-Bafoe and Philip Tovey, "What Does Inculturation Mean?" in *Liturgical Inculturation in the Anglican Communion*, ed. David R. Holeton, Alcuin/GROW Liturgical Study 15 (Bramcote, UK: Grove Books 1990) 14. The authors attribute their definition to

Pedro Arrupe. See Aylward Shorter, *Toward a Theology of Inculturation* (London: Geoffrey Chapman, 1988), 11.
35. "'Down to Earth Worship': Liturgical Inculturation and the Anglican Communion," in Holeton, *Liturgical Inculturation in the Anglican Communion*, 9–10.
36. Mbonigabe, "Indigenization of the Liturgy," 39.
37. Mbonigabe, "Indigenization of the Liturgy," 39.
38. Elisha G. Mbonigabe, "The Indigenization of Liturgy," in Gitari, *Anglican Liturgical Inculturation in Africa*, 26.
39. "The Kanamai Statement Incorporating Reports from the Groups," in Gitari, *Anglican Liturgical Inculturation in Africa*, 40.
40. Mbonigabe, "Indigenization of the Liturgy," 46–47.
41. Mbonigabe, "The Indigenization of Liturgy," 22.
42. Jagessar and Burns, *Christian Worship*, 34.
43. I thank Sheryl Kujawa-Holbrook for sharing with me her prepublished chapter "Prayer Book Revision," in *Oxford Handbook of the Book of Common Prayer*, ed. Paul Bradshaw, Luiz Coehlo, and Ruth A. Meyers (Oxford: Oxford University Press, 2024).
44. Luiz Coelho, "IEAB's 2015 Book of Common Prayer: The Latest Chapter in the Evolution of the Book of Common Prayer in Brazil," *Studia Liturgica*, 49, no. 1 (2019): 33–35.
45. Coelho, "IEAB's 2015 Book of Common Prayer," 41.
46. Musa W. Dube, "Boundaries and Bridges: Journeys of a Postcolonial Feminist in Biblical Studies," in *Resistance and Visions—Postcolonial, Post-Secular and Queer Contributions to Theology and the Study of Religions*, ed. Ulrike Auga et al. (Leuven: Peeters, 2014), 142–43.
47. Storm Swain, "*A New Zealand Prayer Book = He Karakia Mihinare O Aotearoa*: A Study in Postcolonial Liturgy," in *Liturgy in Postcolonial Perspectives: Only One Is Holy*, ed. Cláudio Carvalhaes (New York: Palgrave Macmillan, 2015), 165–66.
48. The term "living liturgy" is from Peter Waggoner, "Prayer Book Revision: Considerations for the Episcopal Church," unpublished paper, April 30, 2023. Use by permission.
49. Swain, "*A New Zealand Prayer Book*," 166.
50. Hirini Kaa, *Te Hāhi Mihinare: The Māori Anglican Church* (Wellington, New Zealand: Bridget William Books, 2020), 164.
51. Jenny Te Paa, "From *Te Rawiri* to the New Zealand Prayer Book," in Hefling and Shattuck, *Oxford Guide to the Book of Common Prayer*, 346.
52. Kaa, *Te Hāhi Mihinare*, 145. Puckey and Williams translated the BCP based on earlier work done by William Yate. Puckey came to New Zealand when he was fourteen and was known as one of the best interpreters of Maori in the fledging mission and formed relationships with influential Maoris from a young age. William Williams was also involved in the translation of the Bible into the Maori language and would later become a bishop.
53. Kaa, *Te Hāhi Mihinare*, 146.
54. Jenny Te Paa, "From *Te Rawiri*," 344–45.
55. The English version can be found in *A New Zealand Prayer Book =He Karakia Mihinare O Aotearoa* (Auckland: Collins, 1989), 479. The Maori version is Storm Swain's translation, see "*A New Zealand Prayer Book*," 170.
56. Jenny Te Paa, "From *Te Rawiri*," 345.

57. Swain, "*A New Zealand Prayer Book*," 168–69.
58. Swain, "*A New Zealand Prayer Book*," 171.
59. See the reflection by Jenny Plane Te Paa, "From 'Civilizing' to Colonizing to Respectfully Collaborating?" *Theology Today* 63, no. 1 (2005): 67–73.
60. Grant LeMarguand, "The Anglican Church of Kenya," in Hefling and Shattuck, *Oxford Guide to the Book of Common Prayer*, 287. The analysis of the Kenyan liturgical texts is drawn from his chapter.
61. "A Kenyan Service of the Holy Communion, 1989," in *Offerings from Kenya to Anglicanism: Liturgical Texts and Contexts Including "A Kenyan Service of Holy Communion,"* ed. Graham Kings and Geoff Morgan (Cambridge: Grove Books, 2001), 7.
62. "A Kenyan Service of the Holy Communion," 13.
63. *Book of Common Prayer*, 362.
64. "A Kenyan Service of the Holy Communion," 14.
65. George Kiarie, "Factors Inhibiting Inculturation of the Holy Communion Symbols in the Anglican Church in Kenya: A Case Study of the Diocese of Thika," *Missionalia* 44, no. 3 (2017): 301–20.
66. Kenneth Ofula, "'The River Between': Negotiating Dual Identities in the Anglican Churches of Kenya," *Studies in World Christianity* 25, no. 1 (2019): 95–113.
67. Esther Mombo, "Anglican Liturgies in Eastern Africa," in Hefling and Shattuck, *Oxford Guide to the Book of Common Prayer*, 285.
68. Mombo, "Anglican Liturgies in Eastern Africa," 282.
69. Jaci Maraschin, "Culture, Spirit, Worship," in Douglas and Kwok, *Beyond Colonial Anglicanism*, 335–36.
70. Coelho, "IEAB's 2015 Book of Common Prayer," 39.
71. Jeffrey Richards, *Imperialism and Music: Britain 1876–1953* (Manchester: Manchester University Press, 2001), cited in Jagessar and Burns, *Christian Worship*, 53.
72. Renie Chow Choy, *Ancestral Feelings: Postcolonial Thought on Western Christian Heritage* (London: SCM Press, 2021), 104. She discusses the impact of English hymns on her mother and her, see 101–16.
73. Lim Swee Hong, "Church Music in Postcolonial Liturgical Celebration," in *Postcolonial Practice of Ministry: Leadership, Liturgy, and Interfaith Engagement*, ed. Kwok Pui-lan and Stephen Burns (Landham, MD: Lexington Books, 2016), 131.
74. Lim, "Church Music in Postcolonial Liturgical Celebration," 130.
75. Israel O. O. Odewole, "Singing and Worship in an Anglican Church Liturgy in Egba and Egba West Dioceses, Abeokuta, Nigeria," *HTS Teologiese Studies* 74, no. 1 (2018): 5, https://hts.org.za/index.php/hts/article/view/4584/11588.
76. "The Kanamai Statement Incorporating Reports from the Groups," 40.
77. Cited in Mbonigabe, "The Indigenization of Liturgy," 28.
78. Mbonigabe, "The Indigenization of Liturgy," 29.
79. See Geoff Morgan, "Aspects of Inculturation in Music, Drama and Protest," in Kings and Morgan, *Offerings from Kenya to Anglicanism*, 43–44.
80. Jagessar and Burns, *Christian Worship*, 62.
81. Kwok Pui-lan, *Postcolonial Politics and Theology: Unraveling Empire for a Global World* (Louisville, KY: Westminster John Knox Press, 2021), 157.

82. Homi K. Bhabha, *The Location of Culture* (London: Routledge, 1994), 36–39.
83. Rowan Strong, "A Vision of Anglican Imperialism: The Annual Sermons of the Society for the Propagation of the Gospel in Foreign Parts 1701–1714," *Journal of Religious History* 30, no. 2 (2006): 176.
84. Strong, "Vision of Anglican Imperialism," 175.
85. R. S. Sugirtharajah, "Salvos from the Victorian Pulpit: Conscription of Texts by Victorian Preachers during the Indian Rebellion of 1857," in *The Bible and Empire: Postcolonial Explorations* (Cambridge: Cambridge University Press, 2005), 66.
86. Jennifer Benjamin Brooks, "The Missionary Connection: White Preaching in the British Colonies of the Caribbean," in *Unmasking White Preaching: Racial Harmony, Resistance, and Possibilities in Homiletics*, ed. Lis Valle-Ruiz and Andrew Wymer (Lanham, MD: Lexington Books, 2022), 19–28.
87. Sarah Travis, *Decolonizing Preaching: The Pulpit as Postcolonial Space* (Eugene, OR: Cascade Books, 2014), 48.
88. Travis, *Decolonizing Preaching*, 48.
89. Harold T. Lewis, "Unapologetic Apologetics: The Essence of Black Anglican Preaching," *Anglican Theological Review* 101, no. 1 (2019): 46.
90. Lewis, "Unapologetic Apologetics," 48.
91. R. S. Sugirtharajah, *Postcolonial Criticism and Biblical Interpretation* (Oxford: Oxford University Press, 2002), 25.
92. R. S. Sugirtharajah, "The Version on Which the Sun Never Sets: The English Bible and Its Authorizing Tendencies," in *Postcolonial Criticism and Biblical Interpretation*, 127–54.
93. Fernando F. Segovia, "Johannine Studies and Geopolitical: Reflections upon Absence and Irruption," in *What We Have Heard from the Beginning: The Past, Present, and Future of Johannine Studies*, ed. Tom Thatcher (Waco, TX: Baylor University Press, 2007), 284. See also his *Decolonizing Biblical Studies: A View from the Margins* (Maryknoll, NY: Orbis Books, 2000).
94. Musa W. Dube, *Postcolonial Feminist Interpretation of the Bible* (St. Louis, MO: Chalice Press, 2000).
95. David H. Smart, "Christopher Wren and the Architectural Context of Anglican Liturgy," *Anglican Theological Review* 77, no. 3 (1995): 290–306.
96. Hilary M. Carey, "Anglican Imperialism and the Gothic Style in Australia," *Journal for the Academic Study of Religion* 23, no. 1 (2010): 8.
97. Carey, "Anglican Imperialism," 6.
98. James Ellis, "Anglican Indigenization and Contextualization in Colonial Hong Kong: Comparative Case Studies of St. John's Cathedral and St. Mary's Church," *Mission Studies* 36, no. 2 (2019): 219–46.
99. Kaa, *Te Hāhi Mihinare*, 118.
100. Kaa, *Te Hāhi Mihinare*, 119.
101. Don S. Armentrout and Robert Boak Slocum, eds., *An Episcopal Dictionary of the Church: A User-Friendly Reference for Episcopalians* (New York: Church Publishing, 2000), 47.
102. Peter Waggoner, "Prayer Book Revision: Consideration for the Episcopal Church," unpublished paper, April 30, 2023.
103. Desmond Tutu, *An African Prayer Book* (New York: Doubleday, 1995), xviii.

CHAPTER

5

The Debates on Human Sexuality

In recent decades, human sexuality has become the most divisive issue in the Anglican Communion, threatening Church schism and breaking the "bonds of affection." Debates about polygamy, marriage and divorce, contraception, and sexual relationships have a long history and can be traced to the first Lambeth Conference of 1867. At that conference, Bishop John Colenso's more open view on polygamy clashed with that of other bishops, who upheld that polygamy should not be permitted in the Church. Human sexuality has been a highly charged subject because it often serves as a marker of cultural differences and has been treated as taboo. The discussion of sexuality touches on many issues, including the boundary between the private and the public, gender roles and relationships, same-sex union and marriage, procreation and family, and colonialism's impact on sexual norms and laws.

The debates on polygamy brought up the entwined issue of the possibility of divorce, as the Church needed to decide whether a polygamous man had to divorce his other wives before being accepted for baptism. In Matthew 5:32 and 19:9, Jesus allowed for divorce and remarriage only for the reason of adultery. Thus, when civil divorce was established in England by the Matrimonial Causes Act in 1857, it caused controversy in the Church, because the Act automatically allowed remarriage.[1] By the end of the nineteenth century, the Church's position was that divorce could only be granted for adultery and remarriage would not be allowed during the lifetime of the other spouse. This was the position at Lambeth 1888.

But as the divorce rate climbed in the twentieth century, the bishops had to rethink their long-standing position, and Lambeth 1920 allowed for provincial autonomy and differences on the matter. While affirming that marriage is a "life-long and indissoluble union" between one man and one woman, the Conference affirmed "the right of a national or regional church within our Communion to deal with cases which fall within the exception" that Jesus has laid down.[2] Lambeth 1930 took a hard line and reiterated that divorcees could not remarry in church, out of concern for the stability of the home and security for women. However, as time went on, each province was left to decide about the remarriage of divorcees in church, the admission to the Eucharist for remarried divorces, and the ordination of divorced and remarried persons.[3]

Traditionally, the primary purpose of marriage was for procreation, and having children was seen as a gift and God's blessing. When the issue of "artificial restriction of the family" was brought up at Lambeth 1908, the bishops judged such measures as "demoralising to character and hostile to national welfare" and called for the discontinuation of the use of artificial means.[4] But the attitude at Lambeth 1930 took a turn after Margaret Sanger and women's groups had publicized birth control for many years. Even though the Conference still reiterated procreation as an important purpose for marriage, it also recognized that sexual instinct is holy, and that sexual intercourse has functions other than procreation. It found that "intercourse between husband and wife as the consummation of marriage has a value of its own within that sacrament, and that thereby married life is enhanced and its character strengthened."[5] Although the bishops preferred abstinence as the better method, they also recognized that sometimes other methods might be used. In 1958, the Lambeth Conference affirmed the use of family planning, saying, "Christians need always remember that sexual love is not an end in itself nor a means to self-gratification, and that self-discipline and restraint are essential conditions of the freedom of marriage and family planning."[6] It saw that family planning could be responsible parenting, taking into account the resources of the family, the population needs of society, and the claims for future generations. Lambeth 1968 reiterated the positions taken in Lambeth 1958, and the Anglican Communion disagreed with Pope Paul VI and the Catholic Church's staunch opposition to contraception by artificial means.[7]

As we have seen, the Church's positions on a range of topics relating to divorce, procreation, and sexual relationships were not set in stone and could change over time. Sometimes past decisions could be reversed because of changing social and political circumstances. Individual provinces could adapt to their situations based on different cultures and social needs. In the following, I will focus on two of the most hotly debated issues—polygamy and homosexuality—to illustrate the complexities of sexual politics in the Communion. Before doing so, I want to highlight how the colonial legacy has invariably colored the debates by discussing the intersection between race, gender, and sexuality, drawing insights from postcolonial theory.

Race, Gender, and Sexuality

European colonialism was premised on the superiority of the white race, who were destined to rule the world because of God's providence. Various theories have been put forth to justify the white race as the pinnacle of humankind. Though the Enlightenment thinkers advocated for reason and equality, figures such as Locke, Kant, and Hume harbored racial biases and prejudices.[8] In the nineteenth century, scholars suggested the novel and faulty theory that human intelligence could be measured by cranial capacity and brain size. They claimed that the brain sizes of people of darker races were smaller, and thus they were less intelligent than white people. During 1880–1920, scientific racism became a dominant discourse, which placed human beings on a hierarchical scale based on biological differences related to heredity. Europeans were placed at the top of this scale, while Africans were generally placed at the lowest end. When evolutionary theory became more accepted by the end of the nineteenth century, people attributed racial differences to cultural development, rather than biology. Although Christianity teaches that all people are equal before God, missionaries had a "double vision," which allowed them to claim the spiritual equality of all humans while maintaining the superiority of British culture. Rebecca C. Hughes, who has studied CMS history in Uganda, writes, "British missionaries ranked different races according to a civilizational model that mapped cultures to different stages of development, with British culture as the zenith."[9]

Anthropologists and historians used the terms "primitive," "backward," or "uncivilized" to describe the cultures of Africans, Pacific Islanders, Oceanians, and indigenous peoples. In *Time and the Other*, cultural anthropologist Johannes Fabian challenges the ways anthropologists have studied and classified other peoples, using various ways of constructing temporality. Anthropologists assumed they lived in the "here and now," while other peoples lived in "there and then." Because of the asymmetry of power, the racial other was denied coevality with the "advanced" and "civilized" Europeans.[10] Postcolonial theorist Homi Bhabha interrogates this assumption of time lag that exists between different races. He cites the work of Franz Fanon, who refused to accept the belatedness of the Black man when compared to the white man. It was clear for Fanon, Bhabha says, that "the black man refuses to occupy the past of which the white man is the future."[11] Instead of accepting the time-lag theory, Bhabha says the debate can open an opportunity to speak of "humanity through the differentiations—gender, race, class—that mark an excessive marginality of modernity."[12]

It is worth remembering that missionaries played a pioneering role in what we now called "social scientific" research of native peoples. They learned the native languages and acquired much data about the customs, rituals, ceremonies, and geographies to further their aims for evangelization.[13] Some missionary literature and anthropological studies invariably painted a sharp contrast between European cultures and native cultures. The submission of women in native societies, in particular, was often taken as symptomatic of the inferiority of their cultures. In the Victorian period, white women were heralded as the angels of the home, who were pure, innocent, gentler, and more religious than men. In sharp contrast, women of the darker races were seen as ignorant, illiterate, and lustful, who needed to be rescued from their sorrowful states. Missionaries tried to uplift the native women by providing education, offering employment in churches and missions, and criticizing practices such as polygamy, *sati*, and the harem. Their attempts in introducing what they perceived to be the ideals of Christian motherhood often encountered resistance because they undermined traditional understanding of manhood and patriarchal authority. As colonized subjects, native men already felt their pride and ego threatened, as colonial discourse described them as effeminate or less manly than white men.

Influenced by their Victorian understanding of gender and sexuality, Europeans looked at sexual practices deviating from monogamous marriage and nuclear family with condescension and scorn. They were intrigued by the accounts of "exotic" customs, such as the rites of puberty, initiation, courtship, polygamy, fertility rites, and purity and taboo in native societies. In *Carnal Knowledge and Imperial Power*, Ann Laura Stoler shows that the management of sexual practices of colonizers and colonized is fundamental to the colonial order and the discourses on sexuality aim to shape bourgeois subjects and police domestic recesses of imperial rule.[14] The introduction of European sexual norms and practices was an important part of the "civilizing mission" that missionaries and colonial officials took upon themselves. The public sphere had to be under control and the private sphere under surveillance. As Bhabha notes, this redrawing of the domestic space as the space for normalizing and policing clearly shows that "the personal-*is*-the political; the world-*in*-the-home."[15]

Missionaries and colonial governments introduced notions of sexuality foreign to Africa and other parts of the world. Kapya John Kaoma says that in precolonial Africa, sexuality had been community-based and seen as joyful and celebratory, as it was associated with procreation. But the missionaries have taught Africans that sex is taboo and should not be discussed in public.[16] This silence around sexuality has hampered sexual education for the young, contributed to the increase of gender-based violence, and hindered the prevention of HIV/AIDS. Kaoma further argues that African societies allowed for sexual diversity and accepted a range of sexual behaviors, other than heterosexuality. He cites the study of historian Marc Epprecht, who argues that Africans expressed no strong shame or guilt about homosexuality. E. E. Evans-Pritchard's study of the Azande in today's Central African Republic indicated that same-gender marriage between men was at par with heterosexual marriages and lesbianism was also cautiously practiced.[17] In Nigeria, sexual minorities paraded annually in the public square as late as the 1970s.[18] These studies challenge the claim that homosexuality is un-African and is foreign to the continent by politicians, scholars, religious leaders, and laypeople. Kaoma says that to "promote acceptance of sexual minorities in African Christianity, the decolonization of human sexuality from colonial and missionary teachings is imperative."[19]

People who have same-sex relationships were not referred to as "homosexuals" until the nineteenth century. The concept of "homosexuality" was derived as part and parcel of the colonial discourse. As Jeffrey Meeks points out, the term can be traced to two related discourses: sexologists' classification of normal and abnormal behaviors which led them outside of their culture, and anthropological accounts of sexual behaviors of people of other cultures, especially those deemed as primitive.[20] These two accounts intersected when homosexuality was labeled as an inversion, a disorder, and a dread. Homosexuality was not acceptable because it was linked to the sexual practices of primitive races and societies, and thus a form of neuropsychological counter-evolution and a historical and cultural regression. This inversion was taboo because as psychiatrist Vernon Rosario points out, it was a retreat from the civilized to the primitive, symbolized by the effeminacy associated with male hysteria and inversion. It had a religious dimension too, as some French doctors associated homosexuality with regression to pre-Christian morality.[21]

The British introduced laws that criminalized homosexuality in the British colonies without much consultation or adaptation. These laws can be traced to the time of Henry VIII when offenses that were formerly tried in church courts had to be heard in secular ones since Henry broke from Rome. A 1533 statute reiterated the criminalization of sodomy and those who committed "detestable and abominable" acts were punishable by death. In the United States, the sodomy law was inherited from colonial laws in the seventeenth century. In the British Raj, the Indian Penal Code that came into force in 1861 criminalized anal sex and oral sex, targeting mainly homosexual individuals. As the British intensified their colonial process in Africa in the nineteenth century, the colonial governments imposed laws that criminalized homosexuality. These laws were imposed because the colonizers "believed laws could inculcate European morality into resistant masses. They brought in the legislation, in fact, because they thought 'native' cultures did not punish 'perverse' sex enough. The colonized needed compulsory re-education in sexual mores."[22] These laws intended to protect and praise "white" virtue while policing and suppressing "native" vices. Although Britain and Wales decriminalized most consensual homosexual conduct in 1967, it took decades for the former British colonies to abolish the sodomy law—Aotearoa New Zealand in 1986, Hong Kong in 1990, and India in 2018.[23] Today, many African countries, among them former British colonies, still criminalize same-sex sexual activities.

After political independence, there was a push to reclaim cultural autonomy and reconnect with heritages that have been suppressed and devalued. In the attempts to indigenize Christianity to the local contexts, the emphasis has been to use local idioms, languages, and concepts to express Christian thought. Archbishop Henry Orombi of Uganda has said, "The younger churches of Anglican Christianity will shape what it means to be Anglican. The long season of British hegemony is over."[24] Bishops from the Global South have increasingly shown pride and confidence in their cultures and contested negative portrayals of their societies in the past. But even as these male religious leaders and theologians are busy reclaiming their "traditional" cultures, they have overlooked or glossed over the androcentric and heteropatriarchal elements embedded in them. As no culture is static or monolithic, we need to discern and distinguish constantly what is liberating and what is oppressive in it.

For decades, feminist theologians from the Global South have challenged patriarchal beliefs and practices in the Church and society. On the one hand, they have to fight against the patronizing attitudes of Western feminists, who speak from their middle-class, white, privileged positions and often have limited knowledge of feminist struggles outside the North Atlantic. On the other hand, they have to challenge their male compatriots, who condemn feminism as a Western import, which threatens family and sexual relationships. Shuttling between tradition and modernity, feminist theologians from the Global South face tremendous pressure and dilemmas. Kenyan Lutheran feminist theologian Musimbi R. A. Kanyoro notes, "The African continent's history of colonialism and Western imperialism causes a dilemma for African women theologians and activists at large. There is always a struggle regarding how to relate to Western culture, indigenous culture, and religious culture, coupled with the daily need to support life against all odds."[25] As one of the pioneers in African women's theology, she developed an "engendered cultural hermeneutics," which argues that inculturation is not enough if it does not take gender into consideration. Her engendered cultural hermeneutics seeks to develop inculturated theology from gender and feminist perspectives, helping to break the long silence surrounding women's oppression. She proposed an engendered communal theology, which is committed to changing oppressive social structures and works to build solidarity with others in the community.[26] Like Kanyoro, Anglican women theologians from the Global South have also articulated their concerns about gender justice and empowerment of women and girls in the Church and society. Even though sex is treated as a taboo subject, sexual minorities in Africa, Asia, and Latin America within the Communion have increasingly challenged heterosexism and demanded equal participation in the life of the Church.

The Cultural Politics of Polygamy

Polygamy was practiced in most societies encountered by missionaries in the nineteenth century, including India, China, Southeast Asia, and Muslim and African countries. It was in Africa that polygamy became most problematic for Anglican missions. There were social, cultural, and economic reasons for polygamy. Traditional African marriages were arranged between families and often involved the exchange of bridewealth in the form of cattle. Multiple wives and a large family served as a sign of wealth, power, and status. In the case when a wife was infertile, taking other wives ensured procreation, without the need to divorce her. Having more children meant more labor and the potential to bring more wealth to the family. Since sexual intercourse with a woman during menstruation and breastfeeding was frowned upon, having multiple wives satisfied the husband's sexual needs. British missionaries found polygamous marriage troubling and against their Christian upbringing. Ironically, colonization increased the number of cases of polygamy because the new wealth from trade with European settlers enabled more Africans to afford to pay the bridewealth to have additional wives. Colonial governments in general did not want to legislate against polygamy and make monogamy the norm for fear of popular resistance. Polygamy decreased when hut taxes were imposed as a strong financial disincentive for Africans to have large plural households.[27]

Missionaries and mission societies frequently raised the question of how to deal with polygamy. Except for a small minority such as Bishop Colenso, who had more open attitudes toward polygamy and advocated for tolerance and slow reform, the majority of missionaries upheld monogamy as the ideal. Bishop Samuel Adjai Crowther of the Diocese of Niger, the first Black bishop in the Anglican Communion, also staunchly opposed polygamy. Consecrated in 1864, Bishop Crowther's evangelistic work in the Niger Delta brought notable success. He argued that polygamy is against the teaching of the Church and bemoaned the fact that African converts rapidly reverted to their polygamous life. Before the Lambeth conference in 1888, Bishop Crowther prepared a memorandum entitled "Notes on the Life of Polygamy in West Africa," in which he attacked the immoral aspects of polygamy, the physical liability to men because of frequent intercourse, and injustice done to women in polygamous marriages. He wrote, "In consequence to the practice of polygamy, injustice is done to many women for non-performance of marriage duty; jealous of, and quarrels with, those who are the favourites are frequent in the house between one wife and another in which the wife is implicated."[28] The husband would severely punish the quarrelsome wife by beating her or use other forms of abuse. Lambeth 1888 took a hard stance against polygamy and said that it is inconsistent with Christ's teaching on marriage. It resolved that "persons living in polygamy be not admitted to baptism, but that they be accepted as candidates and kept under Christian instruction until such time as they shall be in a position to accept the law of Christ."[29] However, the bishops resolved that the wives of polygamists in some cases could be accepted for baptism and left to the local church authorities to decide. They had embraced Bishop Crowther's view that women were involuntary victims of the institution because they did not have the freedom to contract or dissolve a matrimonial alliance. The decisions at Lambeth did not resolve the issue, but rather created further problems, because they implied that a polygamous husband had to divorce all but one of his wives to receive baptism. But the Church during this period opposed divorce in general and this created a dilemma. In the African familial system at the time, women deserted by their husbands had little means of supporting themselves and their children, and some had no choice but to end up in prostitution.

The decision to ban polygamous men from full membership hindered Anglican missions because missionaries wanted to convert leaders of the community, but these wealthy and powerful men were polygamists. Moreover, in response to the Church's ban, several indigenous African churches, such as the Yoruba Independent African Church, were founded, which accepted polygamous members and siphoned a significant number of converts from European missions. In the twentieth century, the matter was brought up repeatedly at various Lambeth Conferences. The archbishop of Canterbury commissioned a survey of the treatment of polygamous converts in the Anglican Communion leading up to Lambeth 1920. The Conference maintained the ban on the baptism of men living in polygamy. Historian Timothy Willem Jones notes that the tone of church proclamations regarding polygamy softened after World War II, when the African countries became decolonized.[30] Lambeth 1958 maintained that monogamy is the divine will, but recognized that "the introduction of monogamy into societies that practice polygamy involves a social and economic revolution and raises problems which the Christian Church has as yet not solved."[31] It also recognized that polygamy is bound up with the limitations for opportunities for women in society and urged the Church to make effort to advance the status of women. The 1968 Conference reaffirmed monogamous lifelong marriage as God's will and acknowledged that polygamy posed "one of the sharpest conflicts between the faith and particular cultures."[32] It also recognized that many problems concerning marriage confronted the Church and asked each province to take into consideration what was being done in other provinces when they reexamined marriage disciplines.

The protracted debates about polygamy aroused the concerns of not only men but women as well, and one of the places to discuss it was the Mothers' Union. The Mothers' Union, an Anglican organization begun in England, spread to Africa and had a strong presence in the continent that continues today. The Union was set up to strengthen Christian marriage and to promote the well-being of families. Esther Mombo notes that in Kenya, the Mothers' Union discussed marriage and polygamy in their early meetings beginning in the late 1950s.[33] The missionaries who founded the Mothers' Union spoke against polygamy and argued that Christian marriage should be based on the teachings of the Bible. The leaders of the Mothers' Union recognized that polygamy was a complicated issue, as there were different forms of marriages in Africa: civil, Christian, Muslim, Hindu, and customary marriages. They noted that many women, both Christian and non-Christian, did not want to be one of the many wives of a husband. They also laid blame on the girls and women who agreed to marry a man who was married already. Although the Mothers' Unions recognized that polygamy had its social and economic causes and could not be easily abolished, they urged the government to do all that was possible to encourage monogamy.

After the 1970s, postcolonial criticism of the Church's policy on polygamy began to emerge as church leaders and theologians wanted to reassert their cultural identity after decolonization. The Anglican archbishops in Africa commissioned Roman Catholic priest and scholar Adrian Hastings in 1972 to write a report on Christian marriage in Africa. As a white priest, Hastings was critical of colonialism and his report shared the views taken by Colenso earlier. Just like Colenso, Hastings thought monogamous marriage is ideal but recommended the reception of people in polygamous marriages to baptism and communion.[34] The Anglican Consultative Council commended the report and asked the African bishops to propose changes to the Lambeth Conference.

Polygamy became a bone of contention as African theologians wanted to develop their indigenous theology and contest the colonial mentality and European domination in theology and church practices. Writing in 1976, Felix Ekechi questioned whether monogamy as the only ideal Christian family life reflects the imposition of European values. He wrote, "The ignorance of African institutions and European cultural arrogance prompted the church and the state to condemn what Africans very much accepted as good for themselves."[35] He charged that Christian missions had treated polygamy with more seriousness than slavery because they saw polygamy as standing in the way of "the Europeanization of the African."[36] He accused Bishop Crowther of presenting a distorted picture of polygamy and the sexual behaviors of polygamists. Even though polygamy would be advantageous to men from a patriarchal viewpoint, he said, many women supported it because it was prestigious to marry a man with more than one wife and multiple wives could share household chores. He said that Africans want to be Christians, but they are "anxious to be African first and foremost."[37] African converts noted that the Bible is not univocal against polygamy, since some of the patriarchs, such as Abraham and Jacob, had multiple wives. Although many African educated men and women prefer monogamy, polygamy is still widely practiced as an acceptable customary form of marriage. Thus, he concluded, "the African 'Christian community,' in its indigenization process, views polygamy as a legitimate African social institution that ought to be recognized, and considers that those who practice it should not be denied church rights."[38]

As I have pointed out above, even as African male religious leaders and theologians want to reclaim their traditional culture in the postcolonial period, they have not included gender in their critical analysis. In contrast to them, African women theologians argue that African cultures are not monolithic and criticize the androcentric biases in the interpretation of African traditions. Mercy Amba Oduyoye, a Ghanaian Methodist theologian and a leader of African women's theology, has looked at African culture through the oral tradition of folktales, stories, and proverbs and offered another perspective. She notes that many folktales and proverbs emphasize competition among cowives and warn men of showing favoritism toward a certain wife. It is the importance of having children that keep men and women from abandoning polygamy.[39] For her, there is a need to reassess the meaning of marriage not only in Africa but throughout the world. It is not whether a marriage is polygamous or monogamous that defines the status of women, rather "it is the dependence and domination mentalities of the women and men sharing marriage that needs transformation."[40] For Esther Mombo, polygamy raises the deeper question of the position of women in a patriarchal society. She argues that the Bible should be interpreted in a way to support the dignity and worth of women and not abuse them. Even though some of the patriarchs and kings in the Hebrew Bible chose to be polygamous, their marriages point to problems of rivalry, jealousy, envy, succession feuds, hatred, and murder. There is ample evidence that the New Testament prefers monogamous marriage.[41] Kanyoro further argues that indigenization is not sufficient if the culture reclaimed reinforces patriarchy and does not lead to the promotion of justice and support for the life and dignity of women. Citing studies that show that polygamy is an institution that oppresses women, she writes: "Polygamy has been the basis of exploitation of women and children's labor because polygamy is justified as a means of enhancing the productivity of property of men. Polygamy also depicts women as weak and in need of the constant protection of men."[42] There are unfortunately not many reports on what women in polygamous marriages have said on the subject. Their stories are filtered through missionary reports or the writings of polygamous men. Depending on the authors' stance, these stories range from women who are happy in the polygamous marriage to women who show ambivalence toward polygamy.[43]

Despite these diverse opinions about polygamy, African Anglican church leaders were determined to push the Communion to lift the ban against polygamy. The ban has created many pastoral and practical problems. Families were broken up, and the wives and children expelled from polygamous marriages became social concerns. In 1988, the East African bishops came to the Lambeth Conference determined to have the ban on admission to the sacraments of polygamists lifted. The strength of representation from Africa at the Conference was keenly felt. Of the 518 bishops who attended, 175 came from Africa, compared to 80 in 1978.[44] The Conference finally reversed the one hundred years' ban and recommended that under certain conditions, "a polygamist who responds to the Gospel and wishes to join the Anglican Church may be baptized and confirmed with his believing wives and children."[45]

As expected, Lambeth Conference's decision brought out different responses. On the one hand, Nigerian churchman and teacher A. O. Nkwoka proclaims: "It was an evangelical victory" because polygamous men can fully join the community of believers in the Church, and this would provide new incentives for evangelistic efforts.[46] By taking this step, he says, the Church has addressed the concerns of some of the early converts in Nigeria who saw "the imposition of monogamy on the African Church as one of the whiteman's oppressive measures and a sign of white supremacy."[47] On the other hand, Western scholars are more circumspect. Jones argues the Lambeth 1988 decisions show that English understanding of gender relationships cannot be replicated in many African and Asian contexts. "Polygamy implicitly provincialised Anglican gender understanding and confounded notions of a 'natural,' universal gender order."[48] Historian Jane Shaw points out that the debates on polygamy, divorce, and contraception show that many issues are local and need to be treated so and they are influenced by the history of colonialism. The fact the Church can change its position, she says, shows that Anglican moral theology and tradition are dynamic, and moral decisions cannot be made in the abstract and must engage with particular situations.[49]

Schism over Homosexuality

The Anglican Communion's long debate on polygamy provides useful background and insights for looking at the cultural politics of the controversy on homosexuality that threatens to divide the Communion. Although the missionaries and mission bodies had insisted on monogamy as the ideal family structure, different marriage patterns and sexual norms continue to exist, showing that it is difficult to prescribe universal norms that fit all cultures. The demographic shift within the Communion means that African bishops have increasingly played significant roles in setting the terms for the Communion. The debate on polygamy also points out there are diverse perspectives on this complex issue, especially when gender and women's concerns are brought into the picture. The cultural politics at the level of the Lambeth Conference was quite different from what was happening at the local level.

The 1978 Lambeth Conference discussed the issue of homosexuality and called for further study and listening. "While we affirm heterosexuality as the scriptural norm, we recognise the need for deep and dispassionate study of the question of homosexuality, which would take seriously both the teaching of Scripture and the results of scientific and medical research."[50] By 1973, the American Psychiatric Association had resolved that homosexuality was not a mental illness or sickness. The Conference continued, "The Church, recognizing the need for pastoral concern for those who are homosexual, encourages dialogue with them."[51] When Lambeth 1988 reversed the ban on the baptism of polygamist converts, it also discussed homosexuality and placed the issue within the context of human rights and pastoral care for people with homosexual orientation. From today's perspective, the wording of the resolution was quite mild and respectful. The Conference did not make any moral judgment but recognized the continuing need for study and taking into account biological, genetic, and psychological research done by other agencies.[52] It also recognized that sociocultural factors might lead to different attitudes in the Communion.

In some of the provinces in the Communion, gay men and lesbians had begun to push for greater recognition and equal participation in the Church since the 1970s. Following the Stonewall Riot in 1969, Louie Crew founded Integrity USA in 1974, a national network of gay and lesbian Episcopalians and their friends and families. The network had local chapters throughout the United States and Canada. In 1977, the first openly lesbian priest Ellen Barrett was ordained in New York. In 1994, after many years of deliberation, the Episcopal Church's General Convention added "sexual orientation" to the nondiscrimination canons for ordination. But the debates lingered on, and some bishops continue to refuse to ordain gay men and lesbians. In Britain, the Lesbian and Gay Christian Movement was founded in 1976. The Church of England has commissioned different reports at various times to advise the Church on homosexuality. These reports elicited heated debates on homosexuality, the ordination of gay men and lesbians, and whether gay priests should remain celibate.[53] While these debates continued, unofficial blessings of same-sex unions had been happening in both the Episcopal Church and the Church of England. LGBTQ persons in Britain, the United States, Canada, and elsewhere had hoped that Lambeth 1998 would adopt resolutions that would be more welcoming to them.

However, Lambeth 1998 was under pressure from the alliance formed between the church leaders of the South and conservative Northerners, who felt that their churches had become too liberal. Miranda K. Hassett, in her detailed study of the crisis in the Anglican Communion, mentions that several pre-Lambeth meetings were held in Kuala Lumpur, Dallas, and Kampala, with the goal to strengthen conservative alliances and to influence the outcome of Lambeth 1998.[54] Even before Lambeth 1998, tensions were high when American Bishop John Spong of the Diocese of Newark was reported as having said that African Christians are "superstitious, fundamentalist Christians" who have "moved out from animism into a very superstitious kind of Christianity" and have yet to face the intellectual revolution of Copernicus and Einstein of the modern world.[55] The African and Southern bishops came to Lambeth already feeling insulted and defensive. Tensions and suspicions between the North and the South could not be contained. An unforgettable scene was that of Nigerian Bishop Emmanuel Chukwuma attempting to exorcise the English deacon Richard Kirker, a gay activist. Kirker's sin was that he was gay. Chukwuma's words to Kirker were direct: "God did not create you as a homosexual. That is our stand. That is why your church is dying in Europe—because it is condoning immorality."[56]

The resolution on human sexuality at Lambeth 1998 (Resolution 1:10) upheld the faithfulness in marriage between a man and a woman and acknowledged that there were vastly diverse opinions about homosexuality within the Communion. It recognized that there are people with homosexual orientation, who seek pastoral care and moral direction from the Church. The Conference committed to listening to the experience of homosexual persons and affirmed that all who are baptized, regardless of their sexual orientation, are full members of the Body of Christ. The Southern bishops had unsuccessfully tried to propose resolutions to recognize "The Kuala Lumpur Statement on Human Sexuality," which labeled homosexual practices as a sin.[57] But they and their Western supporters were able to push for the inclusion of the clause that referred to "homosexual practice as incompatible with Scripture." The resolution also did not advise the blessing of same-sex unions and the ordination of those who engaged in same-sex unions.[58] According to one commentator, Bishop Peter John Lee from the Anglican Church in Southern Africa, Resolution 1:10 of Lambeth 1998 "was as much a third-world reaction to American dominance (in numbers, wealth, pushiness) at Lambeth 1978 and 1988, as it was about sexuality."[59] He said churches in the Third World saw the Episcopal Church as too allied with the U.S. government and supported American expansionism in the world and it has tried to control and manipulate the Communion. The controversy caused by Lambeth 1998 was still roaring when several incidents added fuel to the fire. In 2003 the Diocese of New Hampshire elected Gene Robinson, a gay man in a same-sex relationship, as bishop. The Diocese of Westminster in the Anglican Church of Canada authorized rites for same-sex blessing. In the Church of England, Jeffrey John became the first openly gay man to be nominated as bishop in 2003, though he later had to withdraw due to mounting pressure.

For conservative bishops in Africa, the acceptance of homosexuality would mean giving up biblical authority and long church traditions. In an interview, Archbishop Peter Akinola of Nigeria said, "The missionaries brought us the word of God here and showed us the way of life. We have seen the way of life and we rejoice in it. Now you are telling me this way of life is not right. I have to do something else. Keep it for yourself. I do not want it."[60] As the leader who oversaw a province with nearly 20 million members, Akinola was the most powerful Anglican voice against homosexuality. Seeing that North American churches have deviated from biblical discipline, Akinola invited priests and parishes who rejected the authority of their own bishops to come under the diocesan oversight of the Church of Nigeria. In addition to Nigeria, the churches in Uganda, Kenya, and Rwanda also extended such oversight, which interfered with provincial and diocesan authority. Many churches that rejected same-sex marriage and ordination of LGBTQ persons would later form the Anglican Church in North America in 2009.

Responding to the outcry coming from the Communion, Archbishop Rowan Williams appointed a Commission to explore the polity, relationships, and accountability of the Communion. The Commission produced the Windsor Report in 2004. After discussing the purpose and foundation of the Communion, the principle of the Communion, and future life together, the report discussed the maintenance of the Communion and made several recommendations to prevent a schism. It suggested a moratorium on the consecration of the bishops in same-sex relationships and public rites of blessing same-sex unions. It called for the expression of regrets by the Episcopal Church and the Anglican Church of Canada over the consecration of Gene Robinson and the approval of the use of liturgies for blessing same-sex unions. To foster greater unity and common understanding within the Communion, the report also recommended an Anglican Covenant to be ratified by each church.[61] This Anglican Covenant has failed to strengthen connections among churches in the Communion as I have discussed in chapter two.

The Windsor Report did not resolve the debate, as both liberals and conservatives criticized the report. A year later at the Primates' Meeting in Northern Ireland, the primates requested that the Episcopal Church and the Anglican Church of Canada voluntarily withdraw from the Anglican Consultative Council until the next Lambeth in 2008. Carter Heyward, a lesbian Episcopal priest and theologian, said that the Windsor Report and the primates' action showed that the bishops decided that they would not journey with gays and lesbians and listen to them. The primates wanted the two troubling members of the Communion to go away, treating them as outsiders, which is not conducive to unity or reconciliation. Heyward called upon gay men and lesbians, and the priests among them, to continue to lift their prophetic voices and minister to those who are marginalized.[62] It is difficult for the two sides to come closer together because when race intersects with sexuality, the discussion becomes emotionally charged, especially with memories of the scars of colonial history. In her article "Anglicans in Postcolony," Mary-Jane Rubenstein points out that given the demographic shift in the Anglican Communion, the bishops from the Global South think that they speak for the majority. If the Northern churches refuse to listen to the "younger churches" and are unwilling to change their stance, this amounts to a refusal of relation and would constitute an act of neocolonialism in the global world. Those white bishops who spoke for gay men and lesbians and opposed the Southern bishops' defense of scriptural authority have been labeled racist and imperialist. But Rubenstein argues that the gospel that these Southern bishops are defending was a colonial imposition in the first place.[63]

Esther Mombo, a member of the Commission that drafted the Windsor Report, offered a perspective from the Global South. She writes that while the African bishops have said homosexuality is not an issue in Africa, they have devoted much attention to it. "It appears to me that the issue is among some heterosexual male church leaders whose voices appear to dominate global Anglican church politics at the expense of the far more pressing and urgent issues of mission and ministry."[64] These urgent issues include poverty, ethnic strife, environmental crisis, health concerns, and taking care of people affected by HIV/AIDS. The African bishops have put out a "holier-than-thou" attitude and singled out the sin of homosexuality but glossed over other ethical issues such as the squandering of state and church funds, having affairs outside marriage, and discrimination of other ethnic groups. Some church leaders, she says, are far too busy answering what they claim to be the "Macedonian Call" to evangelize the North and have neglected what is happening in their own backyard. She urges us to look at the deeper dynamics shaping the conflicts and ask, "Who is paying for these voices to be heard? . . . Who is using whom in this debate? For whose benefit is this taking place?"[65]

As tensions remained high after the issuing of the Windsor Report, the design group of Lambeth 2008 decided to change the format of the meeting. The bishops would not vote on resolutions but instead would use the *indaba* process, adapted from Zulu culture, as a way of communal listening and transformation.[66] They would be divided into groups to do Bible studies and hold a series of group discussions about the many issues that divide them. Approximately 650 bishops attended the Conference, but more than 230 boycotted it. About a month before Lambeth 2008, 291 Anglican bishops together with other conservative Anglican clergy and laity attended the Global Anglican Future Conference (GAFCON) in Jerusalem and formed the Fellowship of Confessing Anglicans. Participants issued the Jerusalem Declaration, which claimed that they are orthodox Anglicans who base their faith on the Bible and Anglican teachings and acknowledged that "God's creation of humankind as male and female and the unchangeable standard of Christian marriage between one man and one woman as the proper place for sexual intimacy and the basis of the family."[67] GAFCON has continued to meet several times and developed structures to strengthen global connections. Because of the pandemic, the next Lambeth Conference was postponed till 2022. More than 650 bishops gathered for the meeting, but the primates and bishops from Nigeria, Uganda, Kenya, and Rwanda boycotted it. Instead of deciding on resolutions, the bishops were invited to assent to "Lambeth Calls." The Global South Fellowship of Anglican Churches, a fellowship of confessing Anglicans who emphasize biblical authority, had come to the conference with the intent to force public endorsement of the resolution on homosexuality from 1998 and include this in the Call on Human Dignity. The Call affirmed the validity of the Lambeth 1998 Resolution and that many provinces cannot affirm same-sex marriage. Yet it also recognized that there are provinces that have blessed and welcomed same-sex union or marriage, after much careful deliberation and theological reflection.[68] Lambeth 2022 did not resolve the differences, and the Lambeth Calls are being offered to the churches around the world, inviting them to hear each call, add their voice, and bring them to life in their context.

The debates on homosexuality within the Communion have taken place in changing social norms and laws regarding human sexuality and marriage. In the United States, Massachusetts became the first state to legalize same-sex marriage in 2004, and after many more years of activism and organizing, the United States Supreme Court legalized same-sex marriage in all the states in 2015. South Africa became the first African country to legalize same-sex marriage in 2006, and in Asia, Taiwan took the lead to recognize same-sex marriage in 2019. But in other countries, such as Uganda, conservative politicians have pushed for stiffer punishment for homosexual behaviors. Violent attacks, death threats, and other abuses toward LGBTQ people have increased. Postcolonial theorists remind us to listen to the voices of the subaltern, people who are multiply oppressed and situated at the margins of society. African gay and lesbian activists continue to struggle for human rights, even as some African bishops insist that homosexuality is a Western disease and un-African. Several African LGBTQ Anglicans were bold enough to appear in the documentary *Voices of Witness Africa* to share their stories of secrecy, challenges, and hope.[69] Davis MacIyalla, an Anglican activist and founder of a lesbian and gay rights group in Nigeria, argues that homosexuality is not foreign, as each of the local languages has terms for same-sex practices. The Westerners did not bring homosexuality to Africa, they brought sodomy laws and British penal codes, he says.[70] Other gay and lesbian activists worked with local and international supporters to protest against Uganda's anti-homosexuality bill and fought to repeal other legislation that criminalizes same-sex relations. In the conservative Church of the Province of South East Asia, Leng Lim started *Sanctuary*, the first gay and lesbian Christian fellowship in Singapore in 1992. He has written about his experiences of betrayal and struggle as an Asian gay man and remains active in speaking out against heterosexism after becoming an Episcopal priest.[71]

Interpretating Sexual Politics in the Anglican Communion

Commentators use different interpretations to elucidate sexual politics that have created acrimony and threatened schism in the Communion. Some employ the narrative of a demographic shift of Christianity from the North to the South, popularized by Philip Jenkins's book, *The Next Christendom: The Coming of Global Christianity*.[72] Citing this global shift, critics are quick to point out that the majority of Anglicans now live in the South, while membership in mainline churches has been in decline in Europe and North America. The next Christendom, according to Jenkins, will be defined by the Southern churches, which tend to be theologically more conservative, while the influences of liberal mainline denominations will continue to decline. As an Episcopal layman, he is particularly concerned about the rates of decline in membership and average Sunday attendance in the Episcopal Church. He sounds the alarm that if this trend continues, by mid-century, the Episcopal Church will become a tiny sect rather than a great church or denomination.[73] He further warns that if the Northern churches proclaim a moral stance more in line with progressive secular values, they are heading for a collision course with their Southern counterparts.

Conservative Episcopalians and many Southern Anglicans have used Jenkins's writings to bolster their position. But Jenkins's observations have received much criticism from other astute scholars of world Christianity. Vietnamese American theologian Peter C. Phan has criticized Jenkins's use of the trope "Christendom" to describe Southern Christianity, for the term has exaggerated the power and influences of the South. Phan says that Christianity is still a small minority religion in Asia, and the prospects of Asian Christians forming political and ecclesiastical alliances with their counterparts in Latin America and Africa to build Christendom are remote.[74] Phan also faults Jenkins for his generalization of Southern Christianity as conservative and traditional, in sharp contrast with the more progressive and liberal Northern Christianity.

A case in point is Jenkins's description of the North-South clash over homosexuality in the Anglican Communion in his book. He presents Southern Christianity as generally conservative on this issue, focusing on the action and condemning words of Moses Tay, the archbishop of South East Asia, and Akinola. He does not mention other voices that are more open to homosexuality in the South. Furthermore, he points out that debates on gender and sexuality roiled not only the Anglicans, but also the Methodists, Lutherans, and Presbyterians. This bolsters his argument that conservative Southern Christianity has now become a force encroaching on the more liberal Northern churches.[75] As I have shown above, the view on homosexuality is not as monolithic as Jenkins portrays. For example, Archbishop Tutu was a longtime supporter of the rights of LGBTQ persons. For him, it was inconsistent to fight against apartheid and not for other marginalized groups. "If the church, after the victory over apartheid, is looking for a worthy moral crusade, then this is it: the fight against homophobia and heterosexism," he proclaimed.[76] Tutu's unequivocal support has given LGBTQ Christians and activists around the world much hope and encouragement, including those in the Episcopal Church.[77]

While leaders such as Akinola dominated news media, others point to the diversity of opinions and regional differences in the African continent. In a speech given in Liverpool, England, Bishop Musonda Trevor Selwyn Mwamba of Botswana said, "The African provinces are not a monochrome body as popular belief would suggest. There are different points of view in the various African provinces. To think that there is one view is simplistic and a distortion of the truth." He stated that there are three positions among the Anglican provinces in Africa, and they are influenced by the political climate and social circumstances. The first is the conservative voice, represented by the provinces of Nigeria, Uganda, and Tanzania. This position rejects homosexuality and wants to break relations with those member churches that do not follow church discipline. He notes that the Church in Nigeria supported legislation that outlaws same-sex relations and wants to defend itself from attacks of permissiveness by Muslim adherents. The second is the liberal voice, represented by the province of Southern Africa with Archbishop Njongonkulu Ndungane, who succeeded Tutu, as the public face. This position acknowledges the deep divisions within the Communion and urges member churches to respect provincial autonomy and differences. Concerning human sexuality, the liberal voice says that it is a mystery and much more study and theological reflections are needed. The moderate voice is presented by the Anglican Church in Burundi, which has a more reconciliatory tone. It emphasizes loyalty to scriptural authority and commits to working with other members of the Communion to maintain unity.[78]

The blanket description of Southern Christianity as conservative and traditional not only points to theological divergence but also carries with it vestiges of colonial conceptions of cultural difference. In colonial ideology, the colonized are depicted as "uncivilized," "savage," "childlike," and having yet to catch up with modernity. Some of these colonial stereotypes resurfaced in the homosexuality debate, as evident in Bishop Spong's condescending remarks toward Africans. Yet the binary construction of "tradition" and "modern," or "underdeveloped" and "developed," can also be deployed in subtler ways. For example, Kevin Ward, who has written a book on the history of global Anglicanism, states, "The fact that the conflict has focused so fiercely on homosexuality is itself an indication of the way in which what is essentially a conflict within modern western secular society has spilled over to the rest of the world, itself coming to terms with modernity and the increasing dominance of secularity and its discontents."[79]

His remarks are problematic because he assumes that the South is lagging behind the West and is only "coming to terms with modernity" in a belated way. Chinese American gay priest and lawyer Patrick S. Cheng notes that one of the ways to mark the otherness of gender and sexual deviants, women, colonized people, and the poor is to label them "backward." He challenges this linear construction of time and says, "In recent decades, however, many critical theorists—particularly those in the realm of postcolonial and queer theory—have challenged our obsession with the future. Instead of worshipping at the altar of linear (that is, straight) time, such theorists have encouraged us to spiral backwards and embrace the past."[80] Furthermore, Ward's suggestion of a "dominance of secularity" reflects a Western bias, which is not borne out in many societies in the South and the Middle East. Many scholars in the West have debated on a postsecular world, in which religion reenters the realms of politics and public life. Others have theorized about alternative modernities and argued that Western modernity should not be taken as the norm.

Among various commentators, Kaoma provides a postcolonial perspective that places the sexual politics of the Communion in the colonial and neocolonial contexts. He notes that homosexuality became a hot issue in Africa in the 1990s, partly due to the "globalization of culture wars" by the American Christian Right.[81] For decades, American right-wing Christian groups have used wedge issues such as abortion and homosexuality to gain power and influence in national and local politics. These issues have divided the country and led to heated debates and divisions within the mainline denominations in the United States. But as more and more American people have accepted women's reproductive rights and homosexuality, these American conservatives have exported their culture wars to gain influence in the global arena. They argue that they are conducting spiritual warfare and label homosexuality as un-African, un-Christian, and un-Islamic, citing scriptures as support (Gen. 18–19, Quran 26). They have formed networks in Africa and pushed for stringent laws against homosexual behaviors in several countries in Africa. African conservative religious leaders have used this liaison with the Christian Right and adapted their tactics to serve their political needs. Kaoma writes, "African conservative Christianity transforms and domesticates U.S. sexual rights activism to serve its political agenda, influence local policy, and increase its visibility in both local and global politics."[82]

Opposing these anti-LGBTQ groups are those who champion the rights of sexual minorities in Africa. Kaoma notes that both the conservative and progressive groups are mostly associated with and funded by American groups. The pro-LGBTQ groups, supported by American human rights organizations, do not have the power and clout, like the conservative groups do, to influence public policies and the government. Though they use human rights language to bolster their claims, their messages have been labeled neocolonialist and accused of undermining African traditional values. Kaoma cautions that the globalization of sexual politics has unintended consequences in Africa. In some countries, it has led to rising homophobia and the murder and violence inflicted upon LGBTQ persons. Because of local violence and government surveillance and brutality, sexual minorities have gone underground, making them targets of extortion and harassment.[83]

The controversies over sexual politics demonstrate that cultural difference shaped by race, gender, and sexuality has plagued the Anglican Communion from the beginning. From its start as a colonial church that was largely defined by its English character and Victorian understanding of gender roles and marriage, the Church of England encountered cultural customs and sexual practices very different from its own. The imposition of Western values onto the colonized has been labeled colonial and meets with criticism. But today, in our globalized neoliberal world, sexual politics have become more complicated as new alliances have been forged, and we need to avoid the simple binary of the liberal North versus the traditional South. While Southern church leaders have used the issues of gender and sexuality to accuse the West of neocolonialism, some of them have been willing collaborators of the Christian Right and conservative politicians at home. The control of women's bodies and sexuality and the policing of LGBTQ persons cannot be separated from the growing global right-wing politics, often fought under the pretext of religion to benefit those who wield power.

Some commentators have argued that just as the Communion has allowed for alternative marriage patterns in the Global South, it should not repress those provinces that want to recognize the rights of LGBTQ persons. But this is unlikely to happen in the near future. The debate needs to go beyond managing the conflicts of the Communion, resorting to arguments such as provincial autonomy and respecting differences. There need to be deeper dialogues on the issues of colonial sexual fantasy, the fetishization of desire, the postcolonial construction of manhood, and the internationalizing of sexual identities in a world where neocolonialism and unequal power dynamics dominate. We have to examine the long tradition of heterosexist interpretation of the Bible and theology and the exclusion of the voices of women, LGBTQ persons, and other marginalized persons. If Anglican theological anthropology is based on the belief that we are created in the *imago Dei*, it is imperative to theologize how gender and sexual diversity and difference help us to see a fuller picture of the *imago Dei*. The debate of human sexuality is a threat, but it can also be an opportunity for deeper conversation and communion with the Other and with God.

Notes

1. Jane Shaw, "Bonds of Affection: Debates on Sexuality," in *Anglican Women on Church and Mission*, ed. Kwok Pui-lan, Judith A. Berling, Jenny Plane Te Paa (New York: Morehouse Publishing, 2012), 46.
2. Lambeth Conference 1920, Resolution 67, Anglican Communion, https://www.anglicancommunion.org/resources/document-library/lambeth-conference/1920/resolution-67-problems-of-marriage-and-sexual-morality.aspx.
3. Charlotte Methuen, "The Lambeth Conference, Gender and Sexuality," *Theology* 123, no. 2 (2020): 86.
4. Lambeth Conference 1908, Resolution 41, Anglican Communion, https://www.anglicancommunion.org/resources/document-library/lambeth-conference/1908/resolution-41.aspx.
5. Lambeth Conference 1930, Resolution 13, Anglican Communion, https://www.anglicancommunion.org/resources/document-library/lambeth-conference/1930/resolution-13-the-life-and-witness-of-the-christian-community-marriage.aspx.
6. Lambeth Conference 1958, Resolution 113, Anglican Communion, https://www.anglicancommunion.org/resources/document-library/lambeth-conference/1958/resolution-113-the-family-in-contemporary-society-marriage.aspx.
7. Methuen, "Lambeth Conference," 88.
8. David Theo Goldberg, *Racist Culture: Philosophy and the Politics of Meaning* (Oxford: Blackwell, 1999), 14–40.
9. Rebecca C. Hughes, "'Grandfather in the Bones': Scientific Racism and Anglican Missionaries in Uganda, c. 1900–1930," *Social Sciences and Missions* 33, no. 3–4 (2020): 351.
10. Johannes Fabian, *Time and the Other: How Anthropologist Makes Its Object* (New York: Columbia University Press, 1983).
11. Homi K. Bhabha, *The Location of Culture* (London: Routledge, 1994), 238.
12. Bhabha, *Location of Culture*, 238.
13. See, for example, William Carey, *An Enquiry into the Obligations of Christians to Use Means for the Conversion of Heathens* (1792; repr., London: Carey Kingsgate Press, 1961); Patrick Harries and David Maxwell, eds., *The Spiritual in the Secular: Missionaries and Knowledge about Africa* (Grand Rapids, MI: Eerdmans, 2012).
14. Ann Laura Stoler, *Carnal Knowledge and Imperial Power: Race and the Intimate in Colonial Rule* (Berkeley: University of California Press, 2002), 145.
15. Bhabha, *Location of Culture*, 11. Emphasis in the original.
16. Kapya John Kaoma, *Christianity, Globalization, and Protective Homophobia: Democratic Contestation of Sexuality in Sub-Sahara Africa* (Cham, Switzerland: Palgrave Macmillan, 2018), 30–39.
17. E. E. Evans-Prichard, "Sexual Inversion among the Azande," *American Anthropologist*, New Series 72, no. 6 (1970): 1428–34.
18. Kapya John Kaoma, "Beyond Adam and Eve: Jesus, Sexual Minorities and Sexual Politics in the Church in Africa," *Journal of Theology for Southern Africa* 153 (2015): 9–10; and his "The Paradox and Tension of Moral Claims: Evangelical Christianity, the Politicization and Globalization of Sexual Politics in Sub-Saharan Africa," *Critical Research on Religion* 2, no. 3 (2014): 231.
19. Kaoma, "Beyond Adam and Eve," 9.

20. Jeffrey Weeks, *Against Nature: Essays on History, Sexuality and Identity* (London: Rivers Oram Press, 1991), 11. Sexologist Havelock Ellis found that there was a widespread natural instinct toward homosexual relationships among the "lower races." See Havelock Ellis and John Addington Symonds, *Sexual Inversion* (1897; repr., New York: Arno Press, 1975), 4.
21. Vernon A. Rosario, *The Erotic Imagination: French Histories of Perversity* (New York: Oxford University Press, 1997), 88.
22. "This Alien Legacy: The Origins of 'Sodomy' Laws in British Colonialism," Human Rights Watch, December 17, 2008, https://www.hrw.org/report/2008/12/17/alien-legacy/origins-sodomy-laws-british-colonialism.
23. "This Alien Legacy"; "India: Supreme Court Strikes Down Sodomy Law," Human Rights Watch, September 6, 2018, https://www.hrw.org/news/2018/09/06/india-supreme-court-strikes-down-sodomy-law.
24. Archbishop Henry Luke Orombi, "What Is Anglicanism," *First Things* 175 (2007): 23–28, quoted in Mary-Jane Rubenstein, "Anglicans in the Postcolony: On Sex and the Limits of Communion," *Telos* 143 (Summer 2008): 138.
25. Musimbi R. A. Kanyoro, "Engendered Communal Theology: African Women's Contribution to Theology in the Twenty-First Century," in *Hope Abundant: Third World and Indigenous Women's Theology*, ed. Kwok Pui-lan (Maryknoll, NY: Orbis Books, 2010), 21.
26. Kanyoro, "Engendered Communal Theology," 27.
27. Timothy Willem Jones, "The Missionaries' Position: Polygamy and Divorce in the Anglican Communion, 1888–1988," *Journal of Religious History* 35, no. 3 (2011): 395.
28. Bishop Samuel Adjai Crowther, "Notes on the Life of Polygamy in West Africa, January 1, 1887," 3, quoted in Felix K. Ekechi, "African Polygamy and Western Christian Ethnocentrism," *Journal of African Studies* 3, no. 3 (1976): 339.
29. Lambeth Conference 1888, Resolution 5, Anglican Communion, https://www.anglicancommunion.org/resources/document-library/lambeth-conference/1888/resolution-5.aspx.
30. Jones, "Missionaries' Position," 401.
31. Lambeth Conference 1958, Resolution 120, Anglican Communion, https://www.anglicancommunion.org/resources/document-library/lambeth-conference/1958/resolution-120-the-family-in-contemporary-society-polygamy.aspx.
32. Lambeth Conference 1968, Resolution 23, Anglican Communion, https://www.anglicancommunion.org/resources/document-library/lambeth-conference/1968/resolution-23-marriage-discipline.aspx.
33. Esther Mombo, "The Bible and Polygamy: A Mothers' Union Perspective," *AICMAR Bulletin* 1 (2002): 35-41.
34. Jones, "Missionaries' Position," 405–6.
35. Ekechi, "African Polygamy and Western Christian Ethnocentrism," 333.
36. Ekechi, "African Polygamy and Western Christian Ethnocentrism," 334.
37. Ekechi, "African Polygamy and Western Christian Ethnocentrism," 349.
38. Ekechi, "African Polygamy and Western Christian Ethnocentrism," 349.
39. Mercy Amba Oduyoye, *Daughters of Anowa: African Women and Patriarchy* (Maryknoll, NY: Orbis Books, 1995), 52.
40. Oduyoye, *Daughters of Anowa*, 147.
41. Mombo, "Bible and Polygamy," 43.

42. Kanyoro, "Engendered Communal Theology," 30.
43. Jones, "Missionaries' Position," 407.
44. Vinay Samuel and Christopher Sugden, *Lambeth: A View from the Two Thirds World* (London: SPCK, 1988), 4.
45. Lambeth Conference 1988, Resolution 26, Anglican Communion, https://www.anglicancommunion.org/resources/document-library/lambeth-conference/1988/resolution-26-church-and-polygamy.aspx.
46. A. O. Nkwoka, "The Church and Polygamy in Africa: The 1988 Lambeth Conference Resolution," *Africa Theological Journal* 19, no. 2 (1990): 153.
47. Nkwoka, "Church and Polygamy in Africa," 140.
48. Jones, "Missionaries' Position," 407–8.
49. Shaw, "Bonds of Affection?" 50–51.
50. Lambeth Conference 1978, Resolution 10, Anglican Communion, https://www.anglicancommunion.org/resources/document-library/lambeth-conference/1978/resolution-10-human-relationships-and-sexuality.aspx.
51. Lambeth Conference 1978, Resolution 10, Anglican Communion, https://www.anglicancommunion.org/resources/document-library/lambeth-conference/1978/resolution-10-human-relationships-and-sexuality.aspx.
52. Lambeth Conference 1988, Resolution 64, Anglican Communion, https://www.anglicancommunion.org/resources/document-library/lambeth-conference/1988/resolution-64-human-rights-for-those-of-homosexual-orientation.aspx.
53. Shaw, "Bonds of Affection?" 39–41.
54. Miranda K. Hassett, *Anglican Communion in Crisis: How Episcopal Dissidents and Their African Allies Are Reshaping Anglicanism* (Princeton, NJ: Princeton University Press, 2007), 47–70.
55. Andrew Carey, "African Christians? They're Just a Step Up from Witchcraft," *Church of England Newspaper*, July 10, 1998, quoted in Hassett, *Anglican Communion in Crisis*, 72.
56. James E. Solheim, *Diversity or Disunity: Reflections on Lambeth 1998* (New York: Church Publishing, 1999), 65.
57. "The Kuala Lumpur Statement," Anglican Church League, Sydney, February 10–15, 1997, https://www.acl.asn.au/old/news/KLStatement.html.
58. Lambeth Conference 1998, Resolution 1.10, Anglican Communion, https://www.anglicancommunion.org/resources/document-library/lambeth-conference/1998/section-i-called-to-full-humanity/section-i10 human-sexuality.aspx.
59. Peter John Lee, "Indaba as Obedience: A Post Lambeth 2008 Assessment 'If Someone Offends You, Talk to Him,'" *Journal of Anglican Studies* 7, no. 2 (2009): 153.
60. Ruth Gledhill, "For God's Sake," *The Times* (London), July 5, 2007, https://www.thetimes.co.uk/article/for-gods-sake-mqdmclhwb2b.
61. "The Windsor Report 2004," Anglican Communion, https://www.anglicancommunion.org/media/68225/windsor2004full.pdf.
62. Carter Heyward, "Make Us Prophets and Pastors: An Open Letter to Gay and Lesbian Priests," in *Gays and the Future of Anglicanism: Responses to the Windsor Report*, ed. Andrew Linzey and Richard Kirker (New York: O Books, 2005), 315–25.
63. Rubenstein, "Anglicans in the Postcolony," 144–46.
64. Esther Mombo, "The Windsor Report: A Paradigm Shift for Anglicanism," *Anglican Theological Review* 89, no. 1 (2007): 77.

65. Mombo, "Windsor Report," 77.
66. Peter John Lee describes the Indaba process at Lambeth 2008 in "Indaba as Obedience," 147–61.
67. GAFCON, "The Jerusalem Statement," https://www.gafcon.org/about/jerusalem-statement.
68. Paul Handley, "Lambeth 2022: Everything You Need to Know about the Sexuality Row," *Church Times*, August 5, 2022, https://www.churchtimes.co.uk/articles/2022/5-august/features/features/lambeth-2022-everything-you-need-to-know-about-the-sexuality-row.
69. For information about the documentary, see "Coming Soon, To A Screen Near You," May 20, 2009, Voices of Witness, https://voicesofwitness.blogspot.com/#:~:text=Voices%20of%20Witness%20Africa%2C%20produced%20by%20Cynthia%20Black,and%20tragic%20stories%20of%20fear%2C%20imprisonment%20and%20abuse.
70. Rubenstein, "Anglicans in the Postcolony," 149.
71. You-Leng Leroy Lim, "Webs of Betrayal, Webs of Blessings," in *Q & A: Queer in Asian America*, ed. David L. Eng and Alice Y. Hom (Philadelphia: Temple University Press, 1998), 323–34. See also Leng Lim, Kim-Hao Yap, and Tuck-Leong Lee, "The Mythic-Literalists in the Province of Southeast Asia," in *Other Voices, Other Worlds: The Global Church Speaks Out on Homosexuality, ed. Terry Brown* (New York: Church Publishing, 2006), 58–76.
72. Philip Jenkins, *The Next Christendom: The Coming of Global Christianity*, 3rd ed. (New York: Oxford University Press, 2011).
73. Philip Jenkins, "The Church Vanishes, Part Deux," *Patheos*, October 19, 2014, https://www.patheos.com/blogs/anxiousbench/2014/10/the-church-vanishes-part-deux.
74. Peter C. Phan, "A New Christianity, But What Kind?" *Mission Studies* 21, no. 1 (2005): 75.
75. Jenkins, *Next Christendom*, 250–54.
76. Desmond Tutu, "Foreword," in *Aliens in the Household of God: Homosexuality and Christian Faith in South Africa*, ed. Paul Germond and Steve De Gruchy (Cape Town: D. Philip, 1997), x.
77. Kwok Pui-lan and Eunjin Jeon, "Inspirations of Archbishop Demond Tutu on Global Justice Work," *Anglican Theological Review* 104, no. 3 (2022): 356–58.
78. General Synod Communications, "The Anglican Communion: Crisis and Opportunity," The Anglican Church of Canada, March 26, 2007, https://www.anglican.ca/news/the-anglican-communion-crisis-and-opportunity/3006098.
79. Kevin Ward, *A History of Global Anglicanism* (Cambridge: Cambridge University Press, 2006), 315.
80. Patrick S. Cheng, "Race and Sexuality in the 'Regions Beyond': Towards a Postcolonial Queer Missiology," Pitt Lecture, Berkeley Divinity School at Yale, October 18, 2021, http://www.patrickcheng.net/uploads/7/0/3/7/7037096/transcript_cheng_2021_pitt_lecture_2021_10_19_final.pdf.
81. Kaoma, *Christianity, Globalization, and Protective Homophobia*, 89.
82. Kaoma, "Paradox and Tension of Moral Claims," 234.
83. Kaoma, "Paradox and Tension of Moral Claims," 240.

CHAPTER

6

Women's Leadership in the Global South

The **demographic shift of Anglican churches** to the Global South is largely the work of women in the church. Christian women carry out vital functions and ministries and contribute to the church's vitality and evangelistic efforts. They serve on the vestry, teach Sunday school, visit the sick, organize altar guilds and women's groups, act as evangelists, and reach out to their communities. Missiologist Dana L. Robert argues that "the current demographic shift in world Christianity should be analyzed as a women's movement, based on the fact that even though men are typically the formal, ordained religious leaders and theologians, women constitute the majority of active participants."[1] Her observation is especially pertinent for Anglican churches because the average Anglican today is a woman in her thirties living in sub-Saharan Africa. Women make up the overwhelming majority of members of Anglican churches in Africa.

As I have discussed in the previous chapter, colonial Christianity brought ambivalent legacies to the Global South regarding race, gender, and sexuality. On the one hand, Christian missions provided educational opportunities for women and carried out social reforms against practices such as footbinding, polygamy, concubinage, female infanticide, and *sati*. On the other hand, colonial Christianity emphasized domesticity and female subordination, which reinforced patriarchal traditions in local cultures. In some tribal and indigenous communities, women used to play greater roles in their communities, and their power and influence were curtailed under colonialism. In the current debates on human sexuality, some church leaders want to reinforce traditional gender roles, marriage, and family. They regard women's liberation and the acceptance of homosexuality as Western-imposed agenda that contradicts traditional culture. Some of the women of the Global South have reservations about associating with the feminist movement and other progressive causes, for fear that they will be labeled as "problematically Westernized."[2]

In their struggle for gender equality and leadership, women in the Global South must confront the colonial legacy, patriarchal worldviews in their culture, familial and societal pressure, and gender biases of women in their communities. They have been shuttled between "tradition" and "modernity," as men in their societies and Western scholars and media—feminists among them—seek to define them and their roles. In her influential article, "Under Western Eyes: Feminist Scholarship and Colonial Discourses," Chandra Talpade Mohanty points out that Western scholarship on "third world women" often displays cultural biases and harbors a sense of superiority. Replicating colonial logic, Western feminist discourse constructs third-world women in a monolithic way and portrays them as victims of male violence. This discourse depicts non-Western women as the Other in what is called "third world difference," and focuses on their oppression rather than their strength.[3]

A postcolonial interpretation of Anglican women's leadership in the Global South emphasizes women's agency and their contributions to the church's mission and ministries. It requires a paradigm shift of attention from the work of Western missions and missionaries to local agents and organizations. It also embraces a broad ecclesiology and insists that women and men together make up the church, and shifts the focus from the male bishops, church leaders, and theologians to ordinary female church members and their leaders. While we can easily find books on the Anglican women's movement and leadership in the United Kingdom and the United States,[4] we have very few books on Anglican women in the Global South,[5] and resources about them are scattered as book chapters and articles. This is partly because women in the Global South still find it difficult to gain access to higher education and theological training to tell their own stories. Theological institutions and libraries in the Global South may not have sufficient resources to support their research. Yet Anglican women in the Global South have contributed to the Christian mission and the church, and they have brought important changes to the Anglican Communion, such as women's ordination and mission strategies. This chapter introduces Anglican women's leadership in the Global South, including their work in evangelism and ministry, the Mothers' Union and other women's organizations, women's struggle for ordination, and women's efforts in combating gender-based violence and HIV/AIDS. The discussion is selective because of the vast scope, and it is further limited by the availability of sources.

Women's Work and Ministry

Local women have played important roles in the work of Christian missions and the establishment of Anglican churches in different parts of the world. In some places, the segregation of the sexes and norms of sexual propriety necessitated the sending of female missionaries to reach women. Evangelizing the women was seen as key to bringing their families to Christ. The CMS sent an increasing number of married and single missionaries, and the Church of England Zenana Mission Society (CEZMS) was set up in 1880 specifically to work among Indian women, and the work was expanded to Japan and China. In the mission fields, missionaries trained Bible women to assist them in what was called "women's work for women" in missionary circles. These Bible women taught women and children the Bible, prayers, and hymns, visited homes, counseled the sick, and networked with the community. Christian missions set up schools for girls to train future wives of church workers and female evangelists to assist in evangelistic work. These girls and young women learned the Bible, elementary skills, as well as hygiene and sewing to prepare them for good motherhood. As the missions grew, the girls' schools began to offer more advanced courses, and some became famous for their educational standards. The graduates would work in ministry, education, government, medicine, and other professions to contribute to their societies.

Christian mission offered women opportunities to explore new roles, exercise leadership, and serve as a bridge-builder between the church and their families and communities. As various Anglican and Episcopal mission societies worked in very diverse contexts, I offer three portraits from different regions—China, Tanzania, and Cuba—to illustrate the work of local women and their agency. I highlight the ways that changing social and political situations affected their work and ministry.

In China, Episcopal women missionaries from the United States began their work in the 1840s; since then, CMS sent an increasing number of women and CEZMS began its work in South China in 1884. In the beginning, evangelistic work involved visiting women at their homes and teaching the Bible and catechism, since women were prevented from attending church services by gender-segregated norms. Bible women were trained to assist women missionaries and served as their translators because of the many local Chinese dialects. They helped introduce, communicate, and adapt a foreign religion to a vernacular culture. Because of the high rate of illiteracy, an important function of the Bible women was to teach local women how to read so that they could understand biblical passages and catechism. Bible women also served as role models for the local women and as community leaders.[6] Initially, these Bible women were informally trained, and later short-term courses and training schools were established to teach them the Bible, preaching, history, hygiene, science, and singing. Historian Zhou Yun underscores the importance of Bible women's work: "They were able to act as a bridge between this alien religion and the local society. Their Chinese identity helped to spread the imported religion and transform it into a local one, linguistically and culturally."[7] Sometimes, these Bible women had to overcome resistance from their families and communities to carry out their work.

The changing social and political situation in China affected women's evangelistic and educational work. In traditional China, girls were not educated, though rich families might provide some tutoring for their daughters. The girls' schools established by the missions had a hard time attracting students. At the turn of the twentieth century, Chinese social reformers began to advocate for female education and the abolition of footbinding because, they argued, strong mothers will raise a strong nation. The Chinese became more receptive to Christian girls' schools and some attracted wealthy and non-Christian families, such as St. Mary's in Shanghai and St. Hilda's in Wuchang. Unlike the Bible women who worked in villages and were largely immune from larger political changes, urban schoolgirls in mission schools were more influenced by national crises and turmoil. In the 1920s, when nationalistic fervor denouncing Western imperialism swept across China, students in China organized protests and strikes. St. Hilda forbade students to participate in political demonstrations to protect their safety. Yet the students became socially conscientized and politicized, and when Japan invaded China in 1931, they boycotted Japanese goods and supported war efforts against Japan.[8] Graduates from the girls' schools formed close bonds, which continued after they left schools, and they contributed to society as teachers, leaders of YWCA, and other professions.

In addition to evangelism and education, Chinese Anglican women also organized to serve their communities. Beginning in 1893, Women's Auxiliary mission chapters were established in Chinese Anglican churches in Shanghai, Wuhan, and other dioceses, modeled after the Women's Auxiliary in the American Episcopal Church. With the establishment of the Chung Hua Sheng Kung Hui (Chinese Anglican-Episcopal Church, CHSKH) in 1912, the Women's Auxiliary spread to all nine dioceses and subsequently formed the CHSKH Women's Missionary Service League in 1921. The purpose of the League was to unite women, both local and foreign, to "engage in prayer, contributions, service, and extending the kingdom of Heaven."[9] Evangelism and service to the church became the chief focus of its work. In the larger cities, the League members consisted of middle- and upper-middle-class women. League members raised funds to support mission work and relief for refugees, and victims of drought and other disasters. Some of the branches ran schools for the poor, organized women's literacy classes or night schools, and supported mothers and children. During the Japanese invasion, the League campaigned in support of the war against Japan, raised funds to support wounded soldiers and refugees, and assisted the government in relief work.[10] With the founding of the Peoples' Republic of China and the expulsion of missionaries, the CHSKH stopped its work in 1958.

While Chinese Anglican women served as cultural translators helping the church to adapt to the local context, Christian women in today's Tanzania formed what historian Andreana C. Pritchard has called an "affective spiritual community" for female bonding and evangelistic work.[11] The Universities' Mission to Central Africa (UMCA) was established in 1859 by Anglican members within the Universities of Oxford, Cambridge, Durham, and Dublin in response to David Livingston's call to mission work in Central Africa. UMCA worked with ex-slaves and refugees from the illegal and yet ongoing slave trades. After some initial failed efforts, the UMCA established a base on the East African archipelago of Zanzibar and formed a settlement in Mbweni for those released slaves to live in. They included orphans and children liberated from slavery, and men and women that the British navy rescued from the Indian Ocean slave trades. Many of them were women because women who were single, widowed, or without the protection of males could be vulnerable to enslavement. Separate from home and family members, these female ex-slaves often felt lonely and homesick, and they nurtured a kind of kinship and familial relationship through emotional bonding and spiritual connection with one another and with the British missionary women. This spiritual community tied its members, especially the female evangelists, together across linguistic, ethnic, and generational differences and across geographical space. As a result of these women's inherent mobility and movement between different mission outposts, the community extended to women of different ethnolinguistic groups in the mainland of Tanzania and Malawi between 1860 and 1970.

This building of an affective spiritual community took place "against a backdrop of the campaign to end the slave trade, the transformation of the East Africa economy, widespread Christian evangelism, and the consolidation of colonial rule."[12] After receiving education from the Mbweni Girls' School, some women served as evangelists to teach short lessons to the younger girls, try on the role of pupil-preacher, and assist the missionaries in supervising a large number of children. After marriage, they set up their homes in accordance with the Christian values they were taught to serve as role models for neighbors and onlookers. Some of these women would join their husbands to become evangelists and the couples would travel to serve in the mission stations in the mainland of Tanzania (which was German East Asia at the time) and Malawi. They would help in outreach campaigns, visit women's homes, establish girls' schools, hold Bible studies and sewing circles, and practice daily Christian living to bring new congregants to the UMCA community.[13] They used their Mbweni experiences as a template to cultivate a spiritual community with their students, neighbors, and new inquirers.

World War I disrupted evangelistic work in German East Asia. British missionaries had to flee the mainland for safety and abandon their stations. The Germans arrested many of those who remained, along with many African clergy, teachers, and congregants. In the absence of missionaries, African clerics and local leaders assumed more autonomy and authority during the war. These men and women attended to the spiritual and physical needs of the congregation and worked hard to protect the vulnerable, sometimes at great personal sacrifice. The spiritual network they formed helped them persevere during this trying time.[14] After the war, the colonial rule of German East Asia passed on to the British, and UMCA's mission work expanded because of its association with power and prestige. Female evangelists worked hard along with other local leaders to meet the growing demands and the need for rebuilding the churches. In the 1920s and 1930s, UMCA congregations directed their energy and labor in the creation of a kind of African "civilization," based on Christian modernity, supra-ethnic unity, and racial identity.[15] After independence, their experience of forming a spiritual community helped Anglican women and men negotiate the multiple identities of living as Christians, members of their ethnic groups, and citizens of a new country.

Just as in Zanzibar, the history of slavery formed a backdrop of the work of Christian mission in Cuba, the largest island in the Caribbean. After the Spanish colonized Cuba in the fifteenth century and decimated the indigenous populations, the conquistadors brought the Spanish culture, language, architecture, and Roman Catholicism. Later, mostly during the late eighteenth and nineteenth centuries, the Spaniards imported African slaves as substitutes for the drastically reduced indigenous population to work on the sugar plantations. These Africans brought their culture, music, and religions. While the majority of Cubans are white, about one-quarter are people of mixed ethnic lineage and are identified as mulattoes or mestizos, and about 10 percent are Black. Christian mission encountered this rich mix of diverse cultures, religions, and customs.

The Episcopal Church began mission work in Cuba in the latter part of the nineteenth century. After the United States won the Spanish-American War in 1898, the island, together with Guam, Puerto Rico, and the Philippines, became American territories. In 1901, the General Convention of the Episcopal Church constituted the island as a missionary district. Since Cuba was predominantly Catholic, the Episcopal Church worked among the American colonists and English-speaking residents, while carrying out mission work to native Cubans as well as West Indians of African descent. Just as in other missions, the church saw the establishment of schools as paving the way for the future. Girls' schools were established to prepare future church workers and Christian wives.[16] As the church grew, emphasis was placed on training local Cuban clergy and leaders, who would assist in establishing a domestic church for the Cuban people.

Cuban theologian Clara Luz Ajo Lázaro wrote, "Cuban culture, formed by way of a mixture of different races and the ideals of freedom and sovereignty, has decisively shaped and influenced the faith of Cuban men and women."[17] It is from this mixture that Cuban women developed a spirituality within the process of transculturation, which blends different cultures together in a give-and-take process to form a new reality. For example, women in the Episcopal community of San Felipe Diácono in the province of Matanzas, most of them Black, would go to church as well as practice Santería, a religion of African origin, at home. They are brought up in both traditions and the two traditions mix and intermingle with one another. For these women, Jesus and Mary are considered Orichas (divinities) and have relationships with the Orichas in the Santería tradition. Instead of maintaining doctrinal purity, they have deconstructed the dominant images of Jesus and Mary and recuperated them as figures who walk and share with the humble inhabitants of the village.[18] Women make up the majority of the Episcopal Church of Cuba and they have played pivotal roles and sustained the work of the church during political changes. After the Cuban Revolution in 1959, many priests migrated from Cuba and numerous congregations were left without their shepherds. Women stepped up and took charge and maintained the work of the church.[19]

As we can see in the cases of China, Tanzania, and Cuba, Anglican and Episcopal women have been an integral part of the Christian missions and partners in building the church, as in other places. They served as cultural translators to contextualize Christianity into their own cultures and religions. In some places, women formed spiritual and affective communities across ethnic, linguistic, and generational differences for mutual support and empowerment. The female evangelists were bridge-builders between Western missionary women and the local populace and introduced female education, hygiene, and Christian motherhood. During wars and political upheavals, when male clergy could not function, they served as pillars for the church and maintained its work. They were the unsung heroines, and the stories of these subalterns need to be told to enrich our knowledge of the Anglican tradition and broaden our historical horizons.

The Mothers' Union and Women's Organizations

In order to facilitate women's work and promote women's fellowship, local and international women's organizations have been established. These organizations allow Anglican women to carve out a sphere of influence and leadership, and network with women in other countries. I focus on the Mothers' Union (MU) because it serves as an example of how the inclusion of local women subverted the domination of British and other white women and expanded the mission of the organization. The MU was established in 1876 by an English woman, Mary Summer, the wife of a rector in Hampshire, and later became the largest Anglican laywomen's organization. Influenced by Victorian ideals of domesticity and maternalism, the initial purposes of the MU were to uphold the sanctity of marriage, support responsible motherhood, and "organize in every place a band of mothers who will unite in prayer, and seek by their own example to lead their families in purity and holiness of life."[20] The MU soon spread throughout the United Kingdom and overseas, including Canada, Aotearoa New Zealand, Australia, China, India, and Japan. As Cordelia Moyse, who wrote the definitive work on the history of the MU, points out, the gender ideology of the MU supported British imperialism.[21] Like many British people at the time, MU leaders believed British imperial rule was God's providence and women had special patriotic roles in it. They believed that "women were key to the foundations of empire, because the Christian home was the foundation of British moral superiority and imperial power."[22] At first, overseas members were limited to expatriate white women, but as local women began to join, they brought in local women's concerns and issues in their communities. Therefore, the work of the MU has expanded from marriage and motherhood to include gender equality, HIV/AIDS, economic justice, and other issues affecting women and families. With decolonization, local women demanded to have greater roles in the organization and the indigenization of leadership.

Today, the MU has hundreds of individual MU charities in 84 countries.[23] Among MU's 4 million members, about 1.3 million members are in African dioceses, while the membership in the United Kingdom continues to decline. The examples of the MU in Kenya and South Africa demonstrate how African women have pushed for change and made the MU an indigenous African women's movement. The MU was first established in 1918 in Central Kenya by Mary Stewart Crawford, the wife of the British district commissioner, and membership was initially restricted to white Anglican women.[24] In 1955, the first multiracial branch of MU was founded in Kenya by Gladys Beecher and Lillian Kariuki, the wife of the first African Anglican bishop in Kenya, Obadiah Kariuki. In 1956, after Kariuki and other Kenyan women protested the domination of white women over Black women, the first African women enrolled in the MU. This change took place against the backdrop of the rising consciousness that colonial rule was coming to an end and wider social transformation in the country.

The MU in Kenya gathered women for prayers and fellowship and offer mutual support. Branches were soon established in all the dioceses in Kenya, and they offered training in leadership skills and community work. Following independence in 1963, the MU provided vocational training programs to help women's self-reliance, offered Bible classes, and worked to improve women's literacy. Later, the MU provided women with opportunities for savings and loans to alleviate poverty, since women did not have easy access to financial services. As more women joined the labor force, the MU started organizing nursery schools, mostly on church premises, to take care of the young while women worked. The MU provided a space for women to share and learn about issues in society, thus raising their consciousness. Beginning in the 1990s, the MU in all dioceses focused on the impact of the HIV/AIDS pandemic, especially caring for orphans. As the MU is open to women of different backgrounds, it serves the function of bridging social divisions between members, especially regarding class and ethnicity.

The first MU in South Africa was established by army wives stationed in Bloemfontein in Orange Free State soon after the British occupation in 1900. Just as in Kenya, initial members were made up of British missionaries and other white women.[25] The missionaries saw the potential of MU for nurturing the Christian discipleship of African women. As African women joined the MU and local leadership passed mostly onto Black clergy wives, the MU gatherings adopted features of the Methodist *manyano* (prayer unions) movement. These included fervent extempore prayer and preaching, fundraising activities, and the wearing of a church uniform. Women missionaries and church leadership from England sought to place restrictions on these practices. Branches could only be set up with the consent of the male priest, who was usually a missionary from England. Some male priests wanted to attend MU gatherings to exercise direct control. The MU office in London stipulated that local MU leaders had to be trained under official guidelines.[26] In the 1950s, the colonial hierarchy attempted to place tighter control over African

MU branches. Beverley Haddad, an Anglican priest and scholar, points out that African women resisted the control over them and wearing the uniform became a symbol of resistance. Their MU uniform consisted of a black skirt, hat, girdle, and a white (and/or purple) blouse. The uniform was more than a symbol that gave the women corporate identity, for it was also an expression of Christian commitment, spiritual allegiance, and marital respectability. Even as the church hierarchy sought to abolish the uniform, African women continued to wear them to church, MU meetings, and other festive occasions.[27]

Moyse notes that in no other part of the world did the MU experience such a seismic shift of identity from being a predominantly white organization to one made up largely of Black members, most of whom were Xhosa, Zulus, and Bantus.[28] The implementation of apartheid in 1948 put pressure on South African churches and church groups, including the MU. The MU publicly condemned apartheid from the late 1950s, because the Anglican church, under Archbishop Joose de Blank, was against it. The MU protested the policy, and members of the MU worked to mitigate its damaging effects on family and community life. Even though the MU wanted to maintain a multiracial organization and upheld the spiritual equality of humanity, its branches became racially segregated because of racial geography and apartheid.[29] In 1974, its membership was overwhelmingly African—32,332 African, 3,081 colored, and 783 white—but leadership remained overwhelmingly white. As gender roles changed and women gained greater access to education and occupations, the emphasis of MU on marriage and domesticity met new challenges. There was a push for greater acceptance of divorce and divorcees. White women who saw greater opportunities in the public sphere found MU's emphasis on domesticity no longer appealing and their membership declined.

As the MU became mostly African, some non-African Anglican women wanted to create an organization that would be more inclusive, as the MU would not admit divorcees and unmarried mothers to its membership. The Anglican Women's Fellowship (AWF) was formed in 1968 to "create a fellowship of prayer and service" among women in the Church of Province of Southern Africa (now the Anglican Church in Southern

Africa, ACSA), including members of the MU.[30] Membership was drawn from urban, middle-class, and educated women, especially around Cape Town. In the early days, the AWF used bilingual languages (English and Afrikaans) to appeal to both colored women and white women. AWF attracted colored women, who enjoyed social mobility in society, and they often played an intermediary role between white and African women. In the first two decades, AWF was not able to appeal to many African women, who preferred to stay in the MU with its fervent prayer meetings. Those African women who join the AWF are urban, well-educated, and professionally employed in education, nursing, and banking with English skills. The AWF has built bridges between women of diverse racial groups, reached out to the MU, worked with other women ecumenically, especially on HIV/AIDS issues, and networked with women in the Anglican Communion.[31]

Historians and scholars of religion have different assessments of women's organizations. On the one hand, the MU and AWF allow women to carve out a space for prayers, spiritual support, and fellowship. Women can exercise leadership, fundraise, and have the freedom to plan activities and gatherings. Motherhood has been central to women's personal and cultural identity and their social and economic roles in Africa. Organizations such as the MU enable women to combine their religious convictions with family roles in what Deborah Gaitskell has called "devout domesticity."[32] On the other hand, the emphasis on Christian family, marriage, and motherhood limits women's roles and aspirations. It creates a rift between older women, who make up the membership of women's organizations, and younger women with more progressive outlooks of life. The MU excluded divorcees, unwed mothers, and other women who did not meet the ideals of purity and chastity until the rules were changed later. The focus on heterosexual marriage discriminates against and alienates lesbian, bisexual, and transgender women. As the leadership of the MU, and to a certain extent AWF, are often clergy's wives, there are influences from the clergy and hierarchy. Esther Mombo observes that the segregation of women into their own sphere has liabilities. She writes, "The women's organisations themselves have served the interest of patriarchal ideology to contribute to their isolation and exclusion from leadership roles. It is the men who take up the paid and officially recognised leadership."[33] When the issue of women's ordination was discussed in Kenya in the 1980s, the MU did not agitate for it, because of the assumption that women and men have different gender roles.[34]

In addition to local, provincial, and national women's organizations, the International Anglican Women's Network (IAWN) was formed in 1996 to "strengthen the ministries of women in God's world and to ensure women are influential and equal participants throughout the entire Anglican Communion."[35] The IAWN has accompanied and worked with Anglicans to eradicate gender-based violence, including human trafficking. It advocates the access of women to education and health care, and the eradication of poverty, hunger, and environmental abuse. Its steering group included women from the Global South and Global North, representing different regions of the Communion. Among past IAWN steering group coordinators were Liz Barnes and Pumla Titus from ACSA, Priscilla Julie from the Church of Province of Indian Ocean, as well as women from Canada and Australia.[36] Another opportunity for Anglican women to network is the annual meeting of the United Nations Commission on the Status of Women (UNCSW) held in New York. When the Samoan Anglican leader Taimalelagi Fagamalama Tuatagaloa-Leota served as the Anglican Observer at the United Nations, she organized Anglican women leaders who attended the UNCSW annual meetings. Archdeacon Tai (as she prefers to be called) is an archdeacon in the Anglican Church of Aotearoa, New Zealand and Polynesia, and has leadership experience both in the United Nations and Anglican Communion. When she was appointed in 2001 as the Anglican Observer, she was the first woman and the first layperson to hold that office. Archdeacon Tai worked with representatives of IAWN and other women leaders to increase the number of Anglican women at UNCSW meetings. They also worked and successfully pushed the Anglican Consultative Council in 2005 to pass a resolution to support greater representation of women in decision-making bodies of the Anglican Communion and request the provinces to consider the establishment of women desks. Once the Anglican Consultative

Council has mandated it, women leaders in different provinces began to push for the inclusion of women's voices and perspectives in making decisions and shaping the life of the church.[37]

The Struggle for Women's Ordination

When Li Tim-Oi, a Chinese woman from the former British colony of Hong Kong, was ordained to the priesthood in 1944, she made history as the first woman priest in the Anglican Communion. Bishop Ronald Owen Hall decided to ordain her because of the extenuating circumstances brought about by World War II. Hong Kong was occupied by Japan and no male priests from Hong Kong or southern China could go to Macao to celebrate Eucharist for the Anglican community there. Ordained deaconess in 1941, Li was the only Anglican pastor serving in Macao. Li's ordination was to meet the church's special needs at the time, and most of her male colleagues supported her ordination. In her memoir, she wrote, "Let me say that it is only proper for us, not to discriminate between sexes, but with one heart and one mind bear witness to Christ."[38]

The Chinese Anglican-Episcopal Church, CHSKH, was ahead of the Church of England in terms of women in ministry. CHSKH in 1921 changed its canons to allow women to be elected to the House of Delegates, a move that was far ahead in comparison with the church in Britain and the United States.[39] When the Lambeth Conference of 1920 recommended the order of deaconesses as the "only order of the ministry" for women, the resolutions avoided the use of the word "ordination."[40] But the CHSKH decided in 1924 that the making of deaconesses was an "ordination" and they would enjoy the same rights as male deacons.[41] Historian Philip L. Wickeri notes that the CHSKH was less bound by tradition because "the Chinese churches were short of priests and lay leaders and so they were pushed to give women more authority and responsibility."[42] In addition, women, both Chinese and foreign, had served the church competently and demonstrated that they had leadership and pastoral skills.

The ordination of Li Tim-Oi highlighted the issues of autonomy and authority in the Anglican Communion. Before the ordination, Bishop

Hall wrote to his friend Archbishop William Temple about this decision but did not seek his permission or approval. The ordination was widely reported in the media and created a maelstrom. Bishop Hall was under tremendous pressure from the bishops in CHSKH and Archbishop Geoffrey Fisher, who had succeeded Temple, to suspend Li's license as a priest. In 1946, Li resigned her license, though not her priestly order, because of mounting pressure but she continued her ministry in South China.

Li's ordination prompted discussion on women's ministry in the wider Anglican Communion. In 1947, the Diocese of South China brought the case of women's ordination to the General Synod of the CHSKH and proposed that deaconesses be ordained under the same conditions as deacons for an experimental period of twenty years. The CHSKH referred the matter to the 1948 Lambeth Conference, which rejected it. But the matter galvanized a group of British women and men who formed an Ordination of Women Ad Hoc Committee and submitted a memorandum in support of women's ordination to the Lambeth Conference.[43] This is an example of how changes that happened in the far-flung colony had an impact on the Church of England and beyond. As Stuart Hall has said, colonialism is a double-inscribing process, affecting both the colonized and colonizers.

The question of women's ordination became a critical site for the negotiation of unity and difference in the Anglican Communion. After two decades, Lambeth 1968 opened the door for women's inclusion in the historic three-fold order of ministry and resolved that "those made deaconesses by laying-on of hands with appropriate prayers be declared to be within the diaconate."[44] The resolutions at Lambeth 1968 paved the way for the ordination of Hwang Hsien-Yuin, the vicar of my church when I was a teenager, and Joyce Bennett to be ordained priests in 1971. In the Episcopal Church, eleven women were "irregularly" ordained in Philadelphia in 1974, two years before the Episcopal Church's General Convention authorized women's ordination. American historian Fredrica Harris Thompsett and the British scholar Mary Tanner credited the Diocese of Hong Kong for its pioneering efforts in women's ordination.[45] In 1984, on the occasion of the fortieth anniversary of her ordination, Li Tim-Oi visited the United Kingdom and was warmly received by the then Archbishop of Canterbury Robert Runcie and met with church leaders and people supportive of women's ordination. It was not until 1992 that the Church of England authorized women's ordination and the first thirty-two women were ordained in 1994, half a century after Li's ordination.

After the Episcopal Church, the churches in Canada and Aotearoa New Zealand began to ordain women to the priesthood in 1976 and 1977, respectively. But the struggle for women's ordination in the Global South has been a long and hard journey. Today, some provinces still do not allow women to be priests, such as the provinces of South East Asia, Papua New Guinea, Melanesia, Pakistan, Central Africa, and Nigeria. According to a study, economic development is linked to the democratization of society and greater pressure for social equality and women's ordination.[46] Women in the Global South have many obstacles and hurdles to fulfilling their calling to the priesthood. Opportunities for theological training are limited for women because of a lack of resources and the limited number of theological training facilities. Historically women have been shut out because theological education was linked to ordination. Even when a woman was able to receive the same theological training as men, she would be subjected to stricter scrutiny than her male colleagues. In Africa and elsewhere, traditional culture and colonial Christianity reinforce the belief in women's domesticity and motherhood. Churches debate whether a woman priest should be married and if so, whether she would be able to manage both a parish and a family. Women's biological functions such as menstruating, pregnancy, and lactation have been seen as hindrances to their priestly functions. Some cannot imagine a pregnant or lactating woman at the altar celebrating the Eucharist. In addition to these cultural biases, gender hierarchy and institutional sexism in the churches act against women. Many male church leaders and lay members believed that women should play a supporting role—they can serve in lay ministry or diaconate, but not in priesthood. They cite biblical instructions such as women are not to have authority over men (1 Tim. 2) and Paul's teachings to support their claims. There are also women in the church who have internalized patriarchal teachings and cultural norms and do not support women's ordination and leadership in the church.[47]

The discussion of women's ordination in the Global South took place in broader religious, social, and political changes. The 1978 Lambeth Conference recognized some churches have ordained women and asked churches to recognize the autonomy of other member churches and remain in communion with one another.[48] Women's ordination was discussed in other denominations and ecumenically. The World Council of Churches initiated the Ecumenical Decade of the Churches in Solidarity with Women (1988–1998). More and more women in the Global South were able to receive education and work outside the home, with some occupying leadership positions in government and the professions. Gradually, some qualified women who have received theological training were ready to be ordained. In some cases, women's groups, such as the Circle of Concerned African Women Theologians (hereafter the Circle), strengthened the case for women's ordination by supporting women in theological education and challenging patriarchal theological paradigms.[49] Below I will give a few examples to illustrate the struggle for women's ordination in several provinces.

In the 1970s, some of the Anglican provinces in Africa began to discuss women's ordination, and these attempts were often led by forward-looking bishops. In 1975, Bishop Festo Kivengere of the Church of Uganda led the discussion of women's ordination at the synod. Some bishops argued that the Church of Uganda should wait for the Church of England to decide on the issue. But Bishop Kivengere opposed by saying, "If you wait for the Church of England, you wait till doomsday."[50] Even though the 1970s was a period of political instability in Uganda, Bishop Kivengere ordained several women as deacons in 1979. In 1983, he took the step of ordaining three deacons—Margaret Byekwaso, Grace Ndyabahika, and Debora Micungwe—as priests, even though some of the other dioceses have yet to decide on the issue. As more women have been ordained in the church, Ugandan female clergy spoke out against discrimination in terms of job opportunities and prospects, for they were often employed as school chaplains and in supporting positions and left out of mainstream leadership.[51]

In the then province of Kenya (now the Anglican Church of Kenya), Bishop John Henry Okullu led the discussion of women's ordination at the provincial synod in 1976. While the synod agreed that in principle women could be ordained at an appropriate time, it made several stipulations, such as the candidate should receive theological education and undergo a thorough examination by the bishop. Following the synod, Bishop Okullu sent Lucia Okuthe to a theological college and later made her a deaconess in the diocese serving under male clergy. In 1981, Bishop Okullu ordained Okuthe and later Emily Onyango as the first cohort of women in the diaconate. When the other bishops led by the archbishop of Kenya challenged his move, Bishop Okullu responded that the 1968 Lambeth Conference and the Anglican Consultative Council in 1971 had done away with a separate order of deaconesses. The ordination of Okuthe and Onyango created a paradigm shift in the discourse on women's gender roles and women's ordination. Different dioceses began to enact women's ordination in the mid-1980s, and the provincial synod finally authorized it in 1990.

The struggle for women's ordination in ACSA illustrates the entrenched patriarchal mindsets and practices in the church. Even though ACSA had fought against the country's apartheid laws of segregation, many have not made the connections between racial and gender discrimination. The issue of women's ordination has been discussed since 1960, but the ACSA did not approve it for decades for theological and other cultural reasons.[52] Archbishop Desmond Tutu and his successors openly criticized patriarchy in the church and acknowledged the discrimination against women. Yet it took a long time to dismantle a theology that undergirded sexual and racial discrimination and develop new practices. South African biblical scholar Miranda N. Pillay says there is "the need for the Anglican Church to be intentional about embodying a theology that transcends gender hierarchy in priesthood—and by extension, the laity."[53] In 1989, the Movement for the Ordination of Women was formed, and some dioceses moved ahead to allow women to be ordained. ACSA's provincial synod finally authorized women's ordination in 1992, with the concession that "bishops opposed to the ordination of women could not be compelled to ordain them."[54] Today, many more provinces in Africa have ordained women, but the situation is different from one province and diocese to another.

In the province of the West Indies, the issue of women's ordination is linked to the legacy of race and slavery, gender discrimination, and British imperialism. Color and class play a subtle but important role in the Caribbean society, and though the Anglican church is made up of Black and brown people, it is still associated in people's minds with the upper classes. Traditionally men of color and women of all backgrounds were barred from the ordained ministry. The clergy has come from lighter-colored, upper-class men with European-type features and hair. During the discussion on women's ordination, the laity showed more receptivity, while the male clergy had diverse viewpoints. Though the Diocese of Jamaica voted to approve women's ordination in 1974, it did not ordain the first four women until 1996 after waiting for the agreement of the rest of the province. The Diocese of Barbados also ordained women in the same year. More women have been ordained in Jamaica, Trinidad and Tobago, and elsewhere in the province.[55]

Anglican churches in Asia are small in comparison with other denominations. In the Nippon Sei Ko Kai (Anglican Church in Japan), women gathered to study women's theology and address women's discrimination in the church in the late 1980s. They organized women's groups to push for women's ordination and after much hard work, the church changed its canon to allow women to be priests in 1998.[56] The Episcopal Church in the Philippines used to be part of the Episcopal Church and became autonomous in 1990. The first woman in this church was ordained in 1991. The Church of North India and the Church of South India, which are united churches and part of the Anglican Communion, have women priests, but the Church of Pakistan only allows women to serve as deacons but not priests. The province in South East Asia is more conservative and does not allow women to be ordained as deacons, priests, or bishops.

In 1989 Bishop Barbara Harris, an African American woman, became the suffragan bishop of Massachusetts and the first female bishop in the Anglican Communion. Since then, the issue of women bishops has become a contentious issue, and there are many provinces that would ordain women as deacons and priests, but not bishops. The first woman bishop in the Global South was Bishop Nerva Aguilera of the Episcopal Church of Cuba when she became a suffragan bishop in 2007. She was followed by her colleague Bishop Griselda Delgato who began a diocesan bishop in charge of the Diocese of the Cuban Episcopal Church in 2010. Since then, a small number of provinces in the Global South have ordained women to the episcopate. In 2012 Bishop Ellinah Wamukoya became the first Anglican woman bishop in Africa when she was elected bishop of Swaziland in ACSA, and later Bishop Margaret Vertue was consecrated in False Bay Diocese. The Province of the Episcopal Church of South Sudan ordained Bishop Elizabeth Awut Ngor of the Diocese of Rumbek as bishop in 2016, and five years later, the Anglican Church of Kenya ordained Bishop Emily Onyango and Bishop Rose Okeno. Other provinces in the Global South that have begun to ordain women bishops include the Church of South India (Bishop Pushpa Lilith in 2013), Brazil (Bishop Marinez Rosa dos Santos Bassotto in 2018), and Mexico (Bishop Alba Sally Sue Hernandez in 2022).

Has the ordination of women in the Global South made any difference in the church and society? For the Anglican tradition that emphasizes sacramental and incarnational theology, having a nonwhite woman from the Global South at the altar challenges the symbolic order and subverts the racial and gender ideology of colonial Christianity. Rachele E. Vernon from Jamaica says that the admission of women to the threefold order of ministry does more than change the face of the Anglican priesthood. "Having a woman celebrate at the altar affects the entire concept of holiness and the notion of the sacred. The menstruating woman and the pregnant woman, far from being barred from the altar, become sacraments of Christ's indwelling."[57] The number of ordained women in the Global South is relatively small and they work under the shadow of patriarchal culture and a male-dominated church. Yet they continue to push for greater participation of women in ministry and for theological education that honors women as equals. Some of them are involved in community projects and social problems that plagued their communities, such as violence against women and HIV/AIDS issues.

Fighting Gender-Based Violence and the HIV/AIDS Pandemic

"In the face of the enormity of the crises of gender violence and HIV/AIDS and the particular vulnerability that women and girl-children face in the South African context, the silence of the church on these matters is deadly!" wrote Beverley Haddad in the early 2000s.[58] Anglican female theologians and leaders from the Global South have been outspoken in calling the church to accountability. South Africa has one of the highest rape statistics in the world, even higher than some countries at war, and the country has been an epicenter of the HIV/AIDS pandemic. The erroneous belief that having sex with a virgin will cure HIV/AIDS has been a factor in the rape of babies and children in South Africa.

In 2014, the world was horrified to hear about the kidnapping of 276 mostly Christian schoolgirls by Boko Haram in Nigeria and their being coerced into conversion to Islam and forced marriages. This was, however, not an isolated incident, as there has been an increase in the spate of violence against Nigerian women, affecting one in three women.[59] In South Asia, dowry deaths and honor killings by male family members, who accuse the victims of bringing dishonor upon the family, have been reported. During wars, genocide, and conflicts, women have been beaten, abused, raped, and subjected to unspeakable crimes. Women who were attacked and raped have been abandoned by their husbands and shunned by their communities, exposing them and their children to jeopardy. As a result of poverty and gender discrimination, women and young girls are sold or coerced into prostitution and become victims of sex trafficking. Mass migration and internal displacement dislocate women from their communities and make them vulnerable to attacks, kidnappings, and sexual abuse.

The widespread gender-based violence has caused alarm and prompted responses from the Anglican Communion and ecumenical bodies. At the Lambeth Conference of 2008, the bishops and their spouses held a session on "Equal in God's Sight: When Power Is Abused," and expressed their concern for violence against women. In 2009, at the instigation of IAWN, the Anglican Consultative Council stated its support for the elimination of all forms of violence against women and girls. The primates sent a letter to the churches in 2011 asking them to support initiatives by dioceses and parishes in response to violence against women and girls. The IAWN and the International Anglican Family Network were instrumental in raising consciousness about the issue.[60] In the WCC, the Ecumenical Decade of Churches in Solidarity of Women pointed to violence against women as an urgent issue. At the beginning of the millennium, the WCC initiated the Decade to Overcome Violence from 2001 to 2010 and acknowledged that "gender violence is a sin and encouraged churches, networks and movements to work against all manifestations of this scourge."[61]

From a postcolonial perspective, gender-based violence cannot be separated from the colonial trauma and the sociopolitical changes that have taken place during and after independence struggles in the Global South. Esther Mombo describes some of the causes of appalling violence in Africa at the end of the twentieth century that has inflicted harm and suffering on women and girls. She said when the colonial masters met at the Berlin Conference 1884–85 to redraw the map of Africa, they created political boundaries that cut through ethnic territories, and ethnic groups were separated into two or three countries.[62] During the anti-colonial struggles and the national building period after independence, the concerns of ethnicity, gender, and indigenous peoples' rights have not been adequately dealt with and have been put on the back burner. In the Rwanda genocide, for example, the Hutu militia murdered members of the Tutsi minority group and an estimated 250,000 to 500,000 women were raped. Ethnic rivalries and political infighting waste precious resources and stunt economic growth. Political instability of the Global South is exacerbated by the burden of debts and the imposition of structural adjustment policies by the international financial agencies as I have outlined in chapter 3. These neocolonial policies coupled with the climate crisis have eroded the basic subsistent economy that many women and children rely upon for their survival.

Gender-based violence is the result of women's biological vulnerability and social and cultural factors. As long as a society perpetuates the cultural norms that men have power over women and women are property and objects to satisfy men's needs and desires, women will never be free and feel safe. It is imperative for Anglican churches, through their teaching and practices, to model a renewed community that recognizes women's dignity and equality as children of God. First, we need to evaluate the ways that imperialism and patriarchy have intersected to reinforce male domination and perpetuate the myth that women are impure and the source of evil and death. Second, we have to develop healthy teachings about human sexuality, marriage, and family and dissimilate the knowledge beyond academia to reach the grassroots. The debates on human sexuality that have ripped the Anglican Communion apart point to the need for sexual ethics that recognize the complexities regarding race, gender, economics, and postcolonial realities. Third, we need to examine the church's teaching on sacrifice and suffering. Christian women have been taught to tolerate abuse and suffering and model after Christ who has suffered for us. This kind of teaching has the danger of condoning abuse and legitimizing violence. Careful distinctions must be made between voluntary suffering on behalf of others that is life-giving, and imposed suffering as a result of unequal power and abuse.[63] The church especially cannot use religious excuses and jargon to justify clergy sexual abuse. The ACSA has initiated the Safe Church project.

Gender-based violence is much related to the spread of the HIV/AIDS virus. Since the heaviest burden of the HIV/AIDS pandemic is in sub-Saharan Africa, Anglican female scholars from Africa have addressed the issue and taken action. HIV/AIDS is a stigmatized subject because of its association with sex, shame, sin, purity, and morality. Haddad points out that traditionally women have little say over their bodies and if their husbands practice unsafe sex, they are particularly vulnerable to the virus. They risk further abuse when they reveal that they have been affected. Thus, the HIV/AIDS pandemic cannot be adequately addressed without tackling the issue of men's abuse of power over women, including abuses within the church structures. Haddad calls for a church theology that is prophetic and engendered. "An engendered theology requires a critical social analysis of the patriarchal nature of theology whether traditional, contextual, or liberationist. It needs to be cautious and critical in its use of the Bible as both a source of oppression and liberation for women."[64] The Circle has provided spaces for the development of such an engendered theology and for in-depth learning about the challenges that HIV/AIDS pose to women. Through publications and outreach, members of the Circle have helped churches and faith communities to stand in solidarity with people affected by the virus.[65]

Denise Ackermann, a practical theologian in the Circle and a licensed preacher in ACSA, draws resources from the Bible and church practices to discuss HIV/AIDS. Writing at a time when antiretroviral therapy was not widely available and many were dying from AIDS-related diseases, Ackermann lifted up the biblical tradition of lament. She wrote, "Lament is a form of mourning. . . . Lament is both an individual and a communal act which signals human relationships have gone awry."[66] She mourned for Tamar (2 Samuel 13:1–22) and related Tamar's experience of rape, incest, violence, and betrayal to the abuses of women amid the HIV/AIDS crisis. She said HIV/AIDS is a "gendered pandemic" because it is related to gender relations and the condition of poverty, as most people with HIV are living in developing countries.[67] In order to bring hope to people living with HIV/AIDS, Christian communities must recognize that the church is the Body of Christ, and this body has AIDS. This necessitates the telling of new narratives about Christ's body, suffering, and resurrection, especially when the church celebrates the Eucharist. Ackermann saw a link between "the violated body of Tamar, the abused bodies of women and children, the bodies of people living with HIV and AIDS and the crucified and resurrected body of Jesus Christ whom we remember and celebrate in the bread and wine at the Eucharist."[68] In Jesus's sacrifice, we see the wounds and woundedness of people infected and dying, and in his resurrection, we see hope and new possibility of relationships and love in our broken world. Therefore, Ackermann and other South African female theologians think that the HIV/AIDS pandemic is a kairos moment for the church to find new presence and love of God among us.[69]

A hopeful sign is that African scholars, such as Ezra Chitando, Nyambura J. Njoroge, and others, have challenged elements of toxic masculinity, such as male superiority, the refusal to accept women's leadership, the lack of respect for women's rights, infidelity, and the need to assert male control and prowess. Through reflecting on Jesus's life and other biblical stories, they have articulated a model of redeemed or transformative masculinity to address the prevalence of gender-based violence and HIV/AIDS. Chitando insists that unless men and boys are transformed, violence against women will not stop. He encourages the nurture of "gender equitable men." These men and boys will treat women as equals, care for women's feelings and respect them, remain faithful in relationships, take responsibilities as husbands and fathers, accept women's leadership, and confront sexual and gender-based violence whenever they encounter it.[70] The life of Jesus offers a model of this masculinity. Jesus befriended and taught women, breaking cultural taboos (e.g., speaking to Gentile women and healing the hemorrhaging woman) and advocating justice for women (e.g., forgiving the woman caught in adultery). He was a prophet who challenged all forms of injustice and restored women to dignity and wholeness.[71]

In this chapter, I describe the ministry and leadership roles of Anglican women in the Global South because this herstory has often remained hidden in previous accounts of the Anglican tradition. They were integral partners since the beginning of Anglican missions and the establishment of churches, and over time, they have become the majority of the membership of most churches. Although they work within a male-dominated and hierarchical church structure, they have carved out a women's sphere to organize and exercise their leadership. They have fought for representation in decision-making bodies in the dioceses, provinces, and the Anglican Communion. The ordination of Li Tim-Oi in the former British colony of Hong Kong transformed priesthood in the Communion and opened the doors for women to be ordained and some to become bishops. During the turbulent periods of fighting for independence, national building, and wars and upheavals, they continue to care for their families and communities and contribute to the church. As HIV/AIDS ravages their communities, Anglican female scholars and leaders are at the forefront of calling Anglican churches to provide leadership and pastoral care in addressing the crisis. While the Communion has been torn by debates on women's ordination and episcopacy and sexuality, they pledge to remain in relationships with other sisters in the Anglican Communion to carry out God's reconciling mission in the world.

Notes

1. Dana L. Robert, "World Christianity as a Women's Movement," *International Bulletin of Missionary Research* 30, no. 4 (2006): 180.
2. Uma Narayan, *Dislocating Cultures: Identities, Traditions, and Third-World Feminism* (New York: Routledge, 1997), 1–37.
3. Chandra Talpade Mohanty, "Under Western Eyes: Feminist Scholarship and Colonial Discourses," in *Third World Women and the Politics of Feminism*, ed. Chandra Talpade Mohanty, Ann Russo, and Lourdes Torres (Bloomington: Indiana University Press, 1991), 51–80.
4. For example, Brian Heeney, *The Women's Movement in the Church of England, 1850–1930* (New York: Oxford University Press, 1988); Oonagh Walsh, *Anglican Women in Dublin: Philanthropy, Politics, and Education in Early 20th Century* (Dublin: University College Dublin Press, 2005); Pamela W. Darling, *New Wine: The Story of Women Transforming Leadership and Power in the Episcopal Church* (Cambridge, MA: Cowley, 1994); and Fredrica Harris Thompsett and Sheryl Kujawa-Holbrook, eds., *Deeper Joy: Lay Women in the 20th Century Episcopal Church* (New York: Church Publishing, 2005).
5. Denise Ackermann, Jonathan A. Draper, and Emma Mashinini, eds., *Women Hold Up Half of the Sky: Women in the Church of Southern Africa* (Pietermaritzburg: Cluster Publications, 1991); Andreana C. Prichard, *Sisters in Spirit: Christianity, Affect, and Community Building in East Africa, 1860–1970* (East Lansing: Michigan State University Press, 2017); and Wai Ching Angela Wong and Patricia P. K. Chiu, eds., *Christian Women in Chinese Society: The Anglican Story* (Hong Kong: Hong Kong University Press, 2018).
6. Zhou Yun, "The Making of Bible Women in the Fujian Zenana Mission from the 1880s to the 1950s," in Wong and Chiu, *Christian Women in Chinese Society*, 72–73.
7. Yun, "Making of Bible Women," 78.
8. Judith Liu, "'A Nation Cannot Rise about Its Women': The Social Gospel at St. Hilda's School for Girls, Wuchang, China, 1929–37," in Wong and Chiu, *Christian Women in Chinese Society*, 41–42.
9. Duan Qi, " Study of the Chung Hua Sheng Kung Hui Women's Missionary Service League in the 1930s and 1940s: Drawn from Reports of the Fourth to Seventh WMSL Conferences," trans. Janice Wickeri, in Wong and Chiu, *Christian Women in Chinese Society*, 226.
10. Duan, "Study of the Chung Hua Sheng Kung Hui Women's Missionary Service League," 232–38.
11. Prichard, *Sisters in Spirit*, 4. I would like to thank Emily Badgett for drawing my attention to the work of Universities' Mission to Central Africa in Tanzania.
12. Prichard, *Sisters in Spirit*, 10.
13. Prichard, *Sisters in Spirit*, 119.
14. Prichard, *Sisters in Spirit*, 126–28.

15. Prichard, *Sisters in Spirit*, 149.
16. "Handbooks on the Missions of the Episcopal Church: The West Indies (1926)," Anglican History, http://anglicanhistory.org/wi/missions1926.
17. Clara Luz Ajo Lázaro, "Diversity in the Anglican Tradition: Women and the Afro-Caribbean Church," in *Anglican Women on Church and Mission*, ed. Kwok Pui-lan, Judith A. Berling, and Jenny Plane Te Paa (New York: Morehouse Publishing, 2012), 170.
18. Ajo Lázaro, "Diversity in the Anglican Tradition," 176.
19. Ajo Lázaro, "Diversity in the Anglican Tradition," 171.
20. Cordelia Moyse, *A History of the Mothers' Union: Women, Anglicanism and Globalization, 1876–2008* (Woodbridge: Boydell Press, 2009), appendix 1, 254.
21. Moyse, *History of the Mothers' Union*, 80–86.
22. Cordelia Moyse, "Mother's Union: From Victorian Village to Global Village," in Kwok et al., *Anglican Women on Church and Mission*, 119.
23. "Our Story," Mothers' Union, https://www.mothersunion.org/our-story.
24. The history of the MU from Kenya is from Emily Onyango, "Women Leaders Rising Up: A Case Study of the Anglican Church of Kenya 1844–1985," Mission Theology in the Anglican Communion, November 18, 2016, http://www.missiontheologyanglican.org/article/women-leaders-rising-up-a-case-study-of-the-anglican-church-of-kenya-1844---1945.
25. Moyse, *History of the Mothers' Union*, 90–91.
26. Beverley Haddad, "Church Uniform as an Indigenous Form of Anglicanism: A South African Case Study," *Journal of Anglican Studies* 14, no. 2 (2016): 160.
27. Haddad, "Church Uniform," 161–71.
28. Moyse, *History of the Mothers' Union*, 150.
29. Moyse, *History of the Mothers' Union*, 211–16.
30. Deborah Gaitskell, "Crossing Boundaries and Building Bridges: The Anglican Women's Fellowship in Post-Apartheid South Africa," *Journal of Religion in Africa* 34, no. 3 (2004): 272.
31. Gaitskell, "Crossing Boundaries and Building Bridges," 271–97.
32. Deborah Gaitskell, "Devout Domesticity? A Century of African Women's Christianity in South Africa," in *Women and Gender in Southern Africa to 1945*, ed. Cherryl Walker (Cape Town: D. Philip, 1990), 251–72.
33. Esther Mombo, "Mission and Evangelism," in *Christianity in Sub-Saharan Africa*, ed. Kenneth R. Ross, J. Kwabena Asamoah-Gyadu, and Todd M. Johnson (Edinburgh: University of Edinburgh Press, 2017), 384.
34. Stephen Asol Kapinde and Eleanor Tiplady Higgs, "Global Anglican Discourse and Women's Ordination in Kenya: The Controversy in Kirinyaga, 1979–1992, and Its Legacy," *Journal of Anglican Studies* 20, no. 1 (2012): 26–27.
35. "International Anglican Women's Network," Anglican Communion, https://iawn.anglicancommunion.org.
36. "The Global Voice of Anglican Women," Anglican Communion, https://iawn.anglicancommunion.org/about-us.aspx.
37. Mary Sudman Donavan, "Anglican Women: Empowering Each Other to Further God's Kingdom," *Journal of Anglican Studies* 5, no. 1 (2007): 39–68; Janet Trisk, "Women in the Anglican Communion," in *The Wiley-Blackwell Companion to the Anglican Communion*, ed. Ian S. Markham et al. (Malden, MA: Wiley-Blackwell, 2013), 625.

38. Li Tim-Oi, *Raindrops of My Life: The Memoir of Florence Li Tim-Oi* (Toronto: Anglican Book Center, 1996), 80.
39. The history of the CHSKH is from Philip L. Wickeri, "The Ordination and Ministry of Li Tim Oi: A Historical Perspective on a Singular Event," in Wong and Chiu, *Christian Women in Chinese Society*, 109. The Episcopal Church allowed women to serve as deputies only in 1970; see John L. Kater, "Stirrings: Emerging Women's Ministries in the Church of England and the Episcopal Church and Their Impact on the Chung Hua Sheng Kung Hui (Anglican Church in China)," *Anglican and Episcopal History* 88, no. 4 (2019): 381–82.
40. Lambeth Conference 1920, Resolutions 48–50, Anglican Communion, https://www.anglicancommunion.org/media/127731/1920.pdf.
41. Kater, "Stirrings," 382.
42. Wickeri, "Ordination and Ministry of Li Tim Oi," 109.
43. Kwok Pui-lan, "The Study of Chinese Women and the Anglican Church in Cross-Cultural Perspective," in Wong and Chiu, *Christian Women in Chinese Society*, 29.
44. Lambeth Conference 1968, Resolution 32, Anglican Communion, https://www.anglicancommunion.org/media/127743/1968.pdf.
45. Fredrica Harris Thompsett, ed., *Looking Forward. Looking Backward: Forty Years of Women's Ordination* (New York: Morehouse Publishing, 2014), xii; Mary Tanner, "The Episcopal Ministry Act of Synod in Context," in *Seeking the Truth of Change in the Church: Reception, Communion and the Ordination of Women*, ed. Paul Avis (London: T & T Clark, 2004), 59–60.
46. Benjamin Knoll, "Women's Ordination in the Anglican Communion: The Importance of Religious, Economic, and Political Contexts," Religion in the Public, January 25, 2021, https://religioninpublic.blog/2021/01/25/womens-ordination-in-the-anglican-communion-the-importance-of-religious-economic-and-political-contexts.
47. Kapinde and Higgs, "Global Anglican Discourse and Women's Ordination in Kenya," 25–30; Rachele E. Vernon, "Daughters of Jerusalem, Mothers of Salem: Caribbean Women in the Ministry of the Church," in *Women and Ordination in the Christian Churches: International Perspectives*, ed. Ian Jones, Janet Wootton, and Kirsty Thorpe (London: T & T Clark, 2008), 217–22.
48. Lambeth Conference 1978, Resolution 21, Anglican Communion, https://www.anglicancommunion.org/media/127746/1978.pdf.
49. Kapinde and Higgs, "Global Anglican Discourse and Women's Ordination in Kenya," 37.
50. Esther Mombo, "The Ordination of Women in Africa: An Historical Perspective," in Ian Jones et al., *Women and Ordination in the Christian Churches*, 130.
51. "Uganda: Women Priests Speak of Discrimination," Anglican Communion News Service, September 2, 1996, https://www.anglicannews.org/news/1996/09/uganda-women-priests-speak-of-discrimination.aspx.
52. Phoebe Swart-Russell and Jonathan Draper, "A Brief History of the Movement for the Ordination of Women in the Church of the Province of Southern Africa (CPSA)," in Ackermann, Draper, and Mashinini, *Women Hold Up Half of the Sky*, 220–37.
53. Miranda N. Pillay, "Women, Priests and the Anglican Church in Southern Africa: Reformation of Holy Hierarchies," *Consensus* 38, no. 1 (2017): 2.

54. Pillay, "Women, Priests and the Anglican Church in Southern Africa," 11.
55. Vernon, "Daughters of Jerusalem, Mothers of Salem," 215–24; Joyanne De Four-Babb and Shelley-Ann Tenia, "From the Pantry to the Pulpit: Anglican Clergywomen in the Diocese of Trinidad and Tobago," *Journal of Pan African Studies* 5, no. 2 (2012): 42–66.
56. Miki Mei, "A Church with Newly-Opened Doors: The Ordination of Women Priests in the Anglican-Episcopal Church of Japan," *Japanese Journal of Religious Studies* 44, no. 1 (2017): 37–51.
57. Vernon, "Daughters of Jerusalem, Mothers of Salem," 223.
58. Beverley Haddad, "Gender Violence and HIV/AIDS: A Deadly Silence in the Church," *Journal of Theology for Southern Africa* 114 (2002): 97.
59. La Croix International Staff, "Anglican Archbishop in Nigeria Expresses Concern over Violence against Women," La Croix International, March 20, 2020, https://international.la-croix.com/news/world/anglican-archbishop-in-nigeria-expresses-concern-over-violence-against-women/12038.
60. Samuel van Culen and Andrew Bennett Terry, "Anglican Consultative Councils," in Ian S. Markham et al., *The Wiley-Blackwell Companion to the Anglican Communion*, 115–16.
61. World Council of Churches, *Overcoming Violence: The Ecumenical Decade 2001–2010* (Geneva: World Council of Churches, 2011), 32, http://www.overcomingviolence.org/fileadmin/dov/files/OvercomingViolence.pdf.
62. Esther Mombo, "Reflection on Peace in the Decade to Overcome Violence," *Ecumenical Review* 63, no. 1 (2011): 72.
63. See the discussion in Aruna Gnanadason, *No Longer a Secret: The Church and Violence against Women* (Geneva: World Council of Churches, 1994), 48–54.
64. Haddad, "Gender Violence and HIV/AIDS," 103–4.
65. For example, Isabel Apawo Phiri, Beverley Haddad, and Madipoane Masenya, eds., *African Women, HIV/AIDS and Faith Communities* (Pietermaritzburg: Cluster Publications, 2003); Musa W. Dube and Musimbi Kanyoro, eds., *Grant Me Justice: HIV/AIDS and Gender Readings of the Bible* (Maryknoll, NY: Orbis Books, 2005).
66. Denise M. Ackermann, "Lamenting Tragedy from the Other Side," in *Sameness and Difference: Problems and Potentials in South African Civil Society*, ed. James R. Cochrane and Bastienne Klein (Washington DC: Council for Research in Values and Philosophy, 2000), 220.
67. Denise M. Ackermann, "Tamar's Cry: Re-Reading an Ancient Text in the Midst of an HIV and AIDS Pandemic," in Dube and Kanyoro, *Grant Me Justice*, 35.
68. Ackermann, "Tamar's Cry," 51.
69. Ackermann, "Tamar's Cry," 54.
70. Ezra Chitanto "Introduction," in *Contextual Bible Study Manual on Transformative Masculinity*, ed. Ezra Chitano and Nyambura J. Njoroge (Harare, Zimbabwe: Ecumenical HIV and AIDS Initiative in Africa, 2013), 8. http://ujamaa.ukzn.ac.za/Libraries/manuals/EHAIA_Transformative_Masculinity__English.sflb.ashx.
71. See the discussion in the study guide, *God's Justice: Just Relationships between Women and Men, Girls and Boys Study Materials for Use by Theological Colleges, Seminaries and Training Schemes in the Anglican Communion* (London: Anglican Communion Office, 2019), 48–50, https://www.anglicancommunion.org/media/348551/TEAC-just-relationships-women-men.pdf.

CHAPTER

7

Mission and Interreligious Solidarity

Since the founding of the Society for the Propagation of the Gospel (SPG) in 1701, Anglican mission had been closely related to the expansion of the British Empire and colonialism. The spread of English civilization, Christianity, and commerce went hand in hand. Since the independence struggles of the 1950s and 1960s, the collusion of mission with colonialism has been widely criticized. While this criticism is important, the gaze has been on the work of missionaries and missionary organizations. Beginning in the 1980s, there was a shift in the study of mission, as scholars such as Lamin Sanneh and Andrew F. Walls urged us to pay more attention to Christianity's interaction with local cultures and practices, the translation of the gospel into vernacular languages, and the roles played by local agents and organizations.[1] The field of "World Christianity" emerged, which challenges Eurocentric approaches and commits to the study of Christianity as a worldwide polycentric phenomenon and not an extension of Western church history and its missionary projects.[2]

These changes in the academy influence how we look at the history of Anglican mission. Jesse Zink, a scholar of mission and the world church, reflects on the Anglican understanding of mission from the nineteenth century to the present. The first period saw mission as practiced "over there," when missionaries were sent to evangelize the world. In the Church of England, the SPG, the CMS, and the UMCA sent missionaries to British colonies and other regions. The Episcopal Church formed the Domestic and Foreign Missionary Society in 1821 and worked in Central and

South America, Asia, and the Middle East. While Zink criticizes Anglican mission for its entanglement with "capitalism, colonial power, racism, and Western hegemony,"[3] he also points out that "Anglicanism's global reach is in large measure due to the missionary activity of local and indigenous non-European actors around the world. To focus too much on the link between Anglican mission and imperial interests can obscure other developments that often took place without the knowledge or full understanding of missionaries."[4] He cites as examples missionary efforts initiated by local agents and the phenomena of mass conversion movements in Nigeria, Uganda, and Kenya that often surprised European missionaries.

In the post–World War II period, amid rapid social changes and independence movements, a shift of understanding of mission occurred. In the ecumenical circles, Dutch missiologist J. C. Hoekendijk and other leaders began to argue that the church is not the center of mission because mission is the work of God for the sake of the world. They proposed the phrase *missio Dei* (the mission of God), and the church is privileged to participate in it. Zink points out that the focus of *missio Dei* is not ecclesiology, but eschatology—the bringing of God's shalom and Kingdom in the world. He surmises, "Debates about *missio Dei*, the place of the church in mission, and the relationship between evangelism and social action were the context in which Anglicans sought to chart a post-war missionary path."[5] The Anglican Congress held in Toronto in 1963 adopted the new manifesto, "Mutual Responsibility and Interdependence in the Body of Christ," widely referred to as MRI. Mission is no longer seen as giving but as receiving and sharing with one another. As Canon John Kafwanka, former director of mission for the Anglican Communion Office, writes, "The Anglican Communion could no longer see itself as a European Christianity extended into other parts of the world, but was instead a Communion of autonomous churches, firmly anchored in various traditions and cultures of the world."[6] The postcolonial reality requires the Anglican Communion to treat member churches as equal partners and not replicate colonial relations. In 1971, the ACC adopted the project Partnership in Mission (PIM), which became a guiding model for mutual missions across cultures and socioeconomic divides.[7] Zink has observed that while the intention behind MRI and PIM was good, in practice, the funding of richer provinces for projects in poorer provinces did not challenge the unequal power relations that were part of the colonial legacy in the Anglican Communion.[8] Because of these problems, the Anglican Communion adopted the term "companion" to describe church-to-church relationships, for companionship implies trust, listening, generosity, and solidarity with one another.[9]

After the end of the Cold War, Anglican understanding of mission changed from sending people "over there" to mission "everywhere." As church membership steadily declined in the Church of England and the Episcopal Church, the idea that all people are involved in a "missional" church had a popular reception. Lambeth 1988 launched the Decade for Evangelism, a call proposed by bishops from Africa, the continent that had the largest number of active Anglicans, in response to the deep decline in traditional "Christian" countries.[10] The drive for evangelism extended throughout the worldwide church, including not only Anglican churches, but also the Roman Catholic Church and other mainline denominations. In response to the Decade, churches and para-Christian organizations were encouraged to devise action plans and initiated new programs. The decade's use of the word "evangelism" prompted debates about the relationship between evangelism and mission. Some wanted to focus on the proclamation of the Good News, while others emphasize actions to transform the world and bring in God's shalom.[11] The Church of England published the *Mission-Shaped Church* report in 2004 to encourage churches to incarnate the gospel in the secular and consumerist society.[12] New initiatives such as the emergent church movement in the United States and the Fresh Expressions of the Church movement in Britain were launched.

From a postcolonial perspective, it is important to point out that mission "over there" had colonial undertones, as it was seen as a one-way traffic, going from the Global North to the Global South. Mission "everywhere" broadens the geopolitical imagination and includes missions from South to South and from South to North. Church workers have been sent from the Global South to Britain and North America, especially to work among immigrant communities. Scholars from the Global South and in the diaspora have expanded our understanding of mission and envisioned new patterns of relationships. I will discuss postcolonial visions of mission, interreligious dialogue and solidarity, and the church's responsibilities in the age of migration, when many migrants, refugees, and asylum seekers have had to leave their homelands for economic, political, and social causes.

Postcolonial Visions of Mission

The first Lambeth Conference in 1867 was held in response to controversies arising out of the missional context of the church in Natal in South Africa. One of the resolutions of the Conference said:

> That, in order to the binding of the Churches of our colonial empire and the missionary Churches beyond them in the closest union with the Mother-Church, it is necessary that they receive and maintain without alteration the standards of faith and doctrine as now in use in that Church. That, nevertheless, each province should have the right to make such adaptations and additions to the services of the Church as its peculiar circumstances may require. Provided, that no change or addition be made inconsistent with the spirit and principles of the Book of Common Prayer, and that all such changes be liable to revision by any synod of the Anglican Communion in which the said province shall be represented.[13]

This resolution reflected the understanding of mission as sending missionaries "over there" to form missionary churches. The "Mother-Church" was the center, and the missionary churches were on the periphery, and they had to follow the doctrines emanated from the center. But even so, the resolution contained an important provision that each province could make adaptations and additions to the services of the church as its context required. Cathy Ross notes that this emphasis can also be found in subsequent Lambeth conferences. "There is clear encouragement that 'native Churches' should understand that 'the church is their own and not a foreign Church,' and that 'the Church should be adapted to local circumstances.'"[14] At the 1908 Lambeth Conference, the necessity of self-government and self-support of the churches was discussed. This meant that the native pastorates were expected to assume greater responsibilities and autonomy.

In our postcolonial Anglican Communion, the center-periphery model has been seriously challenged by the Global South, because of shifting demographics. Ross notes, "We know that a majority of Christians are no longer to be found in the West or associated with centres of power. Christianity is increasingly becoming a religion practised as a minority faith without 'Christian' government support."[15] Christianity enjoys phenomenal growth in countries, especially in Africa, that do not enjoy the privilege of "Christendom" as Western Christians used to enjoy in the past. As we have seen in the previous chapters, the authority of the archbishop of Canterbury and other Instruments of Unity in the Anglican Communion have been challenged in the realignment of power over the issues of Anglican identity, human sexuality, and biblical authority and interpretation.

To respond to the postcolonial reality and the divergent voices and perspectives, theologian Christopher Duraisingh calls for "a decolonization of imagination in Christian faith and worship and a reconstruction of the interchurch relationships across the world."[16] The postcolonial imagination challenges the center-periphery model and supports the alternative of decentering the center. This means that we have to "image and articulate reality not in a monologic and eurocentric mode, but rather from a dialogical and a polyphonic perspective."[17] The Anglican Communion will do best, he says, to avoid searching for a stable center or a single metanarrative, which Derrida and other postmodernist thinkers have debunked. The attempts to define "traditional" or "orthodox" Anglican identity often lead to the erection of boundaries and the exclusion and censure of others who are deemed different, deviant, or heretical. Duraisingh exhorts us not to see the world in oppositional binaries, such as white/black, civilized/uncivilized, or the West/the rest, because these binaries often result in hierarchical organizations of reality and relationships. We need to see truth and reality in its particular local context and its multilayered relationships with others because we exist within "a densely woven web of relationality."[18]

Using the postcolonial imagination, Durasingh revisions the church and its mission in terms of the *multivoiced* story of the gospel and the *dialogical* witness. He contrasts the biblical images of Babel (Gen. 11:1–9) and Pentecost (Acts 2:1–11) in conceptualizing the truth of the faith of the church as "multivoiced, processive, and emergent."[19] The image of Babel connotes the search for a singular and monological truth and language to the exclusion of others on the margins. God disrupts such a plan by confusing the language of the people so they cannot understand one another. In contrast, the Pentecost story overturns monologism and challenges the imposition of one rule and one culture by the Roman Empire. It speaks of the richness and the emancipative power of diversity. Only when the gospel is incarnated and unfolded in different cultures and contexts, can one see the fullness and beauty of the gospel. This process continues from the story of the Acts of the Apostles to our present time.

A dialogical approach to Christian witness and mission challenges the "over there" approach, based on a territorial expansion model as the physical extension and numerical increase of the church. The idea of planting the church is still the goal of many mission organizations and churches that have the resources to do so. This understanding of mission assumes that we have the truth to tell, and others need to hear for their own good and salvation. This monologic model and the preoccupation for finding "truth" comes from a Eurocentric epistemology and was universalized and reinforced through the process of colonialism. A dialogical model of mission, as Durasingh says, entails "a genuine openness of listening to the other and the different in such a way that both partners in dialogue are challenged and deepened."[20] Citing the Taiwanese theologian C. S. Song, Duraisingh says mission is not a truth affair, but a love affair—it is to participate in the life of others and to be vulnerable and serve humanity in need as Christ has modeled for us.[21] The postcolonial context and the dialogical model challenge us "to discover an incarnate form of witness to God's love, incarnate *within* human history. A witness from 'within' is the only proper mode of evangelism worthy of a God who does not control history from 'without,' but rather enters into it, suffers within, and transforms it by participating in it fully and really."[22]

Duraisingh believes that the church exists for the sake of the world and that Christian mission is not to propagate a prepackaged and context-free, universalized "gospel," but to discern and witness God's action in history.

For some, such an understanding conflicts with the Great Commission, which charges the disciples to "make disciples of all nations" (Matt. 28:18–20). Within the Anglican churches, the debate on the relationship between evangelism and mission has been ongoing. Some emphasize mission as evangelization, while others see mission as humanization and the pursuit of justice. Sathianathan Clarke, a professor of World Christianity and a presbyter of the Church of South India, helps elucidate the contours of postcolonial mission. He traces the development of the evangelical Lausanne movement, emerging from the Lausanne Conference of World Evangelization in 1974 and the shift of mission understanding in the WCC. He argues that both sides understand mission as the center of Christian identity, yet they have diverse understandings of mission.

On the one hand, the Lausanne movement emphasizes bringing the whole gospel to the whole world, and the new humanity can only be redeemed by Christ's suffering and death. Yet learning from past mistakes in Christian mission, the movement emphasizes "evangelizing of the world for Christ without colonization."[23] It underscores the interchanges between human communities that are noncoercive and dialogical and based on the love of God, the love of the gospel, and the love of the people of God. On the other hand, the WCC emphasizes the "vivification of the world in God without Christianization."[24] Clarke writes, "Here the growth of Christianity is not the main objective of mission passion and engagement. Rather this model of postcolonial mission aims at the unfolding of God's mission, proclaimed and lived out by Jesus Christ, and enlivened by the Holy Spirit to usher life."[25] Working for the fullness of life for human beings and the integrity of creation may not involve Christianizing. Clarke notes that though the understandings of mission are different, both sides highlight the role of the marginalized in God's mission, treating them not as objects of mission, but partners and agents in mission. To mediate the differences between the two sides, Clarke proposes a Trinitarian framework that is expansive and capacious. He writes, "The Trinity opens up possibilities for moving away from the constriction imposed by our 'Jesus only' mission-thinking pattern. One need not sacrifice Jesus Christ. One is merely invited to extract mileage from the expansive relational possibilities inherent in the surplus potential of the Divine Trinity."[26] In this way, we can enthusiastically proclaim the gospel of Jesus Christ and at the same time respect cultural and religious differences made possible by the roominess of the Trinity.

Clarke's Trinitarian theology of mission finds support in the work of Bishop Julio Murray, who wants to emphasize the role of the Spirit in the Trinity. He argues that the traditional understanding of *missio Dei* has not been adequate or sufficient to transform the churches for several reasons. "The theological basis of that concept is founded on the interpretation that emphasizes God the Father who sends his Son to carry out mission," with a lack of focus on the Spirit.[27] Murray cites Acts 1:8—"But you will receive power when the Holy Spirit has come upon you; and you will be my witnesses in . . . all Judea . . . and to the ends of the earth." He says the Spirit empowers us to do God's mission, which he understands to be our testimony to the ways the Spirit is working in our time. He elaborates on why the emphasis on the Spirit is crucial for Latin American churches:

> We must not forget that many of the concepts of mission that have come to us are rooted in Western culture, which should challenge us to seek a missiology rooted in Latin America, as the place where we are called to carry out mission. To move from the idea of mission of God acting through his Son, to considering a concept of mission that recognizes the movement of God in this time, active in the world through the power of God's Spirit, brings with it the introduction of "mission-shaped church.[28]

The above discussion of postcolonial visions of Christian mission provides helpful guides to examine the Five Marks of Mission, which has become a slogan for mission in the Anglican Communion. The 1984 Anglican Consultative Council (ACC) meeting proposed a fourfold definition of mission to bridge the divide between evangelism and social action. This formulation was largely influenced by the development of the Lausanne movement in the 1970s and 1980s. Within evangelical circles, there was the emergent consensus that mission includes both personal evangelization and work for social change. During the same period, the ecumenical movement understood mission as ushering in the Kingdom of God and standing in solidarity with the marginalized and oppressed to fight unjust structures. As Anglican leaders took part in both of these conversations, they brought with them insights when they discussed mission theology in the Anglican Communion. At the 1990 meeting of the ACC, the fifth mark concerning environmental care was added to the original four marks. Affirmed by the 1998 Lambeth Conference, the Five Marks of Mission became popularized and accepted by numerous provinces.[29] There have been modifications to the Five Marks and the current version reads as follows:

The mission of the Church is the mission of Christ

1. To proclaim the Good News of the Kingdom
2. To teach, baptise and nurture new believers
3. To respond to human need by loving service
4. To transform unjust structures of society, to challenge violence of every kind and pursue peace and reconciliation
5. To strive to safeguard the integrity of creation, and sustain and renew the life of the earth[30]

The first three marks are based on "the triad of *kerygma*, *diakonia*, and *koinonia* that has defined mission since Jesus."[31] The other two emphasize the transformation of society and the environment. From a postcolonial perspective, it is important to point out that a small group of African bishops played critical roles at the 1984 ACC meeting. Bishop David Gitari from Kenya and Bishop Benjamin Nwankiti from Nigeria had participated in international conferences on mission and helped shape the ACC report. Gitari was the consultant to the group on mission and ministry and Bishop Benjamin Nwankiti was its secretary. Four years later, Nwankiti chaired the mission section of the 1988 Lambeth Conference, and the report mentioned the fourfold definition.[32] In addition, some of the changes and additions made were influenced or pushed by indigenous Anglicans and leaders from the Global South. The Anglican Church of Canada requested a sixth mark related to peace, conflict transformation, and reconciliation. This attempt was based on the Canadian church's endeavor at reconciliation with the people of the First Nations. It was supported by the church in Burundi, a country involved in post-conflict reconciliation. Instead of adding another mark, the ACC meeting in 2012 added "to challenge violence of every kind and pursue peace and reconciliation" to the original fourth mark.[33] The addition of the fifth mark in 1990 on the environment and care for the earth was influenced by the Justice, Peace, and Integrity of Creation (JPIC) process of the WCC. Many Christian leaders in the Global South have pushed the WCC to recognize over the years the connections between racism, economic inequity, and environmental degradation.[34]

The discussion of mission was a cross-cultural encounter, which enabled Anglican leaders from the Global North and Global South to exchange views and respond to the needs of the time. The Five Marks of Mission try to balance the concerns of the local and the global and to mediate between those who see mission as evangelism or social action. In Clarke's Trinitarian understanding, evangelism and mission are not mutually exclusive but are entwined in hybrid relationships. Clarke writes, "Both motifs are meshed together in the ongoing performance of being Christian and growing Christianity in the world today. If we can conceive of a concealed hyphen between mission and evangelism, we might be able to speak of one without leaving the other behind."[35] Hybridity and searching for the in-between are important postcolonial insights.

The popular reception of the Five Marks of Mission challenges us not to use simple, binary conceptions of conservatives and liberals to understand the faith and practice of global Anglicanism. This is especially unhelpful to appreciating the vitality of young Anglicans, whose Christian identity may be more fluid and not fit into the old classifications. Cathy Ross has edited a book entitled *Life-Widening Mission* and invited young Anglicans to reflect on the five marks. They offer different perspectives from their contexts and ministries. For example, Kwok Keung Chan, a priest from Hong Kong who has worked in youth ministry, reflects on the first mark of proclaiming the good news of the Kingdom. He says that the Kingdom of God is not some distant place to arrive at after death, but "a place among us, where we Christians can love one another as God has loved us."[36] As the Kingdom is here and now, Christians need to live out our witness so that the Kingdom of God can be revealed in our midst. He welcomes the shift of emphasis from "mission to" to "mission with," and offers examples of how the Anglican Church in Hong Kong and Macao has carried out mission through ministry, education, and social service.[37] He notes that the Anglican church used to enjoy privileged status when Hong Kong was a British colony, and since the return to China, the church needs to adjust to the new situation and continue to proclaim the good news in a marginalized position.[38] Vicentia Kgabe, a priest from Johannesburg, South Africa, reflects on the third mark: "To respond to the human need by loving service" from young people's viewpoint. She notes that Anglican churches have often marginalized young people and they are not involved fully in the life of the church and its mission. She insists that churches must respond to young people's needs and help them to be self-reliant and mature in the local church. The church can respond to human needs with and through the young people, as well as adults, in realizing God's Kingdom.[39]

Two aspects are missing in the Five Marks of Mission. The first is Christian unity in mission and working with ecumenical partners. As we have seen above, the formulation of the Five Marks was influenced by conversations in the Lausanne movement and the ecumenical movement. Ecumenical relations are important from a postcolonial point of view because the competition between different branches of Christianity has hampered Christian witness and mission, especially in the non-Western world. Anglicans have participated in the modern ecumenical movement, which emerged in part as a response to the need for unity and common witness in carrying out mission.[40] But the ecumenical movement is in crisis today with the lack of wide support and financial resources. Murray notes that "the leaders of the ecumenical movement have adopted bureaucratic, patriarchal, and business-oriented practices, like managers of any secular business."[41] We need to transform ecumenical partnership so that it is a movement from the grassroots and fully embraces the spirit of "mission-shaped church" and not "church-shaped mission."

Another glaring oversight concerns the relationship with people of other faiths. Both Duraisingh and Clarke emphasize the need for dialogue, mutual learning, and respect for religious differences. In our age when violence, war, and conflicts have been influenced by religious intolerance and strife, interreligious dialogue and learning are critical for peacebuilding. American missiologist Titus Presler has noted that the future of Anglican mission theology will increasingly be defined by the visions and priorities of Global South Anglicans, now the majority in the Anglican Communion. He argues, "Continuing evolution in the theology of religions will influence the respective emphases of evangelization and inter-religious collaboration, especially in relation to Islam."[42]

Interreligious Dialogue and Solidarity

Raimundo Panikkar, the late Catholic theologian who made significant contributions to interreligious dialogue, pointed out that the self-understanding of Christians in relation to other religions can be summarized in five historical periods, though each of them permeated the others.[43] The first was *witnessing* when Christians in the early centuries bore witness to the gospel and the transformation of their lives. They did not imagine they had formed a new religion. The true Christian was a martyr, and they did not fear death in their fidelity to the faith. The next period was *conversion*, as Christianity gradually became the state religion. A true Christian had to be distinguished from the world, experienced a change of heart, and followed a particular style of life. With the Constantinization of Christianity, conversion slowly acquired political connotations, as Christians formed a state and an emerging empire. The period lasted until the Middle Ages and the clash with Islam elicited a new attitude. The third self-understanding, *crusade*, extended from the eighth century till the defeat of the Turkish power in 1571. The Christian empire was under the threat of Islam and the holy places "fell" into Muslim hands. A true Christian was a soldier and a crusader, and Jews were treated as scapegoats. Christianity was taken to be the true religion and other religions were false. The "discovery" of the New World ushered in the new self-understanding as *mission*, which lasted till the end of the modern period. The religious justification for the conquest of the Americas was to make the Amerindians Christian. The true Christian was a missionary, with the duty to convert and save others. During the colonial period, Christianity encountered other religions and saw itself as having a civilizing mission. After the two world wars and the independence of many states, *dialogue* became the "new catchword after the dismantling of the colonial political order."[44] There was an emphasis on indigenization, inculturation, and respect for other religions. Many Christians do not want to conquer or to convert others, but to learn and serve as participants in open dialogue.

In the Roman Catholic Church, Vatican II (1962–1965) issued *Nostra Aetate* (from Latin: in our time, or the Declaration on the Relation of the Church with non-Christian Religions). Promulgated by Pope Paul VI, the Declaration aimed to promote the unity of human beings and recognized the truth in other religions. The Catholic Church created a secretariat on non-Christian religions, which was renamed Pontifical Council for Interreligious Dialogue. Within the WCC, the need to promote interreligious dialogue to foster wider human community was discussed since the Uppsala Assembly in 1968. It has facilitated dialogue among people of different faiths through numerous events. The Anglican response to dialogue has been less formal since it lacks a central agency. Interreligious dialogue depends on the leadership of the bishops and priests at the local level. In the Anglican tradition, dialogue is related to mission, ecumenical relations, and social responsibility in solving issues in the community.[45] The Network for Inter Faith Concerns of the Anglican Communion published the influential report *Generous Love: The Truth of the Gospel and the Call for Dialogue*, which was received by the Lambeth Conference in 2008.[46] It highlights the importance of dialogue within the context of the triune mission of God and underscores diverse experiences and opinions about dialogue within the Anglican Communion. Anglicans are called to participate in the hospitality of the triune God and to journey into deeper understanding with our religious neighbors. "Through his cross and resurrection, Jesus gives us forgiveness, healing and new life, and shapes us into a community which offers these blessings to our neighbours in a pattern of gracious and generous discipleship."[47]

A postcolonial approach to dialogue highlights how the colonial legacy has continued to shape racial, ethnic, and religious relationships today. The divide-and-rule policies of the British Empire in India hardened cultural and religious boundaries and exacerbated religious rivalry. In the so-called scramble for Africa, nations were drawn up by European colonial powers without taking into consideration local histories and cultures, and religions of the people. Interstate and interethnic conflicts break out when religious, racial, ethnic, and linguistic differences are politicized. In the Middle East, the colonial powers encompassed territories and led to intercommunal conflicts because modern boundaries were artificially created as the result of war or by the pencils of colonial mapmakers.[48] In the name of religion, atrocities and violence have been inflicted upon people, and women and children are disproportionately affected.

Interreligious dialogue in the Global South must go beyond the gentlemen's conversation among religious leaders representing diverse religious traditions. Since women are marginalized in many religious traditions, they have seldom been invited as "representatives" of their traditions to join the dialogue. Women's voices have not been sufficiently heard. In addition, as Muslim scholar Najeeba Syeed has pointed out, many events of dialogue have been initiated by Christians and they dominate and set the agenda for the conversation. She writes, "We must de-center Christian scholarship and voices as primary sources of interreligious studies."[49] She also challenges us to scrutinize what constitutes "religion" in interreligious dialogue and learning, because in the academy, scholars have used "Christian-dominated assumptions of 'religion.'"[50] For example, religion has been taken to mean the belief in God or the transcendent, which is not universally true. Anthropologist Talal Asad has argued, "There cannot be a universal definition of religion, not only because its constituent elements and relationships are historically specific, but because that definition is itself the historical product of discursive processes."[51] Therefore, we cannot understand or isolate "religion" apart from its sociopolitical, cultural, and historical context.

In the United States, the Immigration and Nationality Act of 1965 abolished long-standing national-origin quotas, and as a result, immigrants from Asia and other parts of the world have changed the religious landscape of America. In the United Kingdom, as society has become more and more multicultural and multireligious, the general synod of the Church of England debated its relationship with people of non-Christian faiths since the early 1970s.[52] While religious pluralism has been taken more seriously by the Episcopal Church and the Church of England in the latter part of the twentieth century, Anglican Christians in the Global South have had a long history of living among people of other faiths. On the one hand, different religious traditions have coexisted, comingled, and appropriated elements from one another in the cross-fertilization of religions and cultures. A notable example was the Nestorian cross, which had a cross on top of a lotus (the Buddhist symbol of purity), as seen on the Nestorian stele in China dating back to the seventh century.[53] On the other hand, religious differences have exacerbated the conflicts between different racial and ethnic groups, leading to bloodshed and violence. Some of the Anglican churches in South Asia, Africa, and the Middle East have experienced violence and persecution.

I offer a few examples from different parts of the world to illustrate the diversity of relationships with people of other faiths in the Anglican Communion. In East Asia, religious identity is fluid and the boundaries between religions, such as Confucianism, Buddhism, and Daoism, are not rigid, especially in folk religion. Japanese scholar Kayama Hiroto wrestles with how Anglican theology can be an incarnational theology in Asia, respecting the cultures and aspirations of the Asian people. He notes that the Church of England used the via-media approach to accommodate the differences between Roman Catholicism and Puritanism, and he calls this the "third way" of doing theology. "If Anglican theology is a 'third theology' that is not shackled by binary oppositions, we should then refer to this phenomenon, not as Anglicanism, but 'the Anglican Way.'"[54] The "way," he notes, has rich connotations in Chinese culture, as it is the translation of the Chinese character *Dao* in Daoism. For him, Asian Anglicans need not choose between the Anglican tradition and their cultural heritage for

"Anglicans can deploy a notion of via media which is not the assumption of a midpoint between competing claims, but a method of sublating different opinions by providing a new paradigm, integrating them into a new theological framework."[55] Western scholars describe a person with more than one religion as someone with multiple religious belongings. Kayama does not have in mind a person who is both Daoist and Anglican. Rather, he imagines a "third way" in which Christian and Asian cultures and religions can be organically brought together in creative ways.

In other parts of the Communion, searching for the "third way" has been difficult because of intolerance and conflicts between people of different ethnic and religious communities. In South India, religion intersected with caste and class to divide people. Anglican missionaries in India had wanted to confront the caste system, which oppressed and marginalized the Dalits, the so-called untouchables. But the caste system was so entrenched that Anglican churches had to make compromises so as not to alienate people of the higher castes. Since the Dalits constitute the majority of Christians in India and Pakistan, they were looked down upon because of their caste and their adherence to a foreign religion that belonged to the colonizers. After Indian independence in 1947, Anglicans joined the Presbyterian, Wesleyan Methodist, and Congregational denominations to form the Church of South India, which became an ecumenical province of the Anglican Communion. Anglican churches sought to preserve their Anglican missionary heritage in the life and ministry of local congregations. From the period of independence, both the Indian and Pakistan governments restricted missionary work. In the current climate of rising Hindu nationalism, anticonversion laws have been enacted in many Indian states, and there has been an increase in the attacks on Christian communities and organizations.[56]

In Pakistan, Muslim fundamentalism threatens the Christian communities, which are made up mostly of Dalit Christians who are poor and without power. The blasphemy law, an offshoot of the Sharia law, has become a tool of oppression for Christians. Violence against Christians is on the rise and there are incidents targeting Anglican churches and institutions, including the bombing of Christian worship spaces. Pakistani

Christians live in a threatening and precarious situation. In Sri Lanka, Christians live as religious minorities in the Buddhist majority community. Anglican priests such as Laksman Wickremesinghe lived closely with Buddhist monks, incorporated Buddhist symbols and language in explicating the gospel, and appreciated Buddhist meditative practices. The country has been plagued by bloody militarized conflicts between the Tamils and Singhalese. The rise of Buddhist fundamentalism resulted in violence against churches and Christian organizations. In spite of all these difficulties, Anderson H. M. Jeremiah, an Anglican priest who specializes in Christian theology in Asia and Dalit studies, observes, "The Anglican churches in South Asia are growing as they continue to embrace the most vulnerable, poor and marginalised sections in the society. Therein lies the real strength and challenge of Anglicans in South Asia, particularly with the rapid growth of hostile ethno-religious nationalism across the region."[57]

In Southeast Asia, Islamization has made interreligious dialogue difficult in countries such as Malaysia, in which Islam is the official religion and about 60 percent of the population is Muslim. Judy Berinai, an Anglican theological educator in East Malaysia, describes Islamization in her country, which touches on many areas, such as education, media, the role of government, and dietary and dressing practices. She writes, "The Islamic resurgence has created an oppressive atmosphere for the non-Muslim population of Malaysia. Moreover, its impact has increasingly placed them in a subordinate position to that of the vast majority of Muslims who are Malays."[58] Witnessing to Malays is illegal and Christianity is portrayed by Islamic groups as a symbol of Western imperialism and impinging on Malay-Muslim cultures and values. Despite such challenging limitations, Christians bear witness through friendship and solidarity with others as well as modeling Christ's self-giving love in their daily lives.[59] Berinai regards interreligious collaboration as a grassroots effort and challenges Anglican women to come out of their comfort zones to work in solidarity with non-Christians:

> They are called to cooperate with other women for the common good in addressing issues such as social ills, moral decadence, and social and

> communal injustices. It is crucial to have a deeper understanding of one's faith in a pluralistic context. This will help Anglican women to witness Christ more confidently through daily encounters and interactions with neighbors in workplaces, and in the public sphere.[60]

In some parts of Africa, the relationships between Christians and Muslims have been tense because violence and armed conflicts have killed and inflicted pain on many people. Archbishop Josiah Idowu-Fearon from Nigeria, the former secretary general of the Anglican Communion, has lectured extensively on interreligious dialogue and Muslim-Christian relations. Citing Nigeria as an example, he says that British colonial rule has brought together people from Islam, Christianity, and African traditional religions who had little in common to form a nation, which was riddled with ethnic and religious pressure from the nation's beginning. Although Anglicans have lived with Muslims for periods of peace, Islamic political expansion and dominance had led to conflict and tension with many people killed. Christians had been attacked by armed Islamic militants and their lives and properties threatened.[61] The emergence of the extremist group Boko Haram led to the attacks of churches and schools and the horrible abduction of about 276 girls from a secondary school. In such a challenging situation, Nigerian churches have adopted a multidimensional approach to religious conflict: promotion of dialogue and understanding, rehabitating displaced persons, working with civic organizations to strengthen national institutions, and awakening governments to their responsibility in protecting lives and property.[62] In Sudan, the imposition of Islamization, Arabization, and Sharia law on Christians and other non-Muslims has caused civil wars, violence, and bloodshed. The decades of civil wars have taken the lives of millions of people and driven many to become refugees. Women and children had been raped, humiliated, and killed. The Episcopal Church of South Sudan and Sudan have a common vision of working for peace and conflict resolutions. Through the Justice, Peace, and Reconciliation Commission, the churches work to bring peace and reconciliation so that people can live free of violence and hatred.[63] For Anglicans living in these conflict-ridden societies, the challenge is to follow Jesus's commandment of loving one's enemies and continue to serve as bridge-builders and agents of reconciliation. They rely on the support and prayers from other churches in the Anglican Communion in their struggle for a pattern of civic and political life that enables peace and justice for all.

Palestinian Christians have appealed to Christian communities to stand in solidarity with them in the difficult work of bringing justice and peace to the Middle East. Anglican priest and theologian Naim Stifan Ateek, a pioneer of Palestinian liberation theology, argues that conflict resolution and reconciliation must be based on justice. He points out that a Zionist interpretation of the Bible—particularly the Exodus story—has justified the dispossession of the land and oppression of the Palestinian people. Yet he does not condone violence because this will not solve problems but bring misery and disaster. He says that the prophet Micah exhorts us to do justice, to love mercy, and to walk humbly with God (Mic. 6:8). Yet many prefer to be "involved in acts of mercy, but they back from the direct work of doing justice. They love justice from afar. However, the prophetic formula is clear: we must do justice."[64] Ateek surmises that only by acceptance of responsibility, repentance, and restoration of human rights can justice, peace, and reconciliation be achieved. As God has reconciled with us through Christ, he says, we are given the ministry of reconciliation (2 Cor. 5:18–19), however difficult and demanding the task is. He says, "I strongly believe that the Palestinians and Israelis can walk together the way of reconciliation, healing and forgiveness. . . . Once justice is the basis for the resolution of conflict, it is feasible that more innovative possibilities will emerge that can open the way for more creative possibilities for all the people of the land."[65]

The commitment to interreligious dialogue and solidarity in the Global South means crossing boundaries, establishing relationships, and maintaining goodwill for all peoples in trying times. It is a life and death issue when people deploy religion to justify intolerance, violence, killing, and extremism of all kinds. Sri Lankan theologian Jude Lal Fernando urges us to adopt a postcolonial and anti-imperialist approach in problematizing the construction of religio-ethno national identity, which excludes other groups or renders them second-class citizens. He says we have to be mindful of the *geopolitics* of interreligious dialogue and pay attention to what is happening on the ground. For example, a liberal approach to Jewish-Christian dialogue (as in the case of Palestine) and Buddhist-Christian dialogue (as in the case of Sri Lanka) without taking into consideration what the Jewish and Buddhist states have done will not solve problems but add miseries to the dispossessed and disenfranchised.[66] As a result of the colonial legacy, Anglicans have the responsibility to know the ways our past history have caused tense interreligious relations and dream new dreams so that our tradition can be a force for peacebuilding and reconciliation.

The Church in the Age of Global Migration

The shift of mission understanding from "over there" to "everywhere" is influenced by a change in the patterns of migration. Jehu J. Hanciles divides international migration since 1500 into three periods, taking into consideration economic and political factors in the non-Western world. From 1500 to 1850 was the period of European expansion and the Atlantic slave trade; from 1800 to 1960, the period of high imperialism and industrial growth; and from the 1960s to our present moment, the period of global migration.[67] The British saw their colonies in North America as settlement colonies from the start. As other European countries joined their colonial efforts, European migration to other parts of the world increased. In the first three centuries from the late fifteenth century onward, approximately 8 to 9 million Europeans migrated elsewhere.[68] During the period of the transatlantic slave trade, African men and women from West Africa and Western Central Africa were brought to the Americas and other destinations around the Indian Ocean and Arabia. About 11 million Africans were brutally enslaved and transported to the Americas between 1519 and 1867.[69] From the early years of the nineteenth century, European migration to other parts of the world increased considerably. About 55–60 million Europeans left to live overseas between 1815 and 1930, with more than two-thirds headed for North America.[70]

Others migrated to Australia, New Zealand, and South America to form settler communities, which entailed the displacement and genocide of indigenous populations.

After World War II, with the process of decolonization, the volume and velocity of migration accelerated, transforming it into a global phenomenon. The trend of migration has been reversed, with many postcolonial migrants trying, and sometimes risking their lives, to reach Europe and North America. Many of them have to leave to avoid ethnic and religious conflict, persecution, environmental disaster, global financial crisis, cycles of violence, and internal displacement. Citizen rights given to these migrants vary in different Western countries, and the influx of migrants from diverse backgrounds challenges Western political systems and societies.[71] There is a strong anti-immigrant climate in the United States and parts of Europe because of rising nativism, white supremacy, and Islamophobia. But as Hanciles has rightly observed: "If wealthy Western nations are now troubled by a massive and unstoppable influx of nonwhite immigrants, it is partly because non-Western societies were once troubled and overrun by Western migration and colonial expansion."[72]

In 2020, there were around 281 million international migrants, which equates to 3.6 percent of the global population. This number is three times the estimated number in 1970.[73] If migration has become a mode of survival for an increasing number of people in distressed and volatile situations, there is also a gender dimension to it. Female migrant workers remit their hard-earned foreign currencies home by working in the formal or informal labor market and in the sex and entertainment industries. Sociologist Saskia Sassen, who has done important research on global migration, calls this the "feminization of survival," as households and whole communities are increasingly dependent on women for their survival.[74] In addition, there has been a significant increase in displacement of people, both internal and across borders. In 2021, there were 89.3 million people forcibly displaced worldwide, among them 53.2 million internally displaced, 27.1 million refugees, and 4.6 million asylum-seekers.[75]

How might the church carry out its mission and respond to the needs of migrants, refugees, and asylum-seekers in this age of global migration?

Migration means to cross borders and Filipina Catholic theologian Gemma Tulud Cruz invites us to see "borders as theological frontiers." She writes, "Borders serve as indicators of the limits of existence, identity, and belonging."[76] Border-crossing entails leaving the familiar and venturing into the unknown. The theological frontiers we have to cross to develop a theology of migration requires us to challenge our sense of identity and privilege to look at the world through the eyes of migrants, refugees, and asylum-seekers. We must challenge five hundred years of colonial history, which has constructed an unsustainable world system that has forced millions to migrate and seek refuge in other lands. The present cartography of the world with its implicit notions of space, nation, borders, and boundaries cannot be considered natural or divinely ordained! The map of Africa, for example, would be completely different if not for the so-called scramble for Africa. We have to imagine borders as not drawn by colonial desire, power, and might but as constantly being contested and rearticulated by the flesh and blood of people on the move.

In developing a theology of migration, scholars have paid attention to Jesus the migrant. Peter C. Phan says that the incarnation of Jesus as a Jew in Palestine can be seen as a migratory act. In this process, God took on human flesh and went to live in a colonized nation and rub shoulders with people of different racial, ethnic, and national backgrounds, with unfamiliar customs and foreign cultures. The Prologue of John says the Word of God "pitched a tent" among us (John 1:14)—an image that reminds us of the precarious living condition of migrants and refugees. As a baby, Jesus and his family fled from Bethlehem to find safety and refuge in Egypt, when Herod the Great ordered the murder of male infants (Matt. 2:16). The family was uprooted and displaced because of the political and military powers in Roman Palestine. Jesus's ministry took place in the multicultural and migratory context of Galilee, a place steeped in a history of deportation, migration, exile, and return.[78] As an itinerant teacher, Jesus often encountered hostile environments and even his own people rejected him. He said, "Foxes have holes, and birds of the air have nests, but the Son of Man has nowhere to lay his head" (Matt. 8:20). In his travels, Jesus went to the borderland and met with people of different ethnic and religious backgrounds, such as the Syrophoenician woman in the region of Tyre (Mark 7:25–30). He was a border-crosser by speaking to Gentiles, preaching to women, healing the unclean, and mixing with sinners and tax collectors. His itinerant lifestyle and his breaking of cultural and religious codes of honor and status showed that "our belonging to a culture, religious tradition, or biological family should not be absolutized."[79] He started the Jesus movement and formed an alternative community around him to proclaim and usher in the Kingdom of God. As Paul Hertig, a scholar of mission studies, has noted, "Jesus, the migrant Messiah, will eventually call into a community of migrant disciples, who are sent out to the world by faith, without possession and dependent on the hospitality of strangers."[80]

Jesse Zink notes that "the dominant theme of the New Testament is that of displacement, not belonging."[81] Jesus was a refugee in Egypt. He did not prioritize the temple but told the Samaritan woman at the well that the day was coming when God would be worshipped in spirit and in truth, and not on this mountain nor in Jerusalem (John 4:21, 23). Zink notes that the Roman Empire was a transient place as new colonies were often formed consisting of people from around the empire. "The early Christians described themselves as a people without particular place."[82] The First Letter of Peter addressed "the exiles of the Dispersion in Pontus, Galatia, Cappadocia, Asia, and Bithynia" (1:1) and called them "aliens and exiles" (2:11). When Paul preached in Antioch, he referred to the Israelites' sojourn in Egypt and God had chosen and uplifted them (Acts 13:17). Early Christians understood that they were sojourners in this world, migrating to their heavenly home.

Paul, Silas, Timothy, and others in the early church traveled from city to city to spread the gospel. The people of God had not been static or tied to a particular locale or nation. Susanna Snyder, a British Anglican priest and a scholar on migration, offers the image of a "moving body" to describe the church as "inherently 'mobile' or 'shifting': the Body of Christ is not a static institution and rather a moving body."[83] Christianity has been shaped and changed by the migration and intermingling of peoples of diverse cultures, nationalities, languages, and social classes. As Christians migrated from Palestine and the Mediterranean and spread to other parts of the world, the Christian tradition crossed geographical, linguistic, national, and cultural boundaries and has been expressed in diverse and pluralistic forms integrating local cultures and elements. World Christianity as we have come to know it would not be possible without the migration of people throughout history.[84]

The church as a moving body requires new understandings of the church's identity and ministry. Snyder suggests "the notion of *via ecclesiae*, or a way of those called out."[85] She says the Greek term *ekklēsia*, which has often been translated in English as church, consists of *ek* (out) and *caleo* (to call) and means "gathering of the called-out ones." In the Greco-Roman world, *ekklēsia* was the assembly in a particular place of citizens to make free decisions about the welfare of the city-states. *Via ecclesiae* builds on this and suggests

> a repeated movement of the people of God as they are called out, assemble for a while, and then move on as they are called to step out once more. Living church as *via ecclesiae* today means being open to being drawn out of some entrenched habits or practices by those among us with experience of migration, and reassembling to grow and make decisions together as the Body of Christ. This involves repeatedly crossing and inhabiting boundaries between immigrant and non-immigrant, tradition and change, local and global, poor and rich, denomination and faith, unity, and polycentricity, and the mundane and transcendent.[86]

Snyder identifies two important motifs underlying Anglican responses to migration today. The first is incarnate responsibility, which includes providing hospitality and pastoral care to the migrants, refugees, and asylum-seekers; strengthening transnational networks to address the migration crisis; partnership with migrant-led organizations; and political engagement and advocacy to address some of the root causes of migration. The other motif is strange grace, which is "the recognition that human beings often experience divine grace through encounters with the 'other.'"[87] Encountering migrants and refugees from different places, cultures, and religious backgrounds broadens our horizons and breaks us out of our comfortable, self-enclosed world to reimagine divine grace in new ways. The Anglican Communion has formed the Anglican Refugee and Migrant Network to help church communities in responding to migrants, internally displaced people, and refugees and work with other partners, ecumenical agencies, and governments.

Global migration has changed and transformed churches and faith communities in the United States and Europe. According to a study done in 2012, Christians comprised nearly half of the world's international migrants.[88] In the United States, over 60 percent of new immigrants are Christians.[89] Some of these migrants have joined denominational churches, while others have formed immigrant churches. These migrants have brought their cultures and vitality to enliven the Church of England and the Episcopal Church. Yet they are often treated as "strangers in the family" because of their races, theological orientations, worshipping styles, and views about social issues.[90] They struggle to gain trust, recognition, and resources because of racism and stereotypes about migrants, refugees, and asylum-seekers. In response to the influx of new immigrants, especially those from Hong Kong after the protests in the former British colony, the Church of England organized training events to prepare clergy and lay leaders. Meanwhile, the Episcopal Church has to respond to rising anti-immigration sentiments and the huge needs of migrants along the U.S.–Mexico border.

In our globalized and interconnected world, missiologist Allen Yeh says mission is polycentric, which is "from everyone to everywhere."[91] A mission-shaped church exists not for itself but for the healing of the broken and fragmented world and a planet in peril. Anglican mission theology cannot be territorial-bound and focuses on church-planting and numerical increase. The word "parish" is derived from the Greek term *paroikia*, which means stay or sojourn. It is the same word used in the First Peter and Acts.[92] It reminds us that we are sojourners on a pilgrimage with our religious neighbors to seek fuller meaning of life and work for peace and flourishing for all. The global Anglican Communion with members in over 165 countries across national, linguistic, and cultural differences can be a beacon of hope and embrace the strangers and migrants in our midst.

For Jesus has taught us, "just as you did it to one of the least of these brothers and sisters of mine, you did it to me" (Matt. 25:40).

Notes

1. Lamin Sanneh, *Translating the Message: Missionary Impact on Culture* (Maryknoll, NY: Orbis Books, 1989); Sanneh, *Whose Religion Is Christianity? The Gospel Beyond the West* (Grand Rapids, MI: Eerdmans, 2003); and Andrew F. Walls, *The Cross-Cultural Process of Christian History: Studies in the Transmission and Appropriation of Faith* (Maryknoll, NY: Orbis Books, 2002).
2. Jehu J. Hanciles, ed., *World Christianity: History, Methodologies, Horizons* (Maryknoll, NY: Orbis Books, 2021), ix–x.
3. Jesse Zink, "Brief Introductions to Anglican Theology: Christian Mission," *Anglican Theological Review* 104, no. 4 (2022): 448.
4. Zink, "Brief Introductions to Anglican Theology," 449.
5. Zink, "Brief Introductions to Anglican Theology," 454.
6. John Kafwanka, "Partnership in Mission—An Anglican Perspective," in *Call to Unity: For the Sake of Mission*, ed. John Gibaut and Knud Jørgensen (Minneapolis: Fortress, 2015), 160.
7. Titus Presler, "The History of Mission in the Anglican Communion," in *The Wiley-Blackwell Companion to the Anglican Communion*, ed. Ian S. Markham et al. (Malden, MA: Wiley-Blackwell, 2013), 28–29.
8. Zink, "Brief Introductions to Anglican Theology," 455.
9. For a discussion of how Partnership in Mission morphed into Companion Links, see Kafwanka, "Partnership in Mission," 165–70.
10. Andrew Wingate, "Decade of Evangelism," in *Religion Past and Present: Encyclopedia of Theology and Religion*, ed. Hans Dieter Betz et al. (Leiden: Brill, 2019), 3:709. I would like to thank Dominique Deming for her presentation on "Evangelism and Mission: A Decade of Evangelism," at Candler School of Theology, Atlanta, Georgia, March 20, 2023.
11. Zink, "Brief Introductions to Anglican Theology," 458.
12. Church of England's Mission and Public Affairs Council, *Mission-Shaped Church: Church Planting and Fresh Expressions of Church in a Changing Context* (London: Church Publishing, 2004), xiii.
13. Lambeth Conference 1867, Resolution 8, Anglican Communion, https://www.anglicancommunion.org/media/127716/1867.pdf.
14. Cathy Ross, "'Such Unfolding of the Truth of the Gospel': Post-Colonial Reflections on the Missiological Dimension of the Lambeth Conference," in *The Lambeth Conference: Theology, History, Polity and Purpose*, ed. Paul Avis and Benjamin Guyer (London: Bloomsbury T & T Clark, 2017), 300.
15. Ross, "'Such Unfolding of the Truth of the Gospel,'" 309.
16. Christopher Duraisingh, "Toward a Postcolonial Re-visioning of the Church's Faith, Witness, and Communion," in *Beyond Colonial Anglicanism: The Anglican Communion in the Twenty-First Century*, ed. Ian T. Douglas and Kwok Pui-lan (New York: Church Publishing, 2001), 337.
17. Duraisingh, "Toward a Postcolonial Re-visioning," 344–45.

18. Duraisingh, "Toward a Postcolonial Re-visioning," 345.
19. Duraisingh, "Toward a Postcolonial Re-visioning," 352.
20. Duraisingh, "Toward a Postcolonial Re-visioning," 358–59.
21. C. S. Song, *Tell Us Our Names: Story Theology from an Asian Perspective* (Maryknoll, NY: Orbis Books, 1984), 106.
22. Duraisingh, "Toward a Postcolonial Re-visioning," 355.
23. Sathianathan Clarke, "World Christianity and Postcolonial Mission: A Path Forward for the Twenty-First Century," *Theology Today* 71, no. 2 (2014): 200–201.
24. Clarke, "World Christianity and Postcolonial Mission," 201–3.
25. Clarke, "World Christianity and Postcolonial Mission," 202.
26. Clarke, "World Christianity and Postcolonial Mission," 204.
27. Julio E. Murray, "New WCC Affirmation on Mission and Evangelism: Observations from the Episcopal Church of Panama," *International Review of Mission* 102, no. 2 (2013): 205.
28. Murray, "New WCC Affirmation on Mission and Evangelism," 206.
29. Jesse Zink, "Five Marks of Mission: History, Theology, Critique," *Journal of Anglican Studies* 15, no. 2 (2017): 148–55.
30. "Marks of Mission," Anglican Communion, https://www.anglicancommunion.org/mission/marks-of-mission.aspx.
31. Presler, "History of Mission in the Anglican Communion," 31.
32. Zink, "Five Marks of Mission," 151, 154.
33. Ross, "'Such Unfolding of the Truth of the Gospel,'" 304–5.
34. Zink, "Five Marks of Mission," 154–55. I participated in the JPIC process and spoke at the World Convocation on JPIC in Seoul, South Korea, in 1990.
35. Clarke, "World Christianity and Postcolonial Mission," 205.
36. Kwok Keung Chan, "The First Mark of Mission: To Proclaim the Good News of the Kingdom of God," in *Life-Widening Mission: Global Perspectives from the Anglican Communion*, ed. Cathy Ross (Oxford: Regnum Books International, 2012), 15.
37. Chan, "First Mark of Mission," 21–23.
38. Chan, "First Mark of Mission," 19–20.
39. Vicentia Kgabe, "The Third Mark of Mission: To Respond to Human Need by Loving Service," in Ross, *Life-Widening Mission*, 56.
40. Michael Nazir-Ali, "The Anglican Communion and Ecumenical Relations," in Markham, *Wiley-Blackwell Companion to the Anglican Communion*, 569–84.
41. Murray, "New WCC Affirmation on Mission and Evangelism." 208.
42. Presler, "History of Mission in the Anglican Communion," 31. Earlier he proposed ten marks of mission and one of them was the call to work with people of other faiths, see *Horizons of Missions* (Boston: Cowley, 2001), 173–75.
43. Raimundo Panikkar, "The Jordan, the Tiber, and the Ganges: Three Kariological Moments of Christic Self-Understanding," in *The Myth of Christian Uniqueness: Toward a Pluralistic Theology of Religions*, ed. John Hick and Paul F. Knitter (Maryknoll, NY: Orbis Books, 1987), 93–95.
44. Panikkar, "Jordan, the Tiber, and the Ganges," 95.

45. Michael Ipgrave and Clare Amos, "An Untidy Generosity: Anglicans and the Challenge of Other Religions," in *The Oxford Handbook of Anglican Studies*, ed. Mark D. Chapman et al. (London: Oxford University Press, 2015), 427–48.
46. Network for Inter Faith Concerns of the Anglican Communion, *Generous Love: The Truth of the Gospel and the Call to Dialogue* (London: Anglican Consultative Council, 2008).
47. Network for Inter Faith Concerns, *Generous Love*, 10.
48. Kwok Pui-lan, *Postcolonial Politics and Theology: Unraveling Empire for a Global World* (Louisville, KY: Westminister John Knox, 2021), 172–73.
49. Najeeba Syeed, "Interreligious Learning and Intersectionality," in *Asian and Asian American Women in Theology and Religion*, ed. Kwok Pui-lan (Cham, Switzerland: Palgrave Macmillan, 2020), 174.
50. Syeed, "Interreligious Learning and Intersectionality," 174.
51. Talal Asad, *Genealogies of Religion: Discipline and Reasons of Power in Christianity and Islam* (Baltimore, MD: Johns Hopkins University Press, 1993), 29.
52. T. H. N. Kuin, "Perfect Partners or Uneasy Bedfellows: Anglicans and Religious Pluralism in the Late 20th Century," *Studies in Interreligious Dialogue* 7, no. 2 (1997): 177–99.
53. Meng Qingsheng and Li Yang, "Nestorian Stone Tablet Traces Early Christianity in China," CGTN, updated May 19, 2019, https://news.cgtn.com/news/3d3d514e32597a4e34457a6333566d54/index.html.
54. Kayama Hiroto, "A New Perspective for Anglicanism: Mission in Northeast Asia," trans. John Stolzenbach, *Journal of Anglican Studies* 6, no. 2 (2008): 169.
55. Kayama, "New Perspective," 167.
56. See Anderson H. M. Jeremiah, "Anglicans in South Asia: Life in the Midst of Religious Marginality," in *Contemporary Issues in the Worldwide Anglican Communion: Powers and Pieties*, ed. Abby Day (Burlington, VT: Ashgate, 2016), 191–210.
57. Jeremiah, "Anglicans in South Asia," 206.
58. Judy Berinai, "Anglican Women Witnessing in a Muslim Context: Experience in Malaysia," in *Anglican Women on Church and Mission*, ed. Kwok Pui-lan, Judith A. Berling, Jenny Plane Te Paa (New York: Morehouse Publishing, 2012), 186.
59. Albert Sundararaj Walters, "Evangelism and Witnessing in Multi-Religious Malaysia: Towards a Fresh Approach," in *Witnessing Together: Global Anglican Perspectives on Evangelism and Witness*, ed. Muthuraj Swamy and Stephen Spencer (London: Anglican Communion Office, 2019), 65–77.
60. Berinai, "Anglican Women Witnessing in a Muslim Context," 193–94.
61. Josiah Idowu-Fearon, "Anglicans and Islam in Nigeria: Anglicans Encountering Difference," *Journal of Anglican Studies* 2, no. 1 (2004): 40–51. See also the video "'Mr. Dialogue' Bishop Josiah Idowu-Fearon," YouTube, https://www.youtube.com/watch?v=4JqcVb_Gdak.
62. Abiola Mbamalu, "Christian-Muslim Encounter in Nigeria in the Context of Boko Haram," in *Walking Together: Global Anglican Perspectives on Reconciliation*, ed. Muthuraj Swamy and Stephen Spencer (London: Anglican Communion Office, 2019), 49–56.
63. Samuel Enosa Peni Tari, "The Role of the Church in Reconciliation and Peace-Building in South Sudan," in Swamy and Spencer, *Walking Together*, 57–68.
64. Naim Stifan Ateek, *A Palestinian Christian Cry for Reconciliation* (Maryknoll, NY: Orbis Books, 2008), 180.

65. Naim Ateek, "Justice and Reconciliation," in Swamy and Spencer, *Walking Together*, 22.
66. Jude Lal Fernando, "The Geopolitics of Interreligious Dialogue: Political Zionism, Sinhala Buddhist Nationalism, and the Oppressed," in *Transpacific Political Theology: Perspectives and Methods*, ed. Kwok Pui-lan (Waco, TX: Baylor University Press, forthcoming).
67. Jehu J. Hanciles, *Beyond Christendom: Globalization, African Migration, and the Transformation of the West* (Maryknoll, NY: Orbis Books, 2008), 159.
68. Hanciles, *Beyond Christendom*, 39.
69. Hanciles, *Beyond Christendom*, 39.
70. Hanciles, *Beyond Christendom*, 40–41.
71. Ulbe Rosma, Jan Lucassen, and Gert Oostindie, "Introduction: Postcolonial Migrations and Identity Politics: Towards a Comparative Perspective," in *Postcolonial Migrants and Identity Politics: Europe, Russia, Japan, and the United States in Comparison*, ed. Ulbe Rosma, Jan Lucassen, and Gert Oostindie (New York: Berghahn Books, 2012), 1–22.
72. Hanciles, *Beyond Christendom*, 172.
73. "World Migration Report 2022," International Organization for Migration, https://worldmigrationreport.iom.int/wmr-2022-interactive.
74. Saskia Sassen, "Women's Burden: Counter-Geographics of Globalization and the Feminization of Survival," *Journal of International Affairs* 53, no. 2 (2000): 506.
75. "Refugees, Asylum-Seekers, Internally Displaced: Opportunities Not Wars," United Nations, https://www.un.org/en/fight-racism/vulnerable-groups/refugees-asylum-seekers-internally-displaced.
76. Gemma Tulud Cruz, "Between Identity and Security: Theological Implications of Migration in the Age of Globalization," *Theological Studies* 69, no. 2 (2008): 370.
77. Peter C. Phan, "*Deus Migrator*—God the Migrant, Migration of Theology and Theology of Migration," *Theological Studies* 77, no. 4 (2016): 861.
78. Paul Hertig, "Jesus' Migrations and Liminal Withdraws in Matthew," in *God's People on the Move: Biblical and Global Perspectives on Migration and Mission*, ed. vanThanh Nguyen and John M. Prior (Eugene, OR: Pickwick, 2014), 51.
79. Rafael Luciani, "The Itinerant Fraternity of Jesus: Christological Discernment of the Migration Drama," in *Living with(out) Borders: Catholic Theological Ethics on the Migrations of Peoples*, ed. Agnes M. Brazal and María Teresa Dávila (Maryknoll, NY: Orbis Books, 2016), 208.
80. Hertig, "Jesus' Migrations," 49.
81. Jesse Zink, "Anglican Theology in the Midst of a Migration Crisis," *Journal of Anglican Studies* 17, no. 1 (2019): 37.
82. Zink, "Anglican Theology," 37.
83. Susanna Snyder, "Introduction: Moving Body," in *Church in an Age of Global Migration: A Moving Body*, ed. Susanna Snyder, Agnes M. Brazal, and Joshua Ralston (New York: Palgrave Macmillan, 2016), 9.
84. For the major migrations of Christians, see Peter C. Phan, "Christianity as an Institutional Migrant," in *Christianities in Migration: The Global Perspective*, ed. Elaine Padilla and Peter C. Phan (New York: Palgrave Macmillan, 2016), 13–22. See also Jehu J. Hanciles, *Migration and the Making of Global Christianity* (Grand Rapids, MI: Eerdmans, 2021).

85. Susanna Snyder, "Moving the Anglican Communion: Ethics and Ecclesiology in an Age of Migration," in Chapman, *Oxford Handbook of Anglican Studies*, 569. See also her *Asylum-Seeking, Migration, and Church* (Burlington, VT: Ashgate, 2012).

86. Synder, "Moving the Anglican Communion," 569.

87. Synder, "Moving the Anglican Communion," 566.

88. "Faith on the Move—The Religious Faith of International Migrants," Pew Research Center, March 8, 2012, https://www.pewresearch.org/religion/2012/03/08/religious-migration-exec.

89. "The Religious Affiliation of U.S. Migrants: Majority Christian, Rising Share of Other Faiths," Pew Research Center, May 17, 2013, https://www.pewresearch.org/religion/2013/05/17/the-religious-affiliation-of-us-immigrants.

90. Jehu J. Hanciles discusses how African Christian migrants are treated in Europe and the United States in "Migrants as Missionaries, Missionaries as Outsiders: Reflections on African Christian Presence in Western Societies," *Mission Studies* 30, no. 1 (2013): 74–82.

91. Allen Yeh, *Polycentric Missiology: 21st-Century Mission from Everyone to Everywhere* (Downers Grove, IL: IVP Academic, 2016).

92. Zink, "Anglican Theology," 37.

Epilogue

The Future of Anglicanism

In this book I reflect on the Anglican tradition informed by my study and engagement with postcolonial theory. I highlight the issues and concerns of Anglican churches and the contributions of theologians and church leaders from the Global South. The need to reimagine the Anglican Communion and new patterns of relationships among member churches has been heightened because of the controversies besetting the Communion. Before the 2022 Lambeth Conference, Archbishop of Canterbury Justin Welby expressed hope that it would be an occasion for fruitful conversations on the challenges of creating a "postcolonial model" for a Communion created in the era of empire.[1] The Lambeth Calls, prepared for conversation at the conference, acknowledged that "the legacies of colonialism, the trans-Atlantic slave trade, and other abuses of power continue to impact our communities. Some have been enriched and some impoverished. International economic systems, built upon unjust structures of exploitation, have created dehumanizing conditions."[2] The Calls affirm creation is God's gift and exhort the church to respect human diversity and protect the dignity of all creation, cultures, and human beings. In unequivocal terms, the document recognizes the collusion of Anglicanism with colonial power: "We acknowledge the existence and ongoing impact of an imperialist Anglicanism involved in dehumanizing practices predicated upon cultural and racial supremacy. Any Christian commitment to human dignity must celebrate the rich diversities of contextual theologies and take account of Anglicanism's complicity in brutal and extractive colonialisms."[3] This book hopes to contribute to the process of decolonizing our minds and church practices by engaging the works of Anglican theologians who have wrestled with the imprint of colonialism on Anglicanism.

Edward Said's concept of contrapuntal reading offers insights into interpreting Anglican history and theology. Trained as a pianist in classical music, he explains that composers such as Bach used counterpoint to create music in which two or more melodic tunes are played or sung at the same time. As a result of colonialism, Said argues, territories are overlapped and histories intertwined, such that we have to interpret the cultural archive "not univocally but *contrapuntally*, with a simultaneous awareness both of the metropolitan history that is narrated and of those other histories against which (and together with which) the dominating discourse acts."[4] If we use a contrapuntal perspective to analyze history, alternative and new narratives might emerge that counter or complement monophonic or Eurocentric narratives. This book has avoided interpreting the Anglican tradition univocally by focusing on the Church of England or the English heritage. Instead, it is mindful of the polyphonic and multilayered Anglican tradition, which has been shaped by the specific history of colonization, resistance, and postcolonial conditions. The Anglican Communion as we have come to know it today has emerged out of the interactions of Anglicanism with local cultures and the issues arising from such encounters.

The Anglican Communion is a fellowship of churches in which the provinces are autonomous and there is no central authority. The postcolonial process began when the Protestant Episcopal Church in the United States of America separated from the Church of England in 1785 after the American Revolution, making it the first independent church outside of the British Isles. In the nineteenth century, churches in Aotearoa New Zealand and other parts of the world sought autonomy and the authority to elect their own bishops. The first Lambeth Conference in 1867 affirmed the autonomy of the provinces and did not impose a uniform view on polygamy and other issues that had prompted that meeting to be called. As mission work expanded to cover many territories, it was no longer feasible to send missionary bishops or support many local churches. Henry Venn of the CMS proposed the idea of a native pastorate under a native bishop and the principle of three selfs (self-supporting, self-governing, and self-propagating). It was in Sierra Leone that the idea of a native pastorate was first experimented with. Although this process met with barriers and difficulties, the principle of three-selfs never died and became important when former colonies gained independence and wanted to form their own autonomous provinces.

It was in the mission fields that Anglican discussion on Christian unity and ecumenical relations became urgent and necessary. Take the case of China as an example. Anglican missionaries from the United States and United Kingdom arrived in the early nineteenth century and they were later joined by missionaries from Canada. The CMS, the SPG, the CEZMS, the Protestant Episcopal China Mission, and the Church of England in Canada all sent missionaries to work in this vast mission field. Although the missionaries cooperated with one another, there were occasional differences concerning diocesan boundaries and episcopal jurisdiction, and the use of the Prayer Book. British and American bishops and clergy met to resolve their differences and find ways to work collaboratively for evangelism and mission. In 1912, representatives from all the Anglican and Episcopal churches and mission societies gathered in Shanghai to form one national church—the Chung Hua Sheng Kung Hui (Chinese Anglican-Episcopal Church).[5] Earlier, similar steps were taken in 1887 to establish the Nippon Sei Ko Kai (Anglican Church in Japan). The Edinburgh Missionary Conference of 1910 was an important event to promote cooperation between churches and mission societies in advancing Christian mission work. The Chung Hua Sheng Kung Hui was a founding member of the National Christian Council of China in 1922. The model of the national council of churches was replicated in Japan, Korea, and the Philippines. In South Asia, different Protestant denominations, including the Anglican Church, began conversations to move ecumencial relations a step further to form united churches. In a poor country with so many needs and the percentage of Christians in the population so tiny, churches could not carry their work without unity and sharing resources. The Church of South India was established in September 1947, a month after India achieved its independence. Other united churches were formed subsequently: the Church of North India in 1970 and the Church of Pakistan in 1970, and after Bangladesh separated from Pakistan, the church of Bangladesh was formed in 1974. These united churches have to work with each other to solve the differences of polities, recognize each other's ministry, and respect diversity in worship and congregational life. They are members of the Anglican Communion, and their bold experiments have a lot to teach us about the possibilities of working across denominational differences.

The story of the evolution of the Book of Common Prayer tells how a liturgical text meant for use by one nation has become a postcolonial book in today's multicultural Anglican Communion. As a "traveling book," it has been translated, received, and appropriated by Anglicans of many local languages and cultures. After the Episcopal Church was formed, it had to modify the language and prayers of the Prayer Book to adjust to the new political situation. Its Prayer Book of 1789 eliminated state prayers for the king, changed the Eucharistic prayer, and made other revisions.[6] As Ian T. Douglas notes, just as the Anglicans in the postcolonial United States had to determine their governance structure and appropriate liturgical expression in the late eighteenth century, so "Anglicans in the post-colonial realities of Africa, Asia, Latin America, and the Pacific have done for the last five decades."[7] The Church of South India issued *The Book of Common Worship* in 1950 and African theologians and church leaders pushed for the indigenizaton of Anglican liturgy in the 1970s. The newer revisions of the Prayer Book have been bolder in adopting a decolonial approach by creating living liturgies that are inclusive of all the baptized and reflect the cultures and ethos of the community in worship.

Women's ordination in the Anglican Communion first took place in the Diocese of Hong Kong and South China because of the expediency of the war situation. The ordination of Li Tim-Oi stimulated discussion of women's ministry in the churches and paved the way for women's ordination in other parts of the Communion: the Episcopal Church (1974), The Anglican Church of Canada (1976), The Anglican Church in Aotearoa, New Zealand and Polynesia (1977), the Anglican Church of Kenya (1983) and so forth. In the Church of England, the Movement for the Ordination of Women was formed in 1979, but the first women were not ordained till 1994, fully half a century after Li's ordination. As I have shown in chapter 6, ordained and lay women in the Global South have played important leadership roles in the mission and ministry of the church and contributed to the life of the Communion. Today, the average Anglican is an African woman in her thirties. The shift of demographics of Anglicanism to the Global South is in large part the work of women in the churches because they make up the majority of the congregations. While the media has focused on the outspoken bishops and theologians, who are mostly male, it is the rank-and-file Anglican women who carry on the work of the church and help the church grow.

Many are concerned about the future of the Anglican Communion because the heated debates about homosexuality threatened the schism of the church. But if we take a longitudinal view, we will see that many issues in the Communion, such as polygamy and women's ordination, took a long time to deliberate and there is still no uniform view across the Communion. The issue of sexuality has become a wedge issue because of colonial history and the globalization of the American culture wars to other parts of the world. Both liberals and conservatives in America, through church networks and nongovernment agencies, want to influence the opinions of others in the Communion. Some of the church leaders in the Global South claim they represent orthodox Anglicanism and want to discipline Western liberal churches that they perceive as having gone astray. They accuse Western Christians of superimposing their values onto others in a new form of imperialism. The furor and acrimony reveal deep divisions not only because of different theological positions but also because of continued unequal economic and political power dynamics between the Global North and the Global South. For leaders in the Global South, colonial vestiges still linger even though the demographic center of the Communion has shifted to the Global South. Commenting on the rise of GAFCON and the division in the Communion, Michael Doe, the former general secretary of the United Society for the Propagation of the Gospel, writes that there is "the need to move beyond the colonial inheritance in order to recognize both the independence of partners and the need for new patterns of inter-dependence."[8] He also notes that the structures of the Anglican Communion move from colonial paternalism to independence, mutuality, and interdependence: for example, provinces meet on equal grounds in the Anglican Consultative Council. However, the Communion may not be perceived like this because the head office is in London and the Church of England seems to be still in control.[9]

Anglican church leaders in the Global South have gathered and they have formed the Global South Fellowship of Anglican Churches. Some of the bishops have attended GAFCON meetings and they have championed a conservative position on same-sex marriage and the ordination of LGBTQ persons. While it is important to hear the voices from the Global South, it is crucial that the Southern networks not be driven by Northern agenda and funding sources. Churches in the Global South are not monolithic, and we cannot just listen to the primates and bishops, who are mostly men, without hearing from women, LGBTQ persons, and marginalized peoples. It is a global concern that the Christian Right in America has used homosexuality as an issue to divide American churches and would use similar strategies to divide the Communion, as well as churches in the Global South. A disproportionate amount of time and energy has been used in the last two decades on the homosexuality issue, when churches in the Global South face tremendous challenges in responding to poverty, religious persecution, protection of human rights, basic education for girls and young women, environmental disasters, and migration and refugees. If churches in the Global South want to be a prophetic witness in the whole Communion, policing sexuality is a misplaced focus. It is problematic to see conservative leaders lending support to authoritarian politicians, as in the case of Uganda, to criminalize LGBTQ persons and drive them more to the underground. As right-wing political ideologies are gaining ground in the United States, Europe, and parts of Africa and Asia, Anglican churches need to examine whether it has colluded with the state in the past and commit to genuine transformation in the church and society for the sake of the Kingdom.

As we move toward a polycentric Communion that is beyond British colonial hegemony, we have to learn to live in the uneasiness and messiness of conflictual opinions, heated arguments, and diverse theological convictions. American ethicist Kyle Lambelet argues that too often we have seen conflict in the Communion as negative, and scholars have used the descriptions of "crisis," "war," and even "plague" to characterize it. He says

Anglicans have often associated conflict with sin or finitude, but he argues that conflict can be a means of grace: "I wish to make the case for a more positive, theological reception of agonism, or struggle, in the church and suggest that celebrating such struggle might enable a more faithful practice of Christian unity."[10] Drawing from those who have studied conflict and peace, Lambelet says that conflict is part of healthy human relationships and can be used for transformation. He proposes the understanding of conflict-as-communion based on a "Trinitarian account of unity through difference,"[11] which enables us to continue to engage with one another to carry out God's mission in the world.

Christopher Duraisingh encourages us to engage in genuine border crossings in our commitment to stay in a polycentric Communion. As Christ has crossed borders, churches are to "become 'cross-border spaces,' where the 'otherness' of the other may be understood on its own terms, and where new, and holistic, and corporate Christian identities may be formed together in solidarity."[12] The principle of via media, long cherished by Anglicans, can offer tremendous insights in navigating through the treacherous waters of cultural politics today, if understood in a new light. Via media debunks the myth that there is one, stable foundation or source of truth, thus opening up possibilities for dialogue between people on different sides of the fence. Via media entertains the thought that decisions about right or wrong, truth or falsehood are not predetermined or prepackaged, but negotiated in the grayish, ambivalent space of "in-between." While honoring the cultural experiences of people, via media is not complete relativism or moral chaos. It is a kind of disciplined reasoning, seasoned with humility, and sustained by compassion and empathy for oneself and others. Via media has held the Anglo-Catholics and evangelicals, those who emphasize mission as evangelism and social action, and those who accept and reject women's ordination together in the past. I hope it will continue to guide us into the future.

Notes

1. *The Guardian* editorial, "The Guardian View on the Lambeth Conference, Don't Make It about Homosexuality," *The Guardian*, July 25, 2022, https://www.theguardian.com

/commentisfree/2022/jul/25/the-guardian-view-on-the-lambeth-conference-dont-make-it-about-sexuality.
2. "Human Dignity," in *Lambeth Calls*, 14, Lambeth Conference, https://www.lambethconference.org/wp-content/uploads/2022/07/Lambeth-Calls-July-2022.pdf.
3. "Human Dignity," in *Lambeth Calls*, 15. *Lambeth Calls* has been revised after the 2022 Lambeth Conference, and the newest version published in May 2023 has not changed the words cited in notes 2 and 3. See https://www.lambethconference.org/wp-content/uploads/2023/05/The-Lambeth-Calls-English-2023.pdf.
4. Edward W. Said, *Culture and Imperialism* (New York: Alfred A. Knopf, 1993), 51, emphasis in original. For the background of Said's theorization of a contrapuntal perspective, see Wouter Capitain, "From Counterpoint to Heterophony and Back Again: Reading Edward Said's Drafts for *Culture and Imperialism*," *Journal of Musicological Research* 41, no. 1 (2022): 1–22, https://doi.org/10.1080/01411896.2020.1787793.
5. Philip L. Wickeri, "Introduction," in *Christian Encounters with Chinese Culture: Essays on Anglican and Episcopal History in China*, ed. Philip Wickeri (Hong Kong: Hong Kong University Press, 2015), 9–10.
6. Marion J. Hatchett, "The Colonies and the States of America," in *The Oxford Guide to the Book of Common Prayer: A Worldwide Survey*, ed. Charles Hefling and Cynthia Shattuck (Oxford: Oxford University Press, 2006), 176–82.
7. Ian T. Douglas, "Inculturation and Anglican Worship," in Hefling and Shattuck, *Oxford Guide the Book of Common Prayer*, 275.
8. Michael Doe, "From Colonialism to Communion," *Journal of Anglican Studies* 7, no. 2 (2009): 216. The United Society for the Propagation of the Gospel was formed after incorporating the activities of the Universities Mission to Central Africa in 1965. It was renamed the United Society Partners in the Gospel in 2016.
9. Doe, "From Colonialism to Communion," 217.
10. Kyle B. T. Lambelet, "Conflict as Communion: Toward an Agonistic Ecclesiology," *Journal of Anglican Studies* 17, no 2 (2019): 135.
11. Lambelet, "Conflict as Communion," 133.
12. Christopher Duraisingh, "Toward a Postcolonial Re-visioning of the Church's Faith, Witness, and Communion," in *Beyond Colonial Anglicanism: The Anglican Communion in the Twenty-First Century*, ed. Ian T. Douglas and Kwok Pui-lan (New York: Church Publishing, 2001), 363.

Bibliography

Ackermann, Denise M. "Lamenting Tragedy from the Other Side." In *Sameness and Difference: Problems and Potentials in South African Civil Society*, edited by James R. Cochrane and Bastienne Klein, 213–42. Washington, DC: Council for Research in Values and Philosophy, 2000.

———. "Tamar's Cry: Re-Reading an Ancient Text in the Midst of an HIV and AIDS Pandemic." In *Grant Me Justice: HIV/AIDS and Gender Readings of the Bible*, edited by Musa W Dube and Musimbi Kanyoro, 27–59. Maryknoll, NY: Orbis Books, 2005.

Ackermann, Denise M., Jonathan A. Draper, and Emma Mashinini, eds. *Women Hold Up Half of the Sky: Women in the Church of Southern Africa*. Pietermaritzburg: Cluster Publications, 1991.

Adams, Marilyn McCord. "Unfit for Purpose—or, Why a Pan-Anglican Covenant at This Time Is a Very Bad Idea!" *Modern Believing* 49, no. 4 (2008): 23–45.

Asad, Talal. *Genealogies of Religion: Discipline and Reasons of Power in Christianity and Islam*. Baltimore, MD: Johns Hopkins University Press, 1993.

Ateek, Naim Stifan. *A Palestinian Christian Cry for Reconciliation*. Maryknoll, NY: Orbis Books, 2008.

Barton, Mukti. "I Am Black and Beautiful." *Black Theology* 2, no. 2 (2004): 167–87.

Bayne, Stephen Fielding. *Mutual Responsibility and Interdependence in the Body of Christ*. New York: Seabury Press, 1963.

Bhabha, Homi K. *The Location of Culture*. London: Routledge, 1994.

Bobbette, Adam. "Priests on the Shore: Climate Change and the Anglican Church of Melanesia." *GeoHumanities* 5, no. 2 (2019): 554–69.

Boff, Leonardo. *Ecclesiogenesis: The Base Communities Reinvent the Church*. Translated by Robert R. Barr. Maryknoll, NY: Orbis Books, 1986.

Brooks, Jennifer Benjamin. "The Missionary Connection: White Preaching in the British Colonies of the Caribbean." In *Unmasking White Preaching: Racial Harmony, Resistance, and Possibilities in Homiletics*, edited by Lis Valle-Ruiz and Andrew Wymer, 19–28. Lanham, MD: Lexington Books, 2022.

Brown, Stewart J. "Anglicanism in the British Empire, 1829–1910." In *The Oxford History of Anglicanism*, vol. 3, *Partisan Anglicanism and Its Global Expansion, 1829–c.1914*, edited by Rowan Strong, 45–68. Oxford: Oxford University Press, 2017.

Brown, Terry, ed. *Other Voices, Other Worlds: The Global Church Speaks Out on Homosexuality*. New York: Church Publishing, 2006.

Buchanan, Colin Ogilvie, ed. *Modern Anglican Liturgies 1958–1968*. Oxford: Oxford University Press, 1968.

Burridge, Richard A. "Being Biblical? Slavery, Sexuality, and the Inclusive Community." *Sewanee Theological Review* 52, no. 1 (2008): 14–32.

Capitain, Wouter. "From Counterpoint to Heterophony and Back Again: Reading Edward Said's Drafts for *Culture and Imperialism*." *Journal of Musicological Research* 41, no. 1 (2022): 1–22.

Carey, Hilary M. "Anglican Imperialism and the Gothic Style in Australia." *Journal for the Academic Study of Religion* 23, no. 1 (2010): 6–28.

Carey, William. *An Enquiry into the Obligations of Christians to Use Means for the Conversion of Heathens*. London: Carey Kingsgate Press, 1961.

Chan, Kwok Keung. "The First Mark of Mission: To Proclaim the Good News of the Kingdom of God." In Ross, *Life-Widening Mission: Global Perspectives from the Anglican Communion*, 13–30.

Chapman, Mark D. *Anglicanism: A Very Short Introduction*. Oxford: Oxford University Press, 2006.

———. *Anglican Theology*. London: T and T Clark International, 2012.

Chapman, Mark D., Sathianathan Clarke, and Martyn Percy, eds. *The Oxford Handbook of Anglican Studies*. Oxford: Oxford University, 2015.

Charusheela, S., and Eiman Zein-Elabdin, eds. *Postcolonialism Meets Economics*. New York: Routledge, 2004.

Chitano, Ezra, and Nyambura J. Njoroge, eds. *Contextual Bible Study Manual on Transformative Masculinity*. Harare, Zimbabwe: Ecumenical HIV and AIDS Initiative in Africa, 2013.

Choy, Renie Chow. *Ancestral Feelings: Postcolonial Thoughts on Western Christian Heritage*. London: SCM, 2021.

Church of England's Mission and Public Affairs Council. *Mission-Shaped Church: Church Planting and Fresh Expressions of Church in a Changing Context*. London: Church Publishing, 2004.

Clarke, Sathianathan. "World Christianity and Postcolonial Mission: A Path Forward for the Twenty-First Century." *Theology Today* 71, no. 2 (2014): 192–206.

"The Codrington Consensus: Agreed Statement from the Conference on Afro-Anglicanism." *Journal of Religious Thought* 44, no. 1 (1987): 84–93.

Coe, Shoki. "In Search of Renewal in Theological Education." *Theological Education* 9, no. 4 (1973): 233–43.

Coelho, Luiz. "IEAB's 2015 Book of Common Prayer: The Latest Chapter in the Evolution of the Book of Common Prayer in Brazil." *Studia Liturgica*, 49, no. 1 (2019): 26–42.

Crosby, Alfred. *Ecological Imperialism: The Biological Expansion of Europe, 900–1900*. 2nd ed. Cambridge: Cambridge University Press, 2015.

Cruz, Gemma Tulud. "Between Identity and Security: Theological Implications of Migration in the Age of Globalization." *Theological Studies* 69, no. 2 (2008): 357–75.

Daggers, Jenny. *Postcolonial Theology of Religions: Particularity and Pluralism in World Christianity*. New York: Routlege, 2013.

Darling, Pamela W. *New Wine: The Story of Women Transforming Leadership and Power in the Episcopal Church*. Cambridge, MA: Cowley, 1994.

Davies, W. Merlin. *An Introduction to F. D. Maurice's Theology*. London: SPCK, 1964.

Davis, Kortright. "The Codrington Consensus." *Anglican Theological Review* 89, no. 1 (2007): 35–43.

———. "The Legacy of Black Prophetic Moments: Dynastic Monuments versus Dynamic Movements." *Anglican Theological Review* 97, no. 3 (2015): 449–68.

———. "Present and Future Trends in Anglicanism." In *Anglicanism: Present and Future*, edited by Michael P. Hamilton, 25–28. Washington, DC: Washington National Cathedral, 1992.

Day, Abby, ed. *Contemporary Issues in the Worldwide Anglican Communion*. Surrey, England: Ashgate, 2016.

De Four-Babb, Joyanne, and Shelley-Ann Tenia. "From the Pantry to the Pulpit: Anglican Clergywomen in the Diocese of Trinidad and Tobago." *Journal of Pan African Studies* 5, no. 2 (2012): 42–66.

Doe, Michael. "From Colonialism to Communion." *Journal of Anglican Studies* 7, no. 2 (2009): 213–20.

Doe, Norman. "The Instruments of Unity and Communion in Global Anglicanism." In Markham, *Wiley-Blackwell Companion to the Anglican Communion*, 47–66.

Donaldson, Laura E., ed. "Postcolonialism and Scriptural Reading." *Semeia* 75 (1996): 1–240.

Donavan, Mary Sudman. "Anglican Women: Empowering Each Other to Further God's Kingdom." *Journal of Anglican Studies* 5, no. 1 (2007): 39–68.

Dorrien, Gary. "Economic Democracy as Political Theology: The British Anglican Socialist Tradition." *Anglican Theological Review* 102, no. 4 (2020): 539–73.

Douglas, Ian T. "Authority, Unity, and Mission in the Windsor Report." *Anglican Theological Review* 87, no. 4 (2005): 567–74.

Douglas, Ian T., and Kwok Pui-lan, eds. *Beyond Colonial Anglicanism: The Anglican Communion in the Twenty-First Century*. New York: Church Publishing, 2001.

Douglas, Ian T., and Julie Wortman. "Lambeth 1998: A Call to Awareness." *Witness* 81 (September 1998): 24–25.

Douglas, Kelly Brown. *Stand Your Ground: Black Bodies and the Justice of God*. Maryknoll, NY: Orbis Books, 2015.

Dube, Musa W. "Boundaries and Bridges: Journeys of a Postcolonial Feminist in Biblical Studies." In *Resistance and Visions—Postcolonial, Post-Secular and Queer Contributions to Theology and the Study of Religions*, edited by Ulrike Auga et al., 139–56. Leuven: Peeters, 2014.

———. *Postcolonial Feminist Interpretation of the Bible*. St. Louis, MO: Chalice Press, 2000.

Dyer, Mark, et al., eds. *The Official Report of the Lambeth Conference 1998*. Harrisburg, PA: Morehouse Publishing, 1999.

Ekechi, Felix K. "African Polygamy and Western Christian Ethnocentrism." *Journal of African Studies* 3, no. 3 (1976): 329–49.

Ellis, Havelock, and John Addington Symonds. *Sexual Inversion*. New York: Arno Press, 1975.

Ellis, James. "Anglican Indigenization and Contextualization in Colonial Hong Kong: Comparative Case Studies of St. John's Cathedral and St. Mary's Church." *Mission Studies* 36, no. 2 (2019): 219–46.

Equiano, Olaudah. *The Interesting Narrative of the Life of Olaudah Equiano, or Gustavus Vassa, the African*. Chicago: Lakeside Press, 2004.

Evans-Prichard, E. E. "Sexual Inversion among the Azande." *American Anthropologist*, New Series 72, no. 6 (1970): 1428–34.

Fabian, Johannes. *Time and the Other: How Anthropologist Makes Its Object*. New York: Columbia University Press, 1983.

Fanon, Frantz. *The Wretched of the Earth*. Translated by Richard Philcox. New York: Grove Press, 1963.

Fernando, Jude Lal. "The Geopolitics of Interreligious Dialogue: Political Zionism, Sinhala Buddhist Nationalism, and the Oppressed." In *Transpacific Political Theology: Perspectives and Methods*, edited by Kwok Pui-lan. Waco, TX: Baylor University Press, forthcoming.

Fletcher, Brian H. *The Place of Anglicanism in Australia: Church, Society, Nation*. Mulgrave, Australia: Broughton Publishing, 2008.

Gaitskell, Deborah. "Crossing Boundaries and Building Bridges: The Anglican Women's Fellowship in Post-Apartheid South Africa." *Journal of Religion in Africa* 34, no. 3 (2004): 266–97.

———. "Devout Domesticity? A Century of African Women's Christianity in South Africa." In *Women and Gender in Southern Africa to 1945*, edited by Cherryl Walker, 251–72. Cape Town: D. Philip, 1990.

Gibbs, M. E. *The Anglican Church in India 1600–1970*. Delhi: ISPCK, 1972.

Gibson, Paul. "International Anglican Liturgical Consultations: A Review." *Studia Liturgica* 29, no. 2 (1999): 235–50.

Gitari, David, ed. *Anglican Liturgical Inculturation in Africa: The Kanamai Statement "African Culture and Anglican Liturgy."* Alcuin/GROW Liturgical Study 28. Bramcote, UK: Grove Books, 1994.

Glasson, Travis. *Mastering Christianity: Missionary Anglicanism and Slavery in the Atlantic World*. New York: Oxford University Press, 2012.

Gnanadason, Aruna. *No Longer a Secret: The Church and Violence against Women*. Geneva: World Council of Churches, 1994.

Goen, C. C. *Broken Churches, Broken Nation: Denominational Schisms and the Coming of the Civil War*. Macon, GA: Mercer University Press, 1985.

Goldberg, David Theo. *Racist Culture: Philosophy and the Politics of Meaning*. Oxford: Blackwell, 1999.

Gore, Charles, ed. *Lux Mundi: A Series of Studies in the Religion of the Incarnation*. London: John Murray, 1889.

Grau, Marion. *Rethinking Mission in the Postcolony: Salvation, Society and Subversion*. London: T & T Clark, 2011.

Gutiérrez, Gustavo. *A Theology of Liberation: History, Politics, and Salvation*. Translated by Caridad Inda and John Eagleson. Maryknoll, NY: Orbis Books, 1973.

Haddad, Beverley. "Church Uniform as an Indigenous Form of Anglicanism: A South African Case Study." *Journal of Anglican Studies* 14, no. 2 (2016): 156–71.

———. "Gender Violence and HIV/AIDS: A Deadly Silence in the Church." *Journal of Theology for Southern Africa* 114 (2002): 93–106.

———. "Theologising Development: A Gendered Analysis of Poverty, Survival and Faith." *Journal of Theology for Southern Africa* 110 (2001): 5–19.

Hall, Stuart. "The West and the Rest: Discourse and Power." In *Formations of Modernity*, edited by Stuart Hall and Bram Gieben, 275–331. Cambridge: Polity Press, 1992.

———. "When Was 'the Postcolonial'? Thinking at the Limit." In *The Postcolonial Question: Common Skies, Divided Horizon*, edited by Iain Chambers and Lidia Curti, 242–60. New York: Routledge, 1996.

Hanciles, Jehu J. "Anatomy of an Experiment: The Sierra Leone Native Pastorate." *Missiology* 29, no. 1 (2001): 63–82.

———. *Beyond Christendom: Globalization, African Migration, and the Transformation of the West*. Maryknoll, NY: Orbis Books, 2008.

———. *Euthanasia of a Mission: African Church Autonomy in a Colonial Context*. Westport, CT: Praeger, 2002.

———. "Migrants as Missionaries, Missionaries as Outsiders: Reflections on African Christian Presence in Western Societies." *Mission Studies* 30, no. 1 (2013): 64–85.

———. *Migration and the Making of Global Christianity*. Grand Rapids, MI: Eerdmans, 2021.

———, ed. *World Christianity: History, Methodologies, Horizons*. Maryknoll, NY: Orbis Books, 2021.

Harries, Patrick, and David Maxwell, eds. *The Spiritual in the Secular: Missionaries and Knowledge about Africa*. Grand Rapids, MI: Eerdmans, 2012.

Hassett, Miranda K. *Anglican Communion in Crisis: How Episcopal Dissidents and Their African Allies Are Reshaping Anglicanism*. Princeton, NJ: Princeton University Press, 2007.

Heaney, Robert S. *Post-Colonial Theology: Finding God and Each Other Amidst the Hate*. Eugene, OR: Cascade Books, 2019.

Heaney, Robert S., and William L. Sachs. *The Promise of Anglicanism*. London: SCM, 2019.

Heeney, Brian. *The Women's Movement in the Church of England, 1850–1930*. New York: Oxford University Press, 1988.

Hefling, Charles, and Cynthia Shattuck, eds. *The Oxford Guide to the Book of Common Prayer: A Worldwide Survey*. Oxford: Oxford University Press, 2006.

Hertig, Paul. "Jesus' Migrations and Liminal Withdraws in Matthew." In *God's People on the Move: Biblical and Global Perspectives on Migration and Mission*, edited by vanThanh Nguyen and John M. Prior, 46–61. Eugene, OR: Pickwick, 2014.

Heyward, Carter. "Make Us Prophets and Pastors: An Open Letter to Gay and Lesbian Priests." In *Gays and the Future of Anglicanism: Responses to the Windsor Report*, edited by Andrew Linzey and Richard Kirker, 315–25. New York: O Books, 2005.

Holeton, David R., ed. *Liturgical Inculturation in the Anglican Communion*. Alcuin/GROW Liturgical Study 15. Bramcote, UK: Grove Books 1990.

Howe, John. *Anglicanism and the Universal Church*. Toronto: Anglican Book Center, 1990.

Hughes, Rebecca C. "'Grandfather in the Bones': Scientific Racism and Anglican Missionaries in Uganda, c. 1900–1930." *Social Sciences and Missions* 33, no. 3–4 (2020): 347–78.

Huntington, Samuel P. *The Clash of Civilizations and the Remaking of World Order*. New York: Simon & Schuster, 1996.

Idowu-Fearon, Josiah. "Anglicans and Islam in Nigeria: Anglicans Encountering Difference." *Journal of Anglican Studies* 2, no. 1 (2004): 40–51.

Jacob, W. M. *The Making of the Anglican Church Worldwide*. London: SPCK, 1997.

Jagessar, Michael N., and Stephen Burns. *Christian Worship: Postcolonial Perspectives*. London: Routledge, 2011.

Jarvis, Edward. *The Anglican Church in Burma: From Colonial Past to Global Future*. University Park: Pennsylvania State University Press, 2021.

———. *The Anglican Church in Malaysia: Evolving Concepts, Challenging Contexts, Emerging Subtexts*. Cham, Switzerland: Palgrave Macmillan, 2022.

Jenkins, Phillip. *The Next Christendom: The Coming of Global Christianity*. 3rd ed. New York: Oxford University Press, 2011.

Jeremiah, Anderson H. M. "Anglicans in South Asia: Life in the Midst of Religious Marginality." In Day, *Contemporary Issues in the Worldwide Anglican Communion: Powers and Pieties*, 191–210.

Johnson, Todd M., and Gina A. Gurlo. "The Changing Demographics of Global Anglicanism, 1970–2010." In *Growth and Decline in the Anglican Communion: 1980 to the Present*, edited by David Goodhew, 37–53. New York: Routledge, 2017.

———, eds. *World Christian Database*. Leiden: Brill, accessed January 2020.

Jones, Peter. *The Christian Socialist Revival, 1877–1914: Religion, Class, and Social Conscience in Late Victorian England*. Princeton, NJ: Princeton University Press, 1968.

Jones, Timothy. "Waiting for Jubilee: The Campaign for Debt Cancellation." In *British Foreign Policy and the Anglican Church: Christian Engagement with the Contemporary World*, edited by Timothy Blewett, Adrian Hyde-Price, and Wyn Rees, 119–33. Burlington, VT: Ashgate, 2008.

Jones, Timothy Willem. "The Missionaries' Position: Polygamy and Divorce in the Anglican Communion, 1888–1988." *Journal of Religious History* 35, no. 3 (2011): 393–408.

Kaa, Hirini. *Te Hāhi Mihinare: the Māori Anglican Church*. Wellington, New Zealand: Bridget Williams Books, 2020.

Kafwanka, John. "Partnership in Mission—An Anglican Perspective." In *Call to Unity: For the Sake of Mission*, edited by John Gibaut and Knud Jørgensen, 154–72. Minneapolis: Fortress, 2015.

Kanyoro, Musimbi R. A. "Engendered Communal Theology: African Women's Contribution to Theology in the Twenty-First Century." In *Hope Abundant: Third World and Indigenous Women's Theology*, edited by Kwok Pui-lan, 19–35. Maryknoll, NY: Orbis Books, 2010.

Kaoma, Kapya John. "Beyond Adam and Eve: Jesus, Sexual Minorities and Sexual Politics in the Church in Africa." *Journal of Theology for Southern Africa* 153 (2015): 7–28.

———. *Christianity, Globalization, and Protective Homophobia: Democratic Contestation of Sexuality in Sub-Saharan Africa*. Cham, Switzerland: Palgrave Macmillan, 2018.

———. *God's Family, God's Earth: Christian Ecological Ethics of Ubuntu*. Zomba, Malawi: Kachere Series, 2013.

———. "The Paradox and Tension of Moral Claims: Evangelical Christianity, the Politicization and Globalization of Sexual Politics in Sub-Saharan Africa." *Critical Research on Religion* 2, no. 3 (2014): 227–45.

Kapinde, Stephen Asol, and Eleanor Tiplady Higgs. "Global Anglican Discourse and Women's Ordination in Kenya: The Controversy in Kirinyaga, 1979–1992, and Its Legacy." *Journal of Anglican Studies* 20, no. 1 (2012): 22–39.

Kater, John L. "Stirrings: Emerging Women's Ministries in the Church of England and the Episcopal Church and Their Impact on the Chung Hua Sheng Kung Hui (Anglican Church in China)." *Anglican and Episcopal History* 88, no. 4 (2019): 367–83.

Kayama, Hiroto. "A New Perspective for Anglicanism: Mission in Northeast Asia." Translated by John Stolzenbach. *Journal of Anglican Studies* 6, no. 2 (2008): 167–86.

Kaye, Bruce. *An Introduction to World Anglicanism*. Cambridge: Cambridge University Press, 2008.

Kent, John. *William Temple: Church, State, and Society in Britain, 1880–1950*. Cambridge: Cambridge University Press, 1992.

Kgabe, Vicentia. "The Third Mark of Mission: To Respond to Human Need by Loving Service." In Ross, *Life-Widening Mission*, 47–56.

Kiarie, George. "Factors Inhibiting Inculturation of the Holy Communion Symbols in the Anglican Church in Kenya: A Case Study of the Diocese of Thika." *Missionalia* 44, no. 3 (2017): 301–20.

Kings, Graham, and Geoff Morgan, eds. *Offerings from Kenya to Anglicanism: Liturgical Texts and Contexts Including "A Kenyan Service of Holy Communion."* Cambridge: Grove Books, 2001.

Kirkpatrick, Martha. "For God So Loved the World: An Incarnational Ecology." *Anglican Theological Review* 91, no. 2 (2009): 191–212.

Krishnaswamy, Revathi, and John C. Hawley, eds. *The Postcolonial and the Global*. Minneapolis: University of Minnesota Press, 2008.

Kuin, T. H. N. "Perfect Partners or Uneasy Bedfellows: Anglicans and Religious Pluralism in the Late 20th Century." *Studies in Interreligious Dialogue* 7, no. 2 (1997): 177–99.

Kwok, Pui-lan, *Postcolonial Imagination and Feminist Theology.* Louisville, KY: Westminster John Knox Press, 2005.

———. *Postcolonial Politics and Theology: Unraveling Empire for a Global World.* Louisville, KY: Westminster John Knox Press, 2021.

———. "The Study of Chinese Women and the Anglican Church in Cross-Cultural Perspective." In Wong and Chiu, *Christian Women in Chinese Society: The Anglican Story*, 19–35.

Kwok, Pui-lan, Judith A. Berling, and Jenny Plane Te Paa, eds. *Anglican Women on Church and Mission.* New York: Morehouse Publishing, 2012.

Kwok, Pui-lan, and Eunjin Jeon. "Inspirations of Archbishop Demond Tutu on Global Justice Work." *Anglican Theological Review* 104, no. 3 (2022): 350–58.

Lambelet, Kyle B. T. "Conflict as Communion: Toward an Agonistic Ecclesiology." *Journal of Anglican Studies* 17, no 2 (2019): 133–47.

Lambeth Conference. *The Report of the Lambeth Conference 1978.* London: CIO Publishing, 1978.

———. *The Truth Shall Make You Free: The Lambeth Conference 1988.* London: Church House Publishing, 1988.

Lee, Peter John. "Indaba as Obedience: A Post Lambeth 2008 Assessment 'If Someone Offends You, Talk to Him.'" *Journal of Anglican Studies* 7, no. 2 (2009): 147–61.

Lewis, Harold T. "Unapologetic Apologetics: The Essence of Black Anglican Preaching." *Anglican Theological Review* 101, no. 1 (2019): 45–66.

______. *Yet with a Steady Beat: The African American Struggle for Recognition in the Episcopal Church.* Valley Forge, PA: Trinity Press International, 1996.

Li, Tim-Oi. *Raindrops of My Life: The Memoir of Florence Li Tim-Oi.* Toronto: Anglican Book Center, 1996.

Lim, Swee Hong, "Church Music in Postcolonial Liturgical Celebration." In *Postcolonial Practice of Ministry: Leadership, Liturgy, and Interfaith Engagement*, edited by Kwok Pui-lan and Stephen Burns, 123–35, Lanham, MD: Lexington Books, 2016.

Lim, You-Leng Leroy. "Webs of Betrayal, Webs of Blessings." In *Q & A: Queer in Asian America*, edited by David L. Eng and Alice Y. Hom, 323–34. Philadelphia: Temple University Press, 1998.

Lockley, Philip. "Social Anglicanism and Empire: C. F. Andrews's Christian Socialism." *Studies in Church History* 54 (2018): 407–21.

Luciani, Rafael. "The Itinerant Fraternity of Jesus: Christological Discernment of the Migration Drama." In *Living with(out) Borders: Catholic Theological Ethics on the Migrations of Peoples*, edited by Agnes M. Brazal and María Teresa Dávila, 206–12. Maryknoll, NY: Orbis Books, 2016.

Ludlow, John M. *British India: Its Races and History Considered with Reference to the Mutinies of 1857.* London: Macmillan, 1958.

MacCulloch, Diarmaid. "The Myth of the English Reformation." *Journal of British Studies* 30, no. 1 (1991): 1–19.

Makgoba, Thabo. "Politics." In Chapman, *The Oxford Handbook of Anglican Studies*, 372–83.

Markham, Ian S. et al., eds. *Wiley-Blackwell Companion to the Anglican Communion.* Malden, MA: Wiley Blackwell, 2013.

Maurice, Frederick Denison. *The Kingdom of Christ, or, Hints on the Principles, Ordinances, and Constitution of the Catholic Church in Letters to a Member of the Society of Friends*. Vol. 1. 2nd ed. London: James Clark, 1959.

———. *Reconstructing Christian Ethics*. Edited by Ellen K. Wondra. Louisville, KY: Westminster John Knox Press, 1995.

———. *The Religions of the World and Their Relations to Christianity*. 6th ed. London: Macmillan, 1886.

———. *Sermons Preached at Lincoln's Inn Chapel*. Vol. 2. London: Macmillan, 1891.

Mbembe, Achille. *Out of the Dark Night: Essays on Decolonization*. New York: Columbia University Press, 2021.

Mbonigaba, Elisha. "The Indigenization of the Liturgy." In Gitari, *Anglican Liturgical Inculturation in Africa: The Kanamai Statement "African Culture and Anglican Liturgy,"* 20–32.

———. "Indigenization of the Liturgy." In *A Kingdom of Priests: Liturgical Formation of the People of God*, edited by Thomas J. Talley, 39–47. Alcuin/GROW Liturgical Study 5. Bramcote, UK: Grove Books, 1988.

McKinnon, Andrew, and Christopher Craig Brittain. "Anglicans in a Globalizing World: The Contradictions of Communion." In Day, *Contemporary Issues in the Worldwide Anglican Communion*, 113–28.

Memmi, Albert. *The Colonizer and the Colonized*. Translated by Howard Greenfeld. New York: Orion Press, 1965.

Methuen, Charlotte. "The Lambeth Conference, Gender and Sexuality." *Theology* 123, no. 2 (2020): 84–94.

Meyers, Ruth A. "Diversity and Common Worship." In *In Spirit and Truth: A Vision of Episcopal Worship*, edited by Stephanie Budwey et al., 47–57. New York: Church Publishing, 2020.

Miki, Mei. "A Church with Newly-Opened Doors: The Ordination of Women Priests in the Anglican-Episcopal Church of Japan." *Japanese Journal of Religious Studies* 44, no. 1 (2017): 37–51.

Mohanty, Chandra Talpade. "Under Western Eyes: Feminist Scholarship and Colonial Discourses." In *Third World Women and the Politics of Feminism*, edited by Chandra Talpade Mohanty, Ann Russo, and Lourdes Torres, 51–80. Bloomington: Indiana University Press, 1991.

Mombo, Esther. "The Bible and Polygamy: A Mothers' Union Perspective." *AICMAR Bulletin* 1 (2002): 31–45.

———. "The Church and Poverty Alleviation in Africa." In Kwok, Berling, and Te Paa, *Anglican Women on Church and Mission*, 135–49.

———. "Mission and Evangelism." In *Christianity in Sub-Saharan Africa*, edited by Kenneth R. Ross, J. Kwabena Asamoah-Gyadu, and Todd M. Johnson, 376–85. Edinburgh: University of Edinburgh Press, 2017.

———. "The Ordination of Women in Africa: An Historical Perspective." In *Women and Ordination in the Christian Churches: International Perspectives*, edited by Ian Jones, Janet Wootton, and Kirsty Thorpe, 123–43. London: T & T Clark, 2008.

———. "Reflection on Peace in the Decade to Overcome Violence." *Ecumenical Review* 63, no. 1 (2011): 71–76.

———. "The Windsor Report: A Paradigm Shift for Anglicanism." *Anglican Theological Review* 89, no. 1 (2007): 69–78.

Moore-Gilbert, Bart. *Postcolonial Theory: Contexts, Practices, Politics*. London: Verso, 1997.

Morley, David, and Kuan-Hsing Chen, eds. *Stuart Hall: Critical Dialogues in Cultural Studies*. London: Routledge, 1996.

Morris, Jeremy. *F. D. Maurice and the Crisis of Christian Authority*. New York: Oxford University Press, 2005.

Moyse, Cordelia. *A History of the Mothers' Union: Women, Anglicanism and Globalization, 1876–2008*. Woodbridge: Boydell Press, 2009.

Mukherjee, Pablo. "Surfing the Second Waves: Amitav Ghosh's Tide Country." *New Formations* 59 (2006): 144–57.

Murray, Julio E. "The AGAPE Economy: The Church's Call to Action." *Anglican Theological Review* 98, no. 1 (2016): 125–35.

———. "New WCC Affirmation on Mission and Evangelism: Observations from the Episcopal Church of Panama." *International Review of Mission* 102, no. 2 (2013): 205–8.

Mwamba, Musonda Trevor Selwyn. "The Lambeth Conference 2008 and the Millennium Development Goals: A Botswana Perspective." *Journal of Anglican Studies* 7, no. 2 (2009): 229–42.

Narayan, Uma. *Dislocating Cultures: Identities, Traditions, and Third-World Feminism*. New York: Routledge, 1997.

Naughton, Jim, ed. *The Genius of Anglicanism: Perspectives on the Proposed Anglican Covenant*. Chicago: The Chicago Consultation, 2011.

Neill, Stephen C. *Anglicanism*. Harmondsworth: Penguin, 1958.

Network for Inter Faith Concerns of the Anglican Communion. *Generous Love: The Truth of the Gospel and the Call to Dialogue*. London: Anglican Consultative Council, 2008.

Niebuhr, Reinhold. *The Structure of Nations and Empires*. New York: Charles Scribner's Sons, 1959.

Nkwoka, A. O. "The Church and Polygamy in Africa: The 1988 Lambeth Conference Resolution." *Africa Theological Journal* 19, no. 2 (1990): 139–54.

Norman, Edward. *The Victorian Christian Socialists*. Cambridge: Cambridge University Press, 1987.

Odewole, Israel O. O. "Singing and Worship in an Anglican Church Liturgy in Egba and Egba West Dioceses, Abeokuta, Nigeria." *HTS Teologiese Studies* 74, no. 1 (2018): 1–10, https://hts.org.za/index.php/hts/article/view/4584/11588.

Oduyoye, Mercy Amba. *Daughters of Anowa: African Women and Patriarchy*. Maryknoll, NY: Orbis Books, 1995.

Ofula, Kenneth "'The River Between': Negotiating Dual Identities in the Anglican Churches of Kenya." *Studies in World Christianity* 25, no. 1 (2019): 95–113.

Omoyajowo, Akinyele, ed. *The Anglican Church in Nigeria (1842–1992)*. Lagos, Nigeria: Macmillan Nigeria Publishers, 1994.

Panikkar, Raimundo. "The Jordan, the Tiber, and the Ganges: Three Kariological Moments of Christic Self-Understanding." In *The Myth of Christian Uniqueness: Toward a Pluralistic Theology of Religions*, edited by John Hick and Paul F. Knitter, 89–116. Maryknoll, NY: Orbis Books, 1987.

Pelling, Henry. *The Origins of the Labour Party, 1880–1900*. Oxford: Clarendon Press, 1954.

Phan, Peter C. "Christianity as an Institutional Migrant." In *Christianities in Migration: The Global Perspective*, edited by Elaine Padilla and Peter C. Phan, 13–22. New York: Palgrave Macmillan, 2016.

———. "*Deus Migrator*—God the Migrant, Migration of Theology and Theology of Migration." *Theological Studies* 77, no. 4 (2016): 845–68.

———. "A New Christianity, But What Kind?" *Mission Studies* 21, no. 1 (2005): 59–83.

Phiri, Isabel Apawo, Beverley Haddad, and Madipoane Masenya, eds. *African Women, HIV/AIDS and Faith Communities*. Pietermaritzburg: Cluster Publications, 2003.

Pillay, Miranda N. "Women, Priests and the Anglican Church in Southern Africa: Reformation of Holy Hierarchies." *Consensus* 38, no. 1 (2017): 1–13.

Pollard, Jane, Cheryl McEwan, and Alex Hughes, eds. *Postcolonial Economies*. London: Zed Books, 2011.

Porter, Andrew. "Religion and Empire: British Expansion in the Long Nineteenth Century, 1780–1914." *Journal of Imperial and Commonwealth History* 20, no. 3 (1992): 370–90.

Porter, Bernard. *The Lion's Share: A Short History of British Imperialism 1850 to the Present*. 6th ed. New York: Routledge, 2021.

Preston, Ronald H. "The Legacy of the Christian Socialist Movement in England." In *Religion, Economics and Social Thought*, edited by Walter Block and Irving Hexham, 181–201. Vancouver, BC: Frazer Institute, 1986.

Prichard, Andreana C. *Sisters in Spirit: Christianity, Affect, and Community Building in East Africa, 1860–1970*. East Lansing: Michigan State University Press, 2017.

Ramshaw, Gail. *Liturgical Language: Keeping It Metaphoric, Making It Inclusive*. Collegeville, MN: Liturgical Press, 1996.

Ramshaw, Gail, and Gordon Lathrop, eds. *Readings for the Assembly*. Cycles A, B, and C. Minneapolis: Fortress Press, 1995–97.

Robert, Dana L. "Evangelist or Homemaker? Mission Strategies of Early Nineteenth-Century Missionary Wives in Burma and Hawaii." *International Bulletin of Missionary Research* 17, no. 1 (1993): 4–6, 8–10, 12.

———. "World Christianity as a Women's Movement." *International Bulletin of Missionary Research* 30, no. 4 (2006): 180–88.

Rosario, Vernon A. *The Erotic Imagination: French Histories of Perversity*. New York: Oxford University Press, 1997.

Rosma, Ulbe, Jan Lucassen, and Gert Oostindie. "Introduction: Postcolonial Migrations and Identity Politics: Towards a Comparative Perspective." In *Postcolonial Migrants and Identity Politics: Europe, Russia, Japan, and the United States in Comparison*, edited by Ulbe Rosma, Jan Lucassen, and Gert Oostindie, 1–22. New York: Berghahn Books, 2012.

Ross, Cathy. ed. *Life-Widening Mission: Global Perspectives from the Anglican Communion*. Oxford: Regnum Books International, 2012.

———, "'Such Unfolding of the Truth of the Gospel': Post-Colonial Reflections on the Missiological Dimension of the Lambeth Conference." In *The Lambeth Conference: Theology, History, Polity and Purpose*, edited by Paul Avis and Benjamin Guyer, 297–315. London: Bloomsbury T & T Clark, 2017.

Rubenstein, Mary-Jane. "Anglicans in the Postcolony: On Sex and the Limits of Communion." *Telos* 143 (Summer 2008): 133–60.

Rutazibwa, Olivia U., and Robbie Shilliam, eds. *Routledge Handbook of Postcolonial Politics*. New York: Routledge, 2018.

Rutherford, Jonathan. "The Third Space: Interview with Homi Bhabha." In *Identity: Community, Culture, Difference*, edited by Jonathan Rutherford, 207–21. London: Lawrence & Wishart, 1990.

Sachs, William L. *The Transformation of Anglicanism: From State Church to Global Communion*. Cambridge: Cambridge University Press, 1993.

Said, Edward W. *Culture and Imperialism*. New York: Afred A. Knopf, 1993.

———. *Orientalism*. New York: Vintage Books, 1979.

———. *Out of Place: A Memoir*. New York: Alfred A. Knopf, 1999.

Samuel, Vinay, and Christopher Sugden, *Lambeth: A View from the Two Thirds World*. London: SPCK, 1988.

Sanneh, Lamin. *Translating the Message: Missionary Impact on Culture*. Maryknoll, NY: Orbis Books, 1989.

———. *Whose Religion Is Christianity? The Gospel Beyond the West*. Grand Rapids, MI: Eerdmans, 2003.

Sassen, Saskia. "Women's Burden: Counter-Geographics of Globalization and the Feminization of Survival." *Journal of International Affairs* 53, no. 2 (2000): 503–24.

Schüssler Fiorenza, Elisabeth. *In Memory of Her: A Feminist Theological Reconstruction of Christian Origins*. 10th- anniv. ed. New York: Crossroad, 1994.

Scotland, Nigel. "Methodist and the English Labour Movement 1800–1906." *Anvil* 14, no. 1 (1997): 36–48.

Seeley, John Robert. *Ecce Homo: Life and Work of Jesus Christ*. New York: E. P. Dutton, 1908.

———. *The Expansion of England*. Boston: Little, Brown, and Company, 1905.

Segovia, Fernando F. *Decolonizing Biblical Studies: A View from the Margins*. Maryknoll, NY: Orbis Books, 2000.

———. "Johannine Studies and Geopolitical: Reflections upon Absence and Irruption." In *What We Have Heard from the Beginning: The Past, Present, and Future of Johannine Studies*, edited by Tom Thatcher, 281–310. Waco, TX: Baylor University Press, 2007.

Shattuck, Gardiner H., Jr. *Episcopalians and Race*. Lexington: University Press of Kentucky, 2000.

Shenk, Wilbert. "Henry Venn's Legacy." *Occasional Bulletin of Missionary Research* 1, no. 2 (1977): 16–19.

———. "Rufus Anderson and Henry Venn: A Special Relationship?" *International Bulletin of Missionary Research* 5, no. 4 (1981): 168–72.

Smart, David H. "Christopher Wren and the Architectural Context of Anglican Liturgy." *Anglican Theological Review* 77, no. 3 (1995): 290–306.

Snow, Jennifer C. *Mission, Race, and Empire: The Episcopal Church in Global Context*. New York: Oxford University Press, 2023.

Snyder, Susanna. *Asylum-Seeking, Migration and Church*. Burlington, VT: Ashgate, 2012.

———. "Introduction: Moving Body." In *Church in an Age of Global Migration: A Moving Body*, edited by Susanna Snyder, Agnes M. Brazal, and Joshua Ralston, 1–19. New York: Palgrave Macmillan, 2016.

Solheim, James E. *Diversity or Disunity: Reflections on Lambeth 1998*. New York: Church Publishing, 1999.

Song, C. S. *Tell Us Our Names: Story Theology from an Asian Perspective*. Maryknoll, NY: Orbis Books, 1984.

Spencer, Stephen. *Archbishop William Temple: A Study in Servant Leadership*. London: SCM Press, 2022.

———. "History and Society in William Temple's Thought." *Studies in Christian Ethics* 5, no. 2 (1992): 61–73.

———, ed. *Theology Reforming Society: Revisiting Anglican Social Theology*. London: SCM, 2017.

———. *William Temple: A Call to Prophesy*. London: SPCK, 2001.

———. "William Temple's *Christianity and the Social Order* After Fifty Years." *Theology* 95, no. 763 (1992): 32–39.

Spivak, Gayatri Chakravorty. "Can the Subaltern Speak?" In *Marxism and the Interpretation of Culture*, edited by Cary Nelson and Lawrence Grossberg, 271–313. Urbana: University of Illinois Press, 1988.

———. *A Critique of Postcolonial Reason: Toward a History of the Vanishing Present*. Cambridge, MA: Harvard University Press, 1999.

———. "Subaltern Talk: Interview with the Editors." In *The Spivak Reader*, edited by Donna Landry and Gerald MacLean, 287–308. New York: Routledge, 1966.

———. "Three Women's Texts and a Critique of Imperialism." *Critical Inquiry* 12, no. 1 (1985): 243–61.

Stoler, Ann Laura. *Carnal Knowledge and Imperial Power: Race and the Intimate in Colonial Rule*. Berkeley: University of California Press, 2002.

Strong, Rowan. *Anglicanism and British Empire: c.1700–1850*. Oxford: Oxford University Press, 2007.

———. "Rescuing the Perishing Heathens: The British Empire versus the Empire of Satan in Anglican Theology, 1701–1721." *Studies in Church History* 45 (2009): 323–35.

———. "A Vision of Anglican Imperialism: The Annual Sermons of the Society for the Propagation of the Gospel in Foreign Parts 1701–1714." *Journal of Religious History* 30, no. 2 (2006): 175–98.

Strout, Shawn. "Prayer Book Uniformity: Myth or Icon?" *Anglican Theological Review* 105, no. 1 (2023): 24–40.

Sugirtharajah, R. S. *The Bible in the Third World: Precolonial, Colonial, and Postcolonial Encounters*. Cambridge: Cambridge University Press, 2001.

———. ed. *The Postcolonial Bible*. Sheffield: Sheffield Academic Press, 1998.

———. *Postcolonial Criticism and Biblical Interpretation*. Oxford: Oxford University Press, 2002.

———. "Salvos from the Victorian Pulpit: Conscription of Texts by Victorian Preachers during the Indian Rebellion of 1857." In *The Bible and Empire: Postcolonial Explorations*, 60–97. Cambridge: Cambridge University Press, 2005.

Swain, Storm. "*A New Zealand Prayer Book = He Karakia Mihinare O Aotearoa*: A Study in Postcolonial Liturgy." In *Liturgy in Postcolonial Perspectives: Only One Is Holy*, edited by Cláudio Carvalhaes, 165–75. New York: Palgrave Macmillan, 2015.

Swamy, Muthuraj, and Stephen Spencer, eds. *Walking Together: Global Anglican Perspectives on Reconciliation*. London: Anglican Communion Office, 2019.

———, eds. *Witnessing Together: Global Anglican Perspectives on Evangelism and Witness*. London: Anglican Communion Office, 2019.

Swart-Russell, Phoebe, and Jonathan Draper, "A Brief History of the Movement for the Ordination of Women in the Church of the Province of Southern Africa (CPSA)." In Ackermann, Draper, and Mashinini, *Women Hold Up Half of the Sky*, 220–37.

Syeed, Najeeba. "Interreligious Learning and Intersectionality." In *Asian and Asian American Women in Theology and Religion*, edited by Kwok Pui-lan, 171–85. Cham, Switzerland: Palgrave Macmillan, 2020.

Sykes, Stephen, and John Booty. *The Study of Anglicanism*. London: SPCK, 1988.
Tanner, Kathryn. *Christianity and the New Spirit of Capitalism*. New Haven, CT: Yale University Press, 2019.
Tanner, Mary. "The Episcopal Ministry Act of Synod in Context." In *Seeking the Truth of Change in the Church: Reception, Communion and the Ordination of Women*, edited by Paul Avis, 58–74. London: T & T Clark, 2004.
Tawney, R. H. *Religion and the Rise of Capitalism*. New York: Harcourt, Brace, 1926.
Taylor, Charles. *Modern Social Imaginaries*. Durham, NC: Duke University Press, 2004.
Te Paa, Jenny. "From 'Civilizing' to Colonizing to Respectfully Collaborating?" *Theology Today* 63, no. 1 (2005): 67–73.
———. "From *Te Rawiri* to the New Zealand Prayer Book." In Hefling and Shattuck, *Oxford Guide to the Book of Common Prayer*, 343–47.
Temple, William. *Christianity and the Social Order*. New York: Seabury, 1976. First published 1942 by Penguin Books (New York).
———. *The Kingdom of God*. London: Macmillan, 1914.
———. *Mens Creatrix: An Essay*. London: Macmillan, 1917.
Thomas, M. M. "The Meaning of Salvation Today: A Personal Statement." *International Review of Mission* 62, no. 245 (1973): 158–69.
Thompsett, Fredrica Harris, ed. *Looking Forward. Looking Backward: Forty Years of Women's Ordination*. New York: Morehouse Publishing, 2014.
Thompsett, Fredrica Harris, and Sheryl Kujawa-Holbrook, eds. *Deeper Joy: Lay Women in the 20th Century Episcopal Church*. New York: Church Publishing, 2005.
Travis, Sarah. *Decolonizing Preaching: The Pulpit as Postcolonial Space*. Eugene, OR: Cascade Books, 2014.
Trisk, Janet. "Women in the Anglican Communion." In Markham, *The Wiley-Blackwell Companion to the Anglican Communion*, 617–26.
Tutu, Desmond. *An African Prayer Book*. New York: Doubleday, 1995.
———. "Dark Days: Episcopal Ministry in Times of Repression, 1976–1996." *Journal of Theology for Southern Africa* 118 (2004): 27–39.
———. *God Has a Dream: A Vision of Hope for Our Time*. New York: Doubleday, 2004.
———. *No Future Without Forgiveness*. New York: Doubleday, 1999.
Vernon, Rachele E. "Daughters of Jerusalem, Mothers of Salem: Caribbean Women in the Ministry of the Church." In Jones, Wootton, and Thorpe, *Women and Ordination in the Christian Churches: International Perspectives*, 215–24.
Walls, Andrew F. *The Cross-Cultural Process of Christian History: Studies in the Transmission and Appropriation of Faith*. Maryknoll, NY: Orbis Books, 2002.
———. *The Significance of African Christianity*. Edinburgh: St. Colm's Education Center and College, 1989.
Walsh, Oonagh. *Anglican Women in Dublin: Philanthropy, Politics, and Education in Early 20th Century*. Dublin: University College Dublin Press, 2005.
Walters, Albert Sundararaj. "Evangelism and Witnessing in Multi-Religious Malaysia: Towards a Fresh Approach." In Swamy and Spencer, *Witnessing Together: Global Anglican Perspectives on Evangelism and Witness*, 65–77.
Walvin, James. "Slavery, the Slave Trade, and the Churches." *Quaker Studies* 12, no. 2 (2008): 189–95.
Ward, Kevin. *A History of Global Anglicanism*. Cambridge: Cambridge University Press, 2006.

Weeks, Jeffrey. *Against Nature: Essays on History, Sexuality and Identity*. London: Rivers Oram Press, 1991.

Welby, Justin. *Dethroning Mammon: Making Money Serve Grace*. London: Bloomsbury, 2016.

Welch, Pamela. *Church and Settler in Colonial Zimbabwe: A Study in the History of the Diocese of Mashonaland/Southern Rhodesia, 1890–1925*. Leiden: Brill, 2008.

Wickeri, Philip, ed. *Christian Encounters with Chinese Culture: Essays on Anglican and Episcopal History in China*. Hong Kong: Hong Kong University Press, 2015.

White, John. "Christian Responsibility to Reform Society: The Example of William Wilberforce and the Clapham Sect." *Episcopal Review of Theology* 32, no. 2 (2008): 166–71.

Williams, Rowan. "Liberation Theology and the Anglican Tradition." In Rowan D. Williams and David Nicholls, *Politics and Theological Identity: Two Anglican Essays*, 7–26. London: Jubilee Group, 1984.

Wingate, Andrew, Kevin Ward, Carrie Pemberton, and Wilson Sitshebo, eds. *Anglicanism: A Global Communion*. London: Mowbray, 1998.

Wondra, Ellen K. *Questioning Authority: The Theology and Practice of Authority in the Episcopal Church and Anglican Communion*. New York: Peter Lang, 2018.

———. "William Temple." In *Empire and the Christian Tradition: New Readings of Classical Theologians*, edited by Kwok Pui-lan, Dom H. Compier, and Joerg Rieger, 323–35. Minneapolis: Fortress Press, 2007.

Wong, Wai Ching Angela, and Patricia P. K. Chiu, eds. *Christian Women in Chinese Society: The Anglican Story*. Hong Kong: Hong Kong University Press, 2018.

World Council of Churches. *Overcoming Violence: The Ecumenical Decade 2001–2010*. Geneva: World Council of Churches, 2011.

"The World Is Our Host: A Call for Urgent Action for Climate Justice," Good Friday 2015, https://acen.anglicancommunion.org/media/148818/The-World-is-our-Host-FINAL-TEXT.pdf.

Zink, Jesse A. "Anglican Theology in the Midst of a Migration Crisis." *Journal of Anglican Studies* 17, no. 1 (2019): 31–47.

———. "Brief Introductions to Anglican Theology: Christian Mission." *Anglican Theological Review* 104, no. 4 (2022): 444–62.

———. *Christianity and Catastrophe in South Sudan: Civil War, Migration, and the Rise of Dinka Anglicanism*. Waco, TX: Baylor University Press, 2018.

———. "Five Marks of Mission: History, Theology, Critique." *Journal of Anglican Studies* 15, no. 2 (2017): 144–66.

Index